Social forces in urban suicide

THE DORSEY SERIES IN ANTHROPOLOGY AND SOCIOLOGY

EDITOR   ROBIN M. WILLIAMS, JR.   *Cornell University*

BARNOUW   *Culture and Personality*

BELL   *Marriage and Family Interaction*   rev. ed.

BELL & STUB (eds.)   *The Sociology of Education: A Sourcebook* rev. ed.

BREER & LOCKE   *Task Experience as a Source of Attitudes*

GAMSON   *Power and Discontent*

GEORGES (ed.)   *Studies on Mythology*

GOODMAN   *The Individual and Culture*

GOTTLIEB & RAMSEY   *The American Adolescent*

HAGEN   *On the Theory of Social Change: How Economic Growth Begins*

HSU (ed.)   *Psychological Anthropology: Approaches to Culture and Personality*

JACOBS   *Pattern in Cultural Anthropology*

JOHNSON   *Crime, Correction, and Society*   rev. ed.

MARIS   *Social Forces in Urban Suicide*

SALISBURY   *Religion in American Culture: A Sociological Interpretation*

SHOSTAK (ed.)   *Sociology in Action: Case Studies in Social Problems and Directed Social Change*

WILSON   *Sociology: Rules, Roles, and Relationships*

Social forces
in
urban suicide

RONALD W. MARIS, Ph.D.
Assistant Professor of Sociology
Dartmouth College

and

Fellow in Suicidology (1968–69)
Department of Psychiatry and Behavioral Sciences
The Johns Hopkins University School of Medicine

1969

THE DORSEY PRESS, Homewood, Illinois
IRWIN-DORSEY LIMITED, Georgetown, Ontario

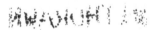

First Printing, March, 1969

Library of Congress Catalog Card No. 69–17167
Printed in the United States of America

To Barbara

Foreword

How it is that I, an antisocial psychologist, should have been asked to write the Foreword to this thoughtful and thoroughly sociological treatise, I leave to the reader's imagination to discern. Perhaps it was that Dr. Maris took pity on my then-lonely neologism, "suicidology," and sought to bring it and me in out of the cold, if only to the new-banked fires of a rekindled sociology of suicide. Therefore, it is clear that I write this not as an expert on what follows, but as one who is interested in all lines of suicidological inquiry and theoretical explication. And I am especially taken with Dr. Maris' appeal to, and use of, logic—implicitly through this volume and explicitly in his final chapter —as the *modus optimus* for pushing to new methodologies and to fresh and innovative insights.

There is a recent new look in the dual fields of suicide and suicide prevention. It is manifested by a number of events, including the establishing of a national center for the study of suicide prevention within the National Institute of Mental Health (in 1966); by the starting of a new journal, the *Bulletin of Suicidology* (in 1967); by the founding of a new multidisciplinary professional group, the American Association of Suicidology (in 1968); and by the publication, in the three-year period 1966 to 1969, of more than one handful of major books in this area— Friedman, Gibbs, Douglas, Resnik, Lifton, Leonard—and now, Maris' substantial volume on the social structure of suicide.

With Dr. Maris, I am one who believes in Whitehead's dictum that a "science that hesitates to forget its founders is lost." We have seen in this country how idolatry of Freud results in conceptual sclerosis, and we read how in the Soviet Union, undilutable fealty—a good trait overdone—to Pavlov, had, at one point, created a monolithic science, which is to say, no science at all. Dr. Maris ends up not destroying Durkheim (as I thought, reading the early pages, he might try to do), but rather supporting him (most appropriately) and honoring him. In analyzing data for Chicago, Maris, like Ruth Cavan before him, brings Durkheim to the heartland of America. Dr. Maris has, in his timely book, presented us not so much with an exegesis of Durkheim, as a transplanting and updating of Durkheim, all in a reasonable and essentially conservative genre. In this, Dr. Maris has demonstrated again the applicability of the sociological method for problems of human pathology and the viability of Durkheim's genius over the space of decades. As a clinically oriented suicidologist, I would hope that Dr. Maris could persuade one of his psychologist friends to write a comparable and companion volume —Psychological Forces in Urban Suicide—so that we might enjoy an equally thoughtful and provocative, empirically based essay on the theoretical modernization of Freud. What a pair of books that would make!

February, 1969   EDWIN S. SHNEIDMAN, Ph.D.
                             Chief, Center for Studies of
                                Suicide Prevention,
                             National Institute of Mental Health

Preface

This book was written because I believe that most human beings are simultaneously repulsed by, and fascinated with, suicide. The immorality, irrationality, and wastefulness of suicide repulses us. Suicide is immoral because it denies social responsibilities in an effort to resolve personal crises. In principle, self-destruction is an act which threatens the very possibility of society. Suicide is irrational because nothing is chosen over something. Finally, suicide is wasteful, since self-inflicted death is always premature and often totally unnecessary. Yet, at the same time, it is nothing short of fascinating that pain, failure, and unhappiness are avoidable through suicide. Philosophers David Hume and Bertrand Russell have argued that one of the most precious of human rights is the right to die. It follows that the fundamental reaction to suicide is ambivalence, an ambivalence of major proportions. Albert Camus has written that whether or not life is worth living is the only truly serious philosophical problem.

Furthermore, I am convinced that suicide is not just another social problem. Acts of deviance hang together, form a system, nest. Very close to the heart of one nest lies suicide. If we can understand the dynamics of suicide, an ultimate reaction to certain social-psychological and physical-chemical forces, then we will also know a great deal about related social problems such as drug addiction, alcoholism, homicide, assault, accidents, mental illness, marital discord, work problems, and prostitution. Thus, on a general level, *Social Forces in Urban Suicide* was worth doing because it speaks to the fundamental ambivalence with which most of us regard our lives, and, second, because knowledge of the causes of suicide may prove a key which unlocks the doors to several related social problems. It is important to realize that these two issues are considered elliptically, not directly, in the pages that follow. The reader must read between the lines to get answers to them.

There are, however, three quite explicit themes: the effect of social structure upon individual behavior, the development of the sociology of suicide as a science, and suicide prevention. In 1960–61 I spent almost all my time reading and thinking about Ludwig Wittgenstein's *Philosophical Investigations,* particularly the private language argument. Does the individual experiencing a toothache alone really understand the meaning of the words he applies to his sensations (after all, he alone has the pain) ? Was there not a time when Albert Einstein, and no one else, understood the language of the general theory of relativity? Is not the artist the only person who really understands his work? How can one possibly make public sense of a religious experience? To make a long story short, I concluded that the very concept of a private language was logically contradictory. As a spin-off of this *ad hoc* conclusion I was impressed that what most of us usually think of as creative acts, individual assertions of a free will, were for the most part in fact a product of social forces. To use George H. Mead's language, I began to believe that the self was primarily a "me," not an "I."

Then, in the fall of 1962, I read Emile Durkheim's *Elementary Forms of the Religious Life.* Here Durkheim made the startling claim that the categories of thought of the Australian aborigines originated from the social organization of their religious life. Finally, in 1963, I read Durkheim's *Suicide.* Again I was struck that suicide, seemingly among the most private of acts, was considered to be the product of a failure of social regulation and integration. As a result of these three stimuli I decided to do an original piece of research on suicide with an eye to determining as best I could the relationship between individual behavior and social forces. *Social Forces in Urban Suicide* presents the results of that research.

In this phase of the research my thinking was strongly influenced by my advisor and friend Louis Schneider, now at the University of Texas. From Schneider, in particular, I gained a fuller appreciation of the meaning of scholarship. I also wish to acknowledge the aid of Bernard Lazerwitz, who helped me operationalize vague ideas and generally tutored me in statistics and research methods. Daniel Glaser was instrumental in my being awarded a National Science Foundation Fellowship and later a National Science Foundation Research Grant (GS-793). My thanks go also to David J. Bordua, Joseph R. Gusfield, and J. E. Hulett, Jr., all of whom carefully went over an early version of the manuscript and made several helpful criticisms. Mr. and Mrs. Larry L. Tifft assisted in the data analysis.

A second theme in *Social Forces in Urban Suicide* is that of "putting Durkheim to bed." When one reads the history of science, one becomes aware of how little accumulation of knowledge there has been in sociology, of how much remains to be done. In the spirit reminiscent of Alfred N. Whitehead this book is dedicated to "forgetting" Durkheim in order that sociology of suicide as a science may not be lost.

It is more difficult to determine my intellectual indebtedness on the second theme. R. P. Stearn's course in the history of science at the University of Illinois was certainly seminal for me. Bennett M. Berger's lectures on sociological theory started me thinking about Whitehead's dictum and introduced me to Max Weber's essay "Science as a Vocation," Robert Beirstedt's "Sociology and Humane Learning," and C. Wright Mill's *The Sociological Imagination*. From Warren Breed I learned that Durkheim's theory of suicide left something to be desired. Although our conclusions were arrived at independently, both Breed and I have found inverse relationships between social status and suicide and have felt that Durkheim underestimated the importance of fatalistic suicide. My colleague at Dartmouth, James A. Davis, has taught me to "think small" and has contributed to my understanding of the role of research methods in the development of social science.

A third and final theme is that of suicide prevention. It is my hope that these research findings on 2,153 Chicago suicides will aid doctors, psychiatrists, public health officials, police, nurses, ministers, and other "gate keepers" to understand the sociology of the completed suicide. With increased understanding, increased control should follow. It is clear to me that previous efforts to prevent suicide have largely failed. Presumably this failure is in part the consequence of basing prevention programs primarily on knowledge about patients and attempted suicides. Too little is known about completed suicides. Hopefully, *Social Forces in Urban Suicide* will help to fill in this lacuna and discharge a small portion of my heavy debt to Edwin S. Shneidman, who has been teacher, counselor, and friend since 1965.

At various times in the last three years I have received editorial suggestions on the manuscript from Irwin Goffman, Daniel N. Gordon, Thomas F. Hoult, Derek L. Phillips, and Thomas P. Wilson. Edmund D. Meyers, Jr., patiently helped me with computer applications. F. D. Yoder, M.D., of the Illinois Department of Public Health; Mr. Leo Ozier of the Bureau of Statistics of the State of Illinois; and Andrew J. Toman, M.D., Cook County Coroner, provided access to the necessary research materials. Mrs. Frank R. Musgrove was accurate and diligent in typing the manuscript. Funds for the typing were granted by the Dartmouth Research Committee. I am especially grateful to Robin M. Williams, Jr., for his numerous and genuinely helpful editorial suggestions. Finally, I wish to thank my wife Barbara and two young daughters who have made many sacrifices in order that this research might be completed.

Baltimore, Maryland   RONALD W. MARIS
February, 1969

Table of contents

Henry and Short's *Suicide and Homicide*. Proposed inadequacies of the Henry and Short hypothesis. Data and methods. Development of the criticisms. Discussion. Conclusions.

Data, methods, and findings. The gold coast area. The skid row area. The suburban area. The Negro area. Conclusion.

Part III. Evaluation and conclusion

Socioeconomic status and the suicide rate. Sex and age. Errors of omission. Race. Alcoholism. Physical and mental health. The strain toward generalization. The relationship between society and individuals. Two methodological problems: *The ecological fallacy. Multivariate analysis.* Conclusions.

Reservations about a unicausal theory of suicide. Relationship between the concept of external constraint and a systematic theory of suicide. A modest systematic theory of suicide. Summary.

Appendixes

Bibliography

Index

PART I

The theoretical background: Durkheim's <u>Suicide</u> and its context

CHAPTER 1

Introduction

Every scientific "fulfillment" raises new "questions"; it *asks* to be "surpassed" and outdated. Whoever wishes to serve science has to resign himself to this fact. Scientific works certainly can last as "gratifications" because of their artistic quality, or they may remain important as a means of training. Yet they will be surpassed scientifically—let that be repeated—for it is our common fate and, more, our common goal.

MAX WEBER
"Science as a Vocation"

It is curious that after 70 years Emile Durkheim's *Suicide* is still *the* sociological treatise on suicide. Curious because as a rule a science which hesitates to forget its founders is lost.[1] One mark of a vital science is the obsolescence of its founders' generalizations resulting from the accumulation and refinement of knowledge.[2] Of course, we still have a lot to learn from Durkheim. But that is not at issue. We still have much to learn from Isaac Newton, but this has not kept Albert Einstein, Neils Bohr, or Werner Heisenberg from going beyond Newton. Can you imagine a modern chemist taking a seminar on Lavosier or Priestly? Some years ago George Lundberg wrote that sociology is perhaps the only science in which a leader of a century ago would not be greatly

---

[1] Alfred North Whitehead, *The Organisation of Thought* (London: Williams & Norgate, 1917).

[2] Robert K. Merton, *On Theoretical Sociology* (New York: The Free Press, 1967), pp. 1–38.

handicapped if he should suddenly come to life again.[3] Although Lundberg's dictum is less true of contemporary sociology, it is still uncomfortably close to the truth. In this book we intend to do what we can to make it untrue of the sociological study of suicide by building on, modifying, and extending Durkheim's *Suicide*.

What follows is not intended to be heretical or irreverent as an end in itself. Indeed much of the empirical investigation of suicide in Chicago supports Durkheim's general theory of suicide. Rather we make the assumption that reverence is not the appropriate response to scientific assertion. It is not appropriate because it is not fruitful. Knowledge accumulates through a dialectical process. Those of us who remember Hegel realize that novelty is often the joint product of theses and antitheses. Robert Bierstedt puts our position well in his article, "Sociology and Humane Learning":

> All I want to suggest is that successive rebuttal and reaffirmation may be as effective in the treatment of one kind of problem as successive approximation is in another and that in the give and take of argument and counterargument we have much to gain. In any event I advocate the theoretical bias on the ground that one of our most imperative needs in contemporary sociology is not more theory, in the sense in which theory has recently been developed, but more theses—that is, positions advanced, taken, defended, lost, and won again in the eternal dialectic that is the life of the mind.[4]

What is needed in the study of suicide, or any other study for that matter, are fresh approaches, new insights.[5]

Durkheim's theory of suicide should be subjected to the same scrutiny that has been so successful in updating and refining his theory of *anomie*. Marshall Clinard's book on *Anomie and Deviant Behavior* shows the conceptual progress which can be made when we apply our collective attention to a particular problem.[6]

---

[3]George A. Lundberg, *Foundations of Sociology* (New York: David McKay Co., Inc., 1964) , p. 157.

[4]Robert Bierstedt, "Sociology and Humane Learning," *American Sociological Review*, Vol. 25 (February, 1960) , p. 8.

[5]For example, see Jack D. Douglas' approach in *The Social Meanings of Suicide* (Princeton, N.J.: Princeton University Press, 1967) .

[6]Marshall B. Clinard (ed.) , *Anomie and Deviant Behavior* (New York: The Free Press, 1964) .

Such a thorough treatment of suicide remains to be done. There are few systematic tests of Durkheim's hypotheses.[7] Fewer still are the critiques of Durkheim's general theory of suicide.[8] We will undertake both of these tasks in the pages that follow.

There is no justification for a faint heart or lack of firm resolve in approaching Durkheim's theory of suicide. His theory, too, was a biased theory. Durkheim was almost fanatically dedicated to a very *ad hoc* conception of social facts—a dedication which blinded him to the causative implications of race, alcoholism, and depressive illness for suicide.[9] He took an ungenerous position on the role of psychological variables in the aetiology of suicide, which is perhaps understandable but not forgivable.[10] There is considerable evidence that Durkheim let conceptual dogma obscure his pioneering empirical observations. All of which means that a critical evaluation of Durkheim's theory of suicide is not only defensible but even imperative.

Why investigate suicide?

Of course, the first question to be asked is "Why study suicide at all?" It would be enough to say that it is interesting. Some people eat razor blades, train lions to jump through hoops, or pump jelly into breakfast rolls. But suicide is more than just interesting. Completed suicides are of sufficient magnitude to constitute a serious social problem. In 1966, about 25,000 Americans killed themselves, a rate a little over 10 per 100,000 population.[11] Many observers feel that this rate is conservative because of the likelihood of underestimation resulting from the stigma associated with being labeled a suicide. A figure closer to 40,000 would probably be more accurate. Even with the conservative estimate, the rate of suicidal deaths exceeds the death rates of

---

[7]Two exceptions are Jack P. Gibbs and Walter T. Martin, *Status Integration and Suicide* (Eugene, Ore.: University of Oregon Books, 1964); and Andrew Henry and James F. Short, Jr., *Suicide and Homicide* (New York: The Free Press, 1954).

[8]Douglas, *op. cit.*, is an exception. Cf. Jack P. Gibbs (ed.), *Suicide* (New York: Harper & Row, 1968), especially the paper by Walter T. Martin, pp. 74–95.

[9]Emile Durkheim, *The Rules of Sociological Method* (New York: The Free Press, 1962).

[10]Emile Durkheim, *Suicide* (New York: The Free Press, 1951), pp. 57–103.

[11]Edwin S. Shneidman and Philip Mandelkorn, *How to Prevent Suicide* (Public Affairs Pamphlet No. 406) (New York, 1967).

tuberculosis, leukemia, rheumatic fever, ulcers, and homicides (taken separately) and approaches that of motor vehicle accidents.

The number of attempted suicides per year is about eight times that of completed suicides.[12] By the time you have read this far someone in the United States will have attempted suicide. If you stop reading here and come back tomorrow to begin again, approximately 60 Americans will have suicided in the interim.[13] Thus, at least 225,000 people in the United States commit an explicit suicidal act in a year, some with fatal consequences. Unfortunately, the incidence of suicidal acts does not stop here. One of the major contributions of Karl Menninger is to demonstrate that suicide is simply the ultimate form of self-destruction which many of us engage in every day to some extent.[14] Alcoholism and many serious automobile accidents have to be regarded as "partial suicides" (penultimate suicides, if you will).[15] The list of self-destructive acts could be extended almost indefinitely. For example, accident-prone persons and cigarette smokers could be added without stretching credulity. What all this amounts to is that suicide is a serious social problem, one worthy of our attention.

Recently suicide has begun to come to the attention of public health officials largely through the efforts of the Los Angeles Suicide Prevention Center and the National Institute of Mental Health's Center for the Study of Suicide Prevention. In the United States in 1968 there were from 70 to 80 suicide prevention centers in operation with about double that number scheduled to open in 1969. In April of 1968 the American Association of Suicidology was founded. The United States Department of Health, Education and Welfare has begun to publish a journal

---

[12]Erwin Stengel, *Suicide and Attempted Suicide* (Great Britain: Penguin Books, C. Nicholls & Co., Ltd., 1964), p. 1.

[13]Shneidman and Mandelkorn, *op. cit.*, p. 1.

[14]Karl Menninger, *Man against Himself* (New York: Harcourt, Brace & World, Inc., 1938).

[15]Robert E. Litman and Norman Tabachinick, "Fatal One-Car Accidents," *The Psychoanalytic Quarterly*, Vol. 36 (1967), pp. 248–59; Joel M. Cantor, "Alcoholism as a Suicidal Equivalent" (unpublished manuscript; Veterans Administration Center, Los Angeles, Calif., 1967); and George E. Murphy and Eli Robins, "Social Factors in Suicide," *The Journal of the American Medical Association*, Vol. 199 (January, 1967), pp. 303–8.

entitled the *Bulletin of Suicidology.* Post-doctoral fellowships for training in suicidology are now offered by the Johns Hopkins University Medical School.

In spite of all this new prevention activity the suicide rate in the United States has remained at about 11 per 100,000 population since 1900. We are not preventing suicide in the United States.[16] During the first 68 years of the 20th century in the United States, life expectancy has increased from about 35 years to about 70 years. Death from scarlet fever, typhoid fever, measles, diphtheria, and whooping cough has been virtually eliminated. Death by tuberculosis and pneumonia is less than one fifth as frequent as it was in 1900. Death by nephritis has been halved. Generally, the crude death rate decreased from 17.2 per 1,000 population to 9.5.

Suicide is becoming an increasingly important factor in the death rate. In fact, if future generations want to lower the death rate, they are well advised to focus on the prevention of suicide and accidents. There is some evidence that not only has suicide failed to decrease over the years but that it has actually begun to increase, especially among the young, females, and nonwhites. For example, the Metropolitan Life Insurance Company has presented data which shows that in the last 10 years the suicide rate has increased 10 percent among white males, 33 percent among nonwhite males, 49 percent among white females, and 80 percent among nonwhite females.[17] These changes are primarily the result of higher rates among younger persons, ages 15–24.

One of the implicit functions of this book is to construct a sociological profile of the completed suicide in order that prevention agencies might direct their programs to the populations making the suicide rate high. Recent surveys of suicide prevention populations in Chicago, St. Louis, and Los Angeles make it painfully clear that completed sucides are not being reached. St.

---

[16]Ronald Maris, "Suicide: The Nondiminishing Rate," *Minnesota Medicine,* Vol. 51, No. 5 (May, 1968), pp. 723–28.

[17]Metropolitan Life Insurance Company, "International Rise in Suicide," *Statistical Bulletin,* Vol. 48 (March, 1967), pp. 4–7. On the other side we must report that the U.S. Department of Health, Education and Welfare claims that in 1966 the suicide rate *decreased* 2 percent over the 1965 rate (see "Final Mortality Statistics, 1966," *Monthly Vital Statistics Report,* Vol. 16, No. 12 [March, 1968]).

Louis found that less than 2 percent of the completed suicides had contacted their suicide prevention center.[18] In general, suicide prevention center populations tend to be called by low lethality types; i.e., those with low suicidal potential. It follows that if we are ever to have any prospect of lowering the suicide rate, more information is needed on the life-style of completed suicides vis-à-vis the life-style of attempted suicides. Then, and only then, can effective programs be developed. Hopefully some of the information needed can be garnered from the pages of this book.

The theoretical and methodological relevance of Durkheim's Suicide

There is at least one other justification for this book which has little or nothing to do with suicide as a social problem. The theoretical and empirical insights in *Suicide* are worthy of attention and development quite apart from their applications to the prevention of suicide. Durkheim's theoretical and methodological innovations could have been made using some other subject than suicide. Paradoxically there is a sense in which *Suicide* would have become a classic even if it had not been about suicide.[19] We take it that it is this sense of *Suicide* which Robert K. Merton alludes to when he calls Durkheim's work "one of the greatest pieces of sociological research ever conducted by anyone."[20] One of the primary reasons for writing or reading a book like this is to learn how to become a sociologist. What Durkheim said about Renouvier, we say about Durkheim:

> If you wish to mature your thought, give yourself over to the meticulous study of a great master; take a system apart, laying bare its innermost secrets. It is what I have done, and my teacher was [Durkheim]."[21]

Suicide can be seen as an indicator of the failure of morality,

---

[18]Richard D. Wetzel, "Suicide Prevention, Inc. of St. Louis," paper presented at the First Annual National Conference on Suicidology, Conrad Hilton Hotel, Chicago, Illinois, March 20, 1968. Cf. Carl I. Wold, "Who Calls the Suicide Prevention Center in Los Angeles?", paper presented at the First Annual National Conference on Suicidology, Chicago, Illinois, March 20, 1968.

[19]Jack P. Gibbs has written that his "impression is that had Durkheim investigated stuttering instead of suicide, sociologists would have followed his lead no less diligently," *Suicide,* p. 7.

[20]Merton, *op. cit.,* p. 63.

[21]Harry Alpert, *Emile Durkheim and His Sociology* (New York: Russell & Russell, Inc., 1961) , p. 26.

of a lack of social integration, of the malfunctioning of the constraining influence of society. In so doing we acknowledge that
several of the seminal concepts in sociology can be traced to or
illustrated in Durkheim's *Suicide*. For example, Durkheim gave
systematic statement, if not birth, to the conception of social
facts as external and constraining, to the notion of collective representations (including particularly the "collective conscience"),
to the empirical generalization concerning the inverse relationship
between social integration and the suicide rate, to the concept of
anomie, and to the role of occupational associations in social order,
just to mention a few concepts.

One measure of an academician is the number of citations his
work receives and the significant research he generates. On both
these indicators Durkheim emerges as a sociologist to be dealt
with. Without being exhaustive we can mention Talcott Parsons'
monumental work, *The Structure of Social Action*; Harry Alpert's
excellent commentary, *Emile Durkheim and His Sociology*; Andrew Henry and James Short, Jr.'s *Suicide and Homicide*; Jack
Gibbs and Walter Martin's *Status Integration and Suicide*; Warren Breed's study of suicide in New Orleans; and most recently,
Jack Douglas' *The Social Meanings of Suicide.*[22]

Durkheim's theory of society was what Merton has called a
"theory of the middle-range."[23] One of the salient attributes of
such a theory is that it integrates systematic empirical data with
generalizations. More specifically theories of the middle range—

1. Consist of assumptions from which specific hypotheses are logically
   derived and tested by empirical observation. (For example, from
   assumptions about *anomie* and deviance it can be hypothesized that
   deviance ensues on a large scale only when common success goals
   are internalized and opportunities to achieve these goals are blocked.
   James Short and Fred Strodtbeck have examined this hypothesis
   empirically in their book *Group Process and Gang Delinquency*.)
2. Can be consolidated into wider networks of theory. (In Chapter 2
   we will see how Durkheim did this with the study of suicide.)

---

[22]Talcott Parsons, *The Structure of Social Action* (New York: The Free Press,
1949), pp. 301–472; Alpert, *op. cit.*; Henry and Short, *op. cit.*; Gibbs and Martin,
op. cit.; Warren Breed, "Occupational Mobility and Suicide Among White Males,"
American Sociological Review, Vol. 28, No. 2 (April, 1963), pp. 179–88; and Douglas,
op. cit.

[23]Merton, *op. cit.*, pp. 38–72.

3. Transcend sheer description or empirical generalization. (Durkheim did not stop his analysis with the observation that the suicide rate varied inversely with social integration but went on to explain why this should be so. It was here that the concepts of social facts, the collective conscience, *anomie*, etc., came into play.)
4. Are logically interrelated sets of propositions. (For example, from the premises that "the more social change, the more *anomie*" and that "the more *anomie*, the higher the suicide rate," Durkheim concluded that "the more social change, the higher the suicide rate.")
5. Help to specify ignorance. (Durkheim's theory of suicide is a limited theory. It shows us what we have to understand *before* prevention of suicide becomes feasible.)

The sociological reader will notice that these attributes of the theory in *Suicide* are very modern. Indeed they form the cornerstone of contemporary systematic theory construction *à la* George Homans, Hans Zetterberg, Llewellyn Gross, *et al.*[24] It follows that the study of Durkheim and suicide may provide a valuable introduction to contemporary sociological theory.

Methodologically Durkheim pioneered in multivariate analysis.[25] For example, Durkheim argued that there was a direct relationship between Protestantism and the suicide rate. It is relatively easy to cast this claim in the form of a fourfold table. If Durkheim was correct, we would expect to get a distribution similar to the following (here we have distributed 200 hypothetical communities):

		Suicide Rate		
		Low	High	
	Protestants	10	90	100
Religion				
	Non-Protestants	85	15	100
		95	105	200

[24]George C. Homans, *Social Behavior: Its Elementary Forms* (New York: Harcourt, Brace & World, Inc., 1961), esp. chaps. 1–4; Hans L. Zetterberg, *On Theory and Verification in Sociology* (New York: The Bedminister Press, 1965); Llewellyn Gross (ed.), *Symposium on Sociological Theory* (Evanston, Ill.: Row, Peterson and Co., 1959); and Llewellyn Gross (ed.), *Sociological Theory: Inquiries and Paradigms* (New York: Harper & Row, 1967).

[25]Hanan C. Selvin, "Durkheim's Suicide: Further Thoughts on a Methodological Classic," in Robert A. Nisbet (ed.), *Emile Durkheim* (Englewood Cliffs, N.J.: Prentice-Hall, Inc., 1965), pp. 113–26.

Having established a zero-order association between religion and the suicide rate, Durkheim next introduces a test variable, such as nationality, to determine if the zero-order relationship is spurious. His model is:

Independent Variable→ Test Variable→ Dependent Variable
(religion)   (nationality)   (suicide rate)

If the major relationship is between nationality and the suicide rate (and not between religion and the suicide rate), then controlling for nationality should explain away the effect of religion on the suicide rate. On pages 152–56 of *Suicide,* Durkheim claims that religion is associated with the suicide rate regardless of nationality. Again using hypothetical data, Durkheim's argument can be illustrated in an eightfold table:

Nationality	Religion	Suicide Rate		
		Low	High	
Bavarian	Protestant	10	90	100
Bavarian	Non-Protestant	85	15	100
Prussian	Protestant	13	87	100
Prussian	Non-Protestant	88	12	100
		196	204	400

Note that the direct relationship between religion and the suicide rate holds when controlling for nationality. Using this *logic* of procedure Durkheim goes through a series of independent and test variables establishing zero-order associations between religion, marital status, education, social class, etc., and the suicide rate.

We conclude that because of its ground-breaking work in multivariate analysis in particular and its empirical support of theoretical claims in general, Durkheim's *Suicide* is a methodological classic as well as a theoretical classic. Thus, it is doubly deserving of our attention.

Overview of the book

This book is concerned primarily with the social structure and
social forces associated with completed suicide. Its focus is on
the social situation of the suicide at the time of his death. We
are in the process of doing the research for a second book on
"suicidal careers," i.e., a study of the social-psychological dynamics
of self-destruction. The present book has two admitted limitations:
First, it says too little about variations in social forces in suicide
over time (because we know too little). Second, it deals almost
exclusively with completed suicides. Given our data (death certificates) and the usual finite supplies of money, time, and energy,
little more could be expected. Still, we realize the need for expanding the research design. Most of our controls are intrasample
comparisons or are derived from secondary sources. In our second
book we will add samples of attempted suicides (especially patients
at the New Hampshire State Hospital and the Johns Hopkins
Hospital), suicide prevention center clients, and natural deaths.
Our present effort should be regarded as a first assault on suicidal
ignorance that attempts to nail down the sociological profile of
a large sample $(N = 2,153)$ of completed suicides committed in
a modern metropolis (Chicago).

We begin in Chapter 2 with a careful exposition of Durkheim's
general theory of society. One fundamental assumption is that
Durkheim's theory of suicide is a special case of his general theory
of society. Thus, it was crucial to get the general exposition right.
We were also aware that while it may be true that a science
which hesitates to forget its founders is lost, it is equally true
that he who forgets the past is condemned to repeat it. Careful
exposition is insurance against setting up straw men. Durkheim
was no fool, but his interpreters sometimes are.

A close reading of Durkheim reveals that he covered himself
well on most points. In fact, his comprehensiveness got him into
logical trouble.[26] For example, in Part III we will ask how *anomie*
and fatalism can both explain the suicide rate. The suicide rate
cannot vary indirectly *and* directly with social integration at the

---

[26]Cf. Walter T. Martin, "Theories of Variation in the Suicide Rate," in Gibbs
(ed.), *Suicide*, p. 79.

same time. Being a great man, Durkheim realized this and put his comments on fatalism in a footnote, apparently hoping that this rather obvious contradiction would be overlooked.[27]

Ludwig Wittgenstein once wrote that if description could be complete, there would be nothing left to explain. One implication of this statement is that the need for explanations is in part generated by incomplete or elliptical exposition. Though Chapter 2 is not a complete description of Durkheim's theory of society or suicide, it avoids a great many pseudo issues. Furthermore, Chapter 2 is significant because one of the stated intentions of this book is to acquaint the reader with Durkheim. From this exposition Durkheim's major hypotheses will be selected for empirical investigation in Part II.

In Chapter 3 there is more stage setting and context building. How novel was Durkheim's theory of suicide? What theories of suicide was he reacting to? Reference is made to the work of Anthony Giddens and Jack Douglas since both have attempted to answer these questions.[28] A brief exposition of the contributions of Halbwachs, Delmas, Esquirol, and de Fleury is presented.

In the remainder of Chapter 3 we ask what are some of the more important extensions of Durkheim's work. Mention must be made of Karl Menninger's development of the psychiatric theory of suicide (following Freud), of Andrew Henry and James Short, Jr.'s social-psychological theory of suicide utilizing the concepts of frustration and aggression, of Jack Gibbs and Walter Martin's formal theory of status integration, of Louis I. Dublin's descriptive statistics of suicide, and finally of Ruth S. Cavan's work on suicide in Chicago (as preparation for our study).[29]

Part II contains an empirical investigation of 2,153 completed suicides in Cook County, Illinois, designed to bring data to bear on Durkheim's hypotheses generated in Part I. Chapter 4 considers the sample design (which is quite rudimentary since we decided on a total sample of suicides from 1959–63) and methods em-

---

[27]It is not clear whether or not Durkheim *consciously* suppressed contradictory evidence. It is also possible that the relationship between social integration and the suicide rate is curvilinear.

[28]Anthony Giddens, "The Suicide Problem in French Sociology," *British Journal of Sociology*, Vol. 16 (March, 1965), pp. 3–18; and Douglas, *op. cit.*

[29]Louis I. Dublin, *Suicide: A Sociological and Statistical Study* (New York: The Ronald Press Co., 1963); and Ruth Shonle Cavan, *Suicide* (New York: Russell & Russell, Inc., 1965).

ployed. Although some tests of significance and measures of association are used, when appropriate, we decided the purposes of
this investigation could best be served by a simple cross-tabulation
of rates of suicide per 100,000 population. In order to lay bare
the idiosyncracies of our sample, we spend some time discussing
the social-demographic characteristics of Cook County and Chicago. Here a first statement of suicide rates is given by year. The
rates of suicide in Cook County are then contrasted with the
rates of other causes of death.

The basic procedure of Chapters 5 through 8 is to examine
Durkheim's hypotheses in light of our data and supporting secondary materials. Although our study is too fragmentary and
limited to provide the foundation for a full-blown systematic
theory of suicide, we do attempt to derive one sociological postulate which we argue should be a part of any systematic theory
of suicide that is formulated. It is our contention that all the
major research results from the Chicago study can be logically
deduced (given the theoretical and operational definitions posited
in Chapter 10 and some standard rules of inference) from the
following proposition:

The suicide rate varies inversely with external constraint. This
postulate is not terribly original (in fact it can be derived directly
from Durkheim), but we believe with George Homans that the
way to explain your research results is to borrow from somebody
else's work, if you can, or invent for yourself, if you must, a set
of general propositions from which the research findings can be
logically deduced.[30] Fortunately, we were able to "borrow" our
postulate from Durkheim. We do have some misgivings about
the explanatory adequacy of this postulate, which we list in
Chapter 9. Thus, while not perfect, the concept of external constraint comes closer to accounting for the findings of our suicide
research than any other single proposition (this probably means
that a *set* of postulates will be needed to explain adequately
variations in the suicide rate).

The study of suicide in Chicago is initiated in Chapter 5 with
a close look at the temporal aetiology of suicide (e.g., the causative
influences of climate or temperature on the suicide rate). This

---

[30]Homans, *op. cit.,* paraphrased from p. 53.

chapter is an exercise in the elimination of what Durkheim would have called "extra-social" variables (e.g., season, mental illness, alcoholism, race, imitation, etc.). Although it may be valuable or interesting to construct a schedule of suicide, we argue that there is something other than the time of day or the weather affecting the scheduling of the suicide rate (in fact it strikes us as ludicrous to argue the contrary). Chapter 5 examines seasonal, diurnal, and hourly variations in the suicide rate, controlling for age, sex, and the work situation of the suicide. Our general conclusion is that "failure of external constraint" (specifically occupational *anomie,* social isolation, marital discord) is a more adequate explanation of the temporal variation in suicide rates than is climate or weather. Temporal variations in suicide can be explained sociologically.

Chapter 6 deals with some core sociological variables—sex, age, race, and marital status—and their relationship to the suicide rate in Cook County. Generally Durkheim's hypotheses are confirmed. For example, age and the suicide rate are related directly; males are three times more likely to commit suicide than females. However, the relationship between age, being male, and the suicide rate tends to be linear (the older the male, the higher the suicide rate), whereas the relationship between age, being female, and the suicide rate tends to be curvilinear (the female suicide rate starts very low, peaks earlier than the male rate, levels off from about ages 35–85 and drops sharply after age 85). These patterns are explained by demonstrating that the older person is more socially and physically isolated, more unregulated, and has a greater wish to die than the younger person. Females have a lower suicide rate because they use less lethal methods to attempt suicide, a fact which in turn reflects their differential motivation to suicide. Females suicides are more likely to be abortive "cries for help."[31]

Controlling for marital status we find that the divorced, widowed, and the unmarried all have higher suicide rates than the married. Apparently children make the big difference in the suicide rate. The more children, the lower the suicide rate. Generally, the more "significant others," the lower the suicide rate.

---

[31]Norman L. Farberow and Edwin S. Shneidman (eds.), *The Cry for Help* (New York: McGraw-Hill Book Co., Inc., 1961).

In Chapter 8 we report a high negative association discovered between population per household and the suicide rate. Apparently one very good way to lower the suicide rate is simply to have someone living with the potential suicide.

Finally, white suicide rates are about twice as high as nonwhite suicide rates. This pattern is explained using the concepts of frustration and aggression. Put grossly, nonwhites perceive their frustration as coming from external sources. Thus, their aggression is more likely to be other-directed rather than self-directed compared with whites. There is one significant exception to the racial patterning of suicide. Young, nonwhite females have a higher suicide rate than young, white females. This anomaly is accounted for by the differential role of the young woman in the nonwhite family: she is much more likely to be the breadwinner than the young white woman. Again we find that the higher the external constraint, the lower the suicide rate. Nonwhite suicides and the suicide of young married persons are exceptions to this generalization. But their suicide rates are low, which is what the explanation predicts.

Both Henry and Short and Durkheim have contended that social status and the suicide rate are related directly. Our Chicago study reveals just the opposite. Suicide rates in Cook County are related negatively to occupation and to social class scores as determined by a United States Census Bureau index based on occupation, education, and income. Warren Breed reached essentially the same conclusion in his New Orleans interview study of suicides. Chapter 7 considers the theoretical implications of this striking inconsistency with Durkheim and Henry and Short.

Since lower status persons are more restrained vertically than upper status persons, some serious questions are raised about our major explanatory postulate concerning external restraint. The problem is resolved by noting that *horizontal* restraint is lower for the lower social classes and that status change may be a more important determinant of suicide than status position. Once we consider the social dynamics of suicide, it becomes theoretically feasible that external constraint "acts at a distance." That is, external constraint is not fully reflected in the social situation of the suicide at the time of death (which is all that death certificates measure), but it is a factor in determining the suicidal career. The social status of the suicide changes (becomes lower) in the years immediately preceding the act of suicide. This suggests that *anomie* and egoism may be the product of fatalism.

Chapter 8 explores the relationships between the suicide rates of community areas in Chicago and selected social characteristics of those areas. Thus, the chapter is not about individual suicides but rather deals with the association of two attributes of communities, their suicide rates and social characteristics. Such a study is worthwhile since Durkheim assumed that the suicide rate could be explained only in relation to other community characteristics (such as the relative constraint of the collective conscience).

The analysis of community characteristics indicates that areas with high suicide rates can be distinguished from areas with low suicide rates on selected social variables. More specifically, the high suicide rate areas have older populations, slightly higher educational and income levels, far more white-collar workers, fewer unemployed, far fewer Negroes, more foreign stock, a much lower population per household, more substandard housing, and slightly more residential mobility.

Among the high suicide rate areas, gold coast and skid row subtypes are discovered and their social attributes outlined. Suburban and Negro subtypes are found in the low suicide rate areas. The analysis of the social characteristics of the subareas suggests that gold coast suicides are predominantly anomic, skid row suicides predominantly egoistic, and suburban and Negro suicides predominantly fatalistic. It is also suggested that fatalistic suicide is rarer than either the anomic or egoistic varieties.

In the concluding part of this book (Part III) we offer a critical evaluation of Durkheim's theory of society based on our research results (Chapter 9) and a set of guidelines for the construction of a systematic theory of suicide (Chapter 10). Although Chapter 9 contests several propositions in Durkheim's theory of suicide, the empirical study of suicide in Chicago was in fact in the main supportive of Durkheim. Nevertheless, some criticisms must be made:

1. Socioeconomic status and the suicide rate have been found to vary inversely. We conclude that Durkheim probably underestimated the importance of fatalistic suicide.

2. Social position is probably not so important a determinant of the suicide rate as social change. Durkheim never extended his notion of *anomie* as the product of sudden social change to social mobility (especially to the relationship between downward mobility and the suicide rate).

3. The relationship of age and sex to the suicide rate is more important and more complicated than Durkheim thought it was. It appears that marital problems are particularly influential on female suicides and occupational problems on male suicides.

4. Durkheim made several errors of omission. Race, alcoholism, physical and mental health, and psychological variables in general all show significant relationships with the suicide rate. Durkheim's theory of suicide could be improved substantially (in predictive power) by adding a concept like Henry and Short's internal restraint to the notion of external restraint.

5. Conceptually, Durkheim had two basic weaknesses:
   a) His strain toward generalization tended to blind him to important details. Thus, his generalizations do not account for his data.
   b) He underestimated the role of individual factors in suicide. Just because data are differently distributed among individuals does not automatically make those data irrelevant to the suicide rate. Social facts are internal and liberating as well as external and constraining. Failure of external constraint is at best a necessary condition of suicide.

6. Methodologically, Durkheim's analysis—
   a) Committed the ecological fallacy. He tried to predict individual suicides solely on the basis of general social conditions like the collective conscience.
   b) Could be improved by a multivariate analysis of the correlates of the suicide rate using modern statistical techniques.

These six points should serve as the foci for new departures in suicide research. They could lead to a significant increment in our present knowledge of suicide.

The final chapter initiates consideration of what form a systematic theory of suicide might take. Fuller explication of the explanatory efficacy of the postulate of external constraint is given. Next we attempt to show how the postulate of external constraint might be related to a systematic theory of suicide. This involves defining and illustrating the concept of sociological theory. Having taken the first steps in the construction of a systematic theory of suicide we beg off on the grounds that our data constitute an inadequate basis for a formal theory of suicide. Until we have more social-psychological histories of suicidal careers, any attempt at a systematic theory of suicide would be premature.

So much for the preliminaries. The time has come to fulfill promises and to get on with the hard work of careful exposition, analysis, interpretation, and criticism. What has gone before should be thought of as a sketch. We shall now attempt to bring that sketch to life, to add color and give attention to detail. We begin in Chapter 2 with a description and interpretation of Durkheim's theory of suicide.

Suggestions for further reading

Bierstedt, Robert. "Sociology and Humane Learning," *American Sociological Review*, Vol. 25 (February, 1960), pp. 3–9. A good general introduction to the major theoretical perspective of our book. Note particularly Bierstedt's plea for cogent, biased theories.

Gibbs, Jack P. (ed.). *Suicide*. New York: Harper & Row, 1968. For readers wishing a recent overview of the past problems and present state of sociological, psychological, and psychoanalytical research on suicide. See particularly pp. 1–121.

Merton, Robert K. *On Theoretical Sociology*, chaps. i, ii. New York: The Free Press, 1967. Considers the development of sociological theory with special attention to the problem of novelty. How does one construct a theory which transcends previous theory? How does knowledge accumulate?

CHAPTER 2

Durkheim's theory of suicide

Selections from Durkheim's theory of society

A fundamental dialogue which runs throughout Durkheim's major works is that between society and individuals.[1] In fact, Talcott Parsons maintains that Durkheim's *basic* problem was in establishing the relationship of the individual to the social group.[2] Thus, the question naturally arises as to Durkheim's meaning of "individuals" and "society." Although Durkheim uses the word "individual" in many senses (at least five), usually he means "the isolated, organico-psychical individual . . . the individual as he would be were he to live in complete isolation."[3] Feral children might serve as an illustration of true individuals. Society, on the other hand, is *qualitatively* different from individuals.[4]

---

[1]Emile Durkheim was born in 1853 and died in 1917. His four most important works were, in the order of their publication: (1) *The Division of Labor in Society (De la Division du travail social)* in 1893 (New York: The Free Press, 1960); (2) *The Rules of Sociological Method (Les Régles de la méthode sociologique)* in 1895 (New York: The Free Press, 1962); (3) *Suicide (Le Suicide)* in 1897 (New York: The Free Press, 1963); and (4) *The Elementary Forms of the Religious Life (Les Formes élémentaires de la vie religieuse)* in 1912 (New York: Collier Books, 1961). A fifth book which we found extremely helpful was *Sociology and Philosophy (Sociologie et Philosophie)*, first published in 1924 (New York: The Free Press, 1953).

[2]Talcott Parsons, *The Structure of Social Action* (New York: The Free Press, 1949), p. 306.

[3]Harry Alpert, *Emil Durkheim and His Sociology* (New York: Russell & Russell, Inc., 1961), pp. 135–36.

[4]*Ibid.*, p. 157.

Society is not simply an aggregate of individuals. (It will be re-called that Max Weber carefully distinguishes social action from aggregate action.) When individuals *associate* with one another, the consequence of their associations (society) derives from individuals but also transcends them. Throughout Durkheim's writings we are told that social facts *have their own existence* independent of their individual manifestations; that society is a specific reality which has its own characteristics distinct from those of the individuals who comprise it; that collective tendencies exist external to the individual; and that there is a heterogeneity between individual states and social states.[5]

To use a homey example, individuals are to society what gears are to a clock. Imagine, if you will, taking the various individual gears, springs, screws, etc., that are parts of clocks and laying them, one by one, in a pile. Clearly the resultant heap is not a clock! Nor are societies simply the sum of their individuals. Clocks and societies have to be organized, their parts integrated in rather specific patterns, *before they can be* clocks or societies.

Thus, Durkheim chooses to call society a "collective represen-tation."[6] By far the most lucid statement of the concept of collec-tive representation occurs in *Sociology and Philosophy*.[7] In this essay Durkheim argues that individual representations (known to philosophers as "sense data") of the external world have an existence apart from *the thing* perceived, i.e., they persist in the absence of the object which gave rise to them. For example, one may remember distinctly the face of a friend whom he has not seen for years. To the degree that individual representations resemble one another, e.g., white snow and white paper, they *can* be associated to form the *concept* of whiteness. Concepts, such as whiteness, exist nowhere in the external world. Individual repre-sentations and concepts (associated individual representations) make up what Durkheim calls the "psychic" world.[8]

When Durkheim says that social facts are external and con-

---

[5]The above were taken from the following references, in the order given: Durk-heim, *Les Régles de la méthode sociologique*, pp. xiv–xix, 19, 57; Durkheim, *Le Suicide*, pp. 346–73; Durkheim, *De la Division du travail social*, p. 341; and Durkheim, *Sociologie et Philosophie*, pp. 45–48.

[6]Durkheim, *Suicide*, p. 317.

[7]Durkheim, *Sociology and Philosophy*, pp. 1–34.

[8]*Ibid.*, p. 24.

straining, a statement that will be examined in some detail below, he is affirming for the social world what is true for the psychic world. Collective representations derive from the association of thoughts and actions (especially thoughts) in the same way that concepts derive from the association of individual representations. As has been shown above, in this association a qualitative difference is affected.

If one can say that to a certain extent collective representations are exterior to individual minds, it means that they do not derive from them as such but from the association of minds, which is a very different thing. No doubt in the making of the whole each contributes his part, but private sentiments do not become social except by combination under the action of the *sui generis* forces developed in association. In such a combination, with the mutual alterations involved, *they become something else.* A chemical synthesis results which concentrates and unifies the synthesized elements and by that transforms them. Since this synthesis is the work of the whole, its sphere is the whole. The resultant surpasses the individual as the whole the part. It is *in* the whole as it is *by* the whole. In this sense it is exterior to the individuals. No doubt each individual contains a part, but the whole is found in no one. In order to understand it as it is one must take the aggregate in its totality into consideration. It is that which thinks, feels, wishes, even though it can neither wish, feel, nor act except through individual minds. We see here also how it is that society does not depend upon the nature of the individual personality.[9]

In the way that water is not simply the sum of two parts hydrogen and one part oxygen, society is something different from the sum of the individuals that make it up. No one individual has, or can have, all the same interests as the society in which he lives.

To be sure, it is likewise true that society has no other active forces than individuals; but individuals by combining form a psychical existence of a new species, which conseqently has its own manner of thinking and feeling. Of course the elementary qualities of which the social fact consists are present in germ in individual minds. But the social fact emerges from them only when they have been transformed by association since it is only then that it appears.[10]

Furthermore, society is not represented by the attributes of the *average* individual.

[9]*Ibid.,* pp. 25–26.
[10]Durkheim, *Suicide,* p. 310.

. . . it is a profound mistake to confuse the collective type of society, as is so often done, with the average type of its individual members. The morality of the average man is only of moderate intensity. He possesses only the most indispensable ethical principles to any decided degree, and even these are far from being as precise and authoritative as in the collective type, that is in society as a whole.[11]

It should be mentioned in passing that Durkheim did not believe that sociology was opposed to psychology per se but to individual psychology. Individual psychology was "the science of individual mentality." Whatever psychology was in the late 19th century France, Durkheim's concept of psychology is not appropriate for contemporary Western psychology. Indeed, "the *science of individual* mentality" is very nearly a logical contradiction since all science ultimately is alien to individuality. In any case, if we are careful to equate sociology with collective psychology then one aspect of the conflict between sociology and psychology, mentioned especially throughout *The Rules of Sociological Method,* dissolves.[12]

Some paragraphs ago a promise was made to elaborate on Durkheim's famous *dictum* that social facts are external and constraining. In several places throughout *Suicide* Durkheim alludes to the concept of externality:

Collective tendencies have an existence of their own; they are forces as real as cosmic forces, though of another sort; they likewise, *affect the individual from without,* though through other channels.

Not only have we admitted that the social states of mind are qualitatively different from individual ones, but that they are in a sense *exterior to individuals.*

It is not true that society is made up only of individuals; it also includes material things . . . . The social fact is sometimes so far materialized as to become *an element of the external world.*

Of course it is true that not all *social consciousness achieves such externalization and materialization.* Not all the aesthetic spirit of a nation is embodied in the work it inspires; not all the morality is formulated in clear precepts. The greater part is diffused . . . . And all these eddies, all these fluxes and refluxes occur without a single modification of the main legal and moral precepts, immobilized in their sacrosanct forms.

---

[11]*Ibid.,* p. 317.
[12]Durkheim, *Sociology and Philosophy,* p. 34 (fn.) .

We do not wish to be reproached further, after this explanation, with wishing to substitute the exterior for the interior in sociology. We start from the exterior because it alone is immediately given, but only to reach the interior.

Therefore, there is not one of all the single centers of consciousness who make up the great body of the nation, to whom the collective current is not almost wholly exterior, since each contains only a spark of it.[13]

Clearly, society is external to individuals in two senses. First, in the sense that social phenomena assume such material and visible embodiments as codes of law, religious dogma, monuments, buildings, rules of etiquette, books, statistical regularities, etc.[14] But these concrete embodiments of the social serve only as indicators of externality in its second and most essential connotation, viz, what Parsons calls its "epistemological sense." Legal codes and suicide statistics are only manifestations of social reality, not social reality itself. Social reality is an analytical abstraction.[15] The social element is psychic, not material. Or as stated in Chapter 9 the social is an ideal type, not a real type.[16]

One of the distinguishing attributes of Parsons' treatment of Durkheim in *The Structure of Social Action* is that the evolution of Durkheim's major concepts is stressed. Among the trends mentioned by Parsons is that of the increasing "psychicality" of the social in Durkheim's later works. For example, Parsons notices that externality became less and less "external" (in the first sense of "external," not the second).[17] For example, on page 389 of *The Elementary Forms of the Religious Life,* one of the latest of his major works, Durkheim states that "society exists and lives only in and through individuals." Parsons calls our attention to an even more convincing passage in which Durkheim concludes that society "consists exclusively of ideas and sentiments."[18]

Having touched on the nature of the externality of society, the constraining or coercive aspect of society remains to be discussed. Harry Alpert, in the best general commentary on Durk-

---

[13]Durkheim, *Suicide.* The preceding six quotations are found in the following six locations: pp. 309, 313, 313, 315, 315 (fn.) , 316.

[14]Alpert, *op. cit.,* p. 161.

[15]Parsons, *op. cit.,* pp. 350 (fn.) , 357.

[16]*Ibid.,* pp. 358, 388. Cf. P. Sorokin, *Contemporary Sociological Theories* (New York: Harper & Bros., 1928) , p. 464.

[17]Parsons, *op. cit.,* pp. 388, 442.

[18]Durkheim, *Les Formes élémentaires de la vie religieuse,* p. 521.

heim and his sociology which we have discovered,[19] writes that:

> Society as organization is not only unity, but also regulation [on page 192 Alpert contends that *constrainte* is best translated as "regulation," not as "constraint," because "constraint" implies an evaluative connotation that Durkheim did not intend; we agree]. It is a system of order, a regime of discipline, and hence, in its regulatory aspect involves both a complex of rules by which order is maintained and a complex of forces and mechanisms whereby these rules are enforced. Social life is *nomic* life (if we may use this adjective in its primitive connotation of "pertaining to rules of laws") and society is a state of *nomia*. The antithesis of, and the alternative to social living is, as political philosophers such as Hobbes so clearly understood, lawlessness, the "state of nature" characterized by the *bellum omnium contra omnes*. Who speaks of society, then, must speak of control. Social order is disciplinary and restraining.[20]

In much the same way that individuals have a superego, society has a collective conscience. In fact, Durkheim contends that the conscience of the individual is only the internalized collective conscience of the individual's group. The collective conscience is the totality of beliefs and sentiments common to citizens of the same society. It is the totality of social likenesses.[21]

The constraint of the collective conscience is manifested especially in repressive law.[22] Following Parsons, we claim that repressive law is an index of the collective conscience, whereas restitutive law is an index of social differentiation.[23] Repressive law, which is most common in more primitive societies, is characterized by a relatively inflexible meting out of punishment. Criminal acts offend society (i.e., tend to compromise society's controlling function) and in so doing threaten its existence.[24] Under repressive law there tends to be an isomorphism between the seriousness of the crime and the sanction it draws.[25] That is to say, repressive law is like the law of the Torah; i.e., it calls for "an eye for an eye and a tooth for a tooth." It is inflexible in the sense that

---

[19]Cf. Robert Nisbet (ed.), Émile Durkheim (Englewood Cliffs, N.J.: Prentice-Hall, Inc., 1965).

[20]Alpert, *op. cit.,* pp. 190 ff.

[21]Durkheim, *The Division of Labor in Society,* pp. 79, 80–81 (fn.), 396 (fn.). Cf. Alpert, *op. cit.,* p. 180.

[22]*Ibid.*

[23]Parsons, *op. cit.,* p. 318.

[24]Durkheim, *The Division of Labor in Society,* p. 99.

[25]Punishment sometimes *exceeds* the seriousness of the crime.

each criminal offense has its just recompense which no arbitration can mitigate. Repressive law is an affair of the heart (i.e., passionate), not of the mind.[26] It could be said that repressive law reflects moral indignation, an offense to the collective conscience, and, thus, is marked by passion; in contrast, restitutive law reflects the perspective of the Kantian ethic, and, thus, is marked by a rational response designed to maintain or to restore the social equilibrium originally engendered by increasing social density and the division of labor.

Repressive law presumes a fundamental strain between the desires of individuals and the dictates of the collective conscience. The tensions between private desire and common interest tend to be extreme and highly visible. Durkheim finds it appropriate to designate the cohesion deriving from repressive law as "mechanical." Social integration is mechanical because society is made up of groups of loosely federated individuals held together not by common interest or structural interdependency but by a superimposed moral code to which no one individual subscribes in its entirety.[27]

Restitutive law, law "without punishment," increases as the division of labor in society increases.[28] As men fulfill more determinate domestic, economic, administrative, or governmental functions, they become more dependent upon one another. Whereas mechanical solidarity presumes a relative homogenization of the population, organic solidarity presumes an increasing human differentiation induced by rising social density.

"Solidarité" refers to a type of relation between the whole and its parts. Since "solidarity" has ethical connotations, perhaps the best translation of *"solidarité"* would be "cohesion." Durkheim conceives of society as an integer; i.e., as a whole.[29] An "integrated" social situation, one in which individuals are strongly attached by a sense of moral obligation or structural interdependency (or both) to society's governing body of rules, will tend

---

[26]Durkheim, *The Division of Labor in Society*, p. 112.

[27]Alpert, *op. cit.*, p. 176: " . . . the test of social integration is the capability of a group to function as a whole."

[28]The reader should be reminded that both restitutive and repressive law are ideal types. No actual legal system is entirely restitutive or repressive; no legal system is devoid of all punishment.

[29]Alpert, *op. cit.*, pp. 176, 178.

to be characterized by strong sanctions for obedience to them (this is especially true of mechanical solidarity).[30]

Restitutive laws pertain predominantly to relations between individuals, not between individuals and society as in repressive law.[31] Organic solidarity, as opposed to mechanical solidarity, suggests the metaphor of the living being.[32] Seen as a living being, society is composed of various functionally interdependent groups and individuals. From this situation, caused by the functional necessity of adjusting to population growth, a structurally induced cooperation ensues in the form of a rising division of labor.[33]

Whereas repressive law requires punishment for deviation from the law, restitutive law is more an affair of the mind, requiring a restoration of the conditions existing prior to the criminal violation. Negative organic solidarity is concerned with negative or "abstentive" relations deriving from real and personal rights. It is called "negative" because it does not lead individuals to move toward common ends but merely requires maintenance of order. "Real rights" refer to the differential access of persons to *things,* while "personal rights" refer to the law which delineates what people cannot do without violating the rights of others, i.e., it deals with the restrictions upon interpersonal relationships. Positive organic solidarity states relations of cooperation originating from functional interdependence.[34]

Everything which is a source of solidarity is moral.[35] In fact, the social is nothing other than the moral.[36] Thus, morality is the source of constraint, of regulation, of obligation. The heart of Durkheim's discussion of morality occurs in the celebrated passage on *anomie* in *Suicide*[37] and in a short, but extremely rich, essay entitled "The Determination of Moral Facts."[38]

Unlike animals, men have the dubious ability to have "felt

---

[30]Parsons, *op. cit.,* p. 403.

[31]Durkheim, *The Division of Labor in Society,* p. 115. Cf. Alpert, *op. cit.,* p. 181.

[32]Parsons, *op. cit.,* p. 311.

[33]Durkheim, *The Division of Labor in Society, passim.*

[34]*Ibid.,* pp. 112–13, 116.

[35]The reader should be aware that Parsons takes issue with the equivocation of the social and the moral (pp. 390–93). He holds that Durkeim's *argumentum per eliminationem* causes him mistakenly to identify the moral with the social.

[36]Durkheim, *Suicide,* pp. 252, 309.

[37]*Ibid.,* pp. 246–54.

[38]Durkheim, *Sociology and Philosophy,* pp. 35–62.

needs" in addition to "genuine" (i.e., physical) needs. For example, while an animal is concerned simply with satisfying its hunger pangs, a man may develop compulsive eating habits based on nonorganic grounds. Chronic overeating can be looked at as a kind of *anomie* of the will. Without externally imposed restraint to his passions, Durkheim claims that man's desires would know no limit.[39] He would be in a state of *anomie* or deregulation.

Unlimited desire logically entails dissatisfaction since no realizable goal is being pursued. Furthermore, though Durkheim does not emphasize this point, unlimited desire also entails anarchy when coupled with a pervasive lack of external regulation. Since man in his nonsocial condition has an insatiable appetite —a morbid desire for the infinite which leads to unhappiness—in order to achieve happiness or satisfaction he must be regulated from without. The only force outside of the individual which is capable of such regulation is society. Durkheim concludes that the characteristic attribute of man is that the bond he accepts is not physical but moral; i.e., social.[40]

Moral facts are characterized by obligation and desirability.[41] To be moral is to observe a collection of rules of conduct conducive to the common good. As Immanuel Kant put it in his categorical imperative, we are to act so that we could also will that our maxim (a "maxim" is the subjective principle of volition; the objective principle is the practical law) should become a universal law. Durkheim goes beyond Kant in insisting that morality cannot merely be imposed upon a recalcitrant mankind; we must *desire* to be regulated.[42]

Thus, morality results from the subordination of individual interests to general interests.[43] Furthermore, it is the existence of morality deriving from the social order that makes individual interests possible.[44] Without moral rules there could be no society

---

[39]Durkheim, *Suicide,* pp. 249 ff.

[40]*Ibid.,* p. 252.

[41]Durkheim, *Sociology and Philosophy,* pp. 35–36.

[42]*Ibid.,* pp. 44–45.

[43]*Ibid.,* pp. 37–40.

[44]Durkheim, *The Division of Labor in Society,* pp. 13–14. "But once the group is formed, a moral life appears naturally carrying the mark of the particular conditions in which it has developed. For it is impossible for men to live together, associating in industry, without acquiring a sentiment of the whole formed by their union,

and there could be only the most brutish of individual existence.

The role of the division of labor in maintaining morality is explained in what Durkheim calls "the categorical imperative of the moral conscience," viz, to make yourself fulfill a determinate function.[45] Fulfilling a determinate function promotes organic solidarity which in turn maintains the socio-moral order.

It is interesting to note that Durkheim saw in the occupational group the single most important mechanism for promoting social solidarity.[46] In the preface to the second edition of *The Division of Labor,* Durkheim states his conclusions on the regulation of *anomie* put forth initially in the final pages of *Suicide,* viz, that "human passions stop only before a moral power that they respect." He then claims that the economic, the administrative, the military, the religious, and the familial institutions have lost much of their power to regulate human passions. Durkheim concludes that the societal function of regulation can best be exercised by occupational groups since there is a "multitude of individuals whose lives are passed almost entirely in the industrial and commercial world."[47] The essence of Durkheim's argument is contained in the following passage:

> What we especially see in the occupational group is a moral power capable of containing individual egos, of maintaining a spirited sentiment of common solidarity in the consciousness of all the workers, of preventing the law of the strongest from being brutally applied to industrial and commercial regulations (and, presumably, to noncommercial relations).[48]

Finally, before leaving this general level and advancing to an exposition of Durkheim's theory of suicide, it should be mentioned that although Durkheim disclaims the effective regulatory power of contemporary religion, nonetheless, he retains the view that religion is the womb of the moral life since God is seen as

---

without attaching themselves to that whole, preoccupying themselves with its interests, and taking account of it in their conduct . . . the subordination of particular interests to the general interest is, indeed, the source of all moral activity." Cf. Parsons, *op. cit.,* p. 334: "Individuality is a product of the collective conscience."

[45]*Ibid.,* p. 43.
[46]*Ibid.,* entire preface to 2d ed. Cf. Durkheim, *Suicide,* pp. 296–322.
[47]*Ibid.,* pp. 3, 4, 16–18.
[48]*Ibid.,* p. 10.

the symbol for society[49] and since religion gave rise to society.[50] As we will see below, orthodox religion apparently has some prophylactic effect on the suicide rate.

Durkheim's theory of suicide

It should be noted that Durkheim is not attempting to account for the aetiology of individual suicides, though he often does so inadvertently.[51] For example, Durkheim admits that imitation of other suicides does account for some individual suicides, but he claims that it does not account for the social suicide rate.[52] Consistent with his interpretation of sociology as collective psychology, Durkheim attempts to explain only the social suicide *rate,* usually the number of suicides per 100,000 population, not controlling for age or sex.[53] In itself the social suicide rate (i.e., the rates used most often by Durkheim) is a crude indicator of suicide since its parameter is the population of a particular society *as a whole.* Durkheim often ignores this important consideration, though, of course, he is not ignorant of the need for population controls in order to reflect true rates. His general conclusion is that the social suicide rate of any population is explicable only in reference to the consequences of varying degrees of social cohesion, not the attributes of the individuals who make up the population.

Sometimes men who kill themselves have had family sorrow or disappointments to their pride, sometimes they have had to suffer poverty, and sickness, at others they have had some moral fault with which they reproach themselves, etc. But we have seen that these individual peculiarities could not explain the social suicide rate; for the latter varies in considerable proportions, whereas the different combinations of circumstances which constitute the immediate antecedents of individual cases of suicide retain approximately the same frequency. They are therefore not the determining causes of the act which they precede.[54]

[49]Durkheim, *Sociology and Philosophy,* p. 52.

[50]Durkheim, *Elementary Forms of the Religious Life,* p. 466: ". . . nearly all the great social institutions have been born in religion . . . it is obviously necessary that the religious life be the eminent form and, as it were, the concentrated expression of the whole of the collective life."

[51]Anthony Giddens, "The Suicide Problem in French Sociology," *British Journal of Sociology,* Vol. 16 (March, 1965) , see p. 6 for what Durkheim was arguing against.

[52]Durkheim, *Suicide,* p. 129.

[53]*Ibid.,* pp. 48, 147.

[54]*Ibid.,* p. 297. Cf. pp. 213-14.

Durkheim's methodology for arriving at causal factors determining the suicide rate consists of: (1) eliminating the extrasocial factors from causative contention; and (2) proceeding via an inductive schema of generalizations of increasing scope to establish an all-encompassing empirical generalization from which the more particularistic generalizations can be deduced. The rule of thumb for increasing generalization is to discover the common denominator of the more particularistic generalizations.

For example, based on statistics (i.e., frequency counts usually converted to crude rates) from Belgium, Germany (especially Berlin, Wein, and Hamburg), the United States, Italy, and France (especially Paris), Durkheim concludes that various extrasocial factors—such as insanity, alcoholism, race, heredity, climate, season, and imitation—show no "significant" association with the social suicide rate.[55] A typical "measure of association" (we should say of the *lack* of association) would be that between the suicide rate and heredity. Durkheim argues that if heredity determined the suicide rate then suicide should affect males and females equally.[56] But it does not, since statistics show that suicide is predominantly a male phenomenon. Thus, heredity is not associated significantly with the suicide rate.

Having disposed of the extrasocial factors to his satisfaction, Durkheim proceeds to compound lower level generalizations of the "greater than," or ordinal scale, variety from his statistics. Some of the more important first-level generalizations[57] are listed below, roughly in the order of their appearance in *Suicide*. (For the sake of brevity the symbol $>$ is employed to mean "tend to be more likely to commit suicide than.")

h1. City dwellers $>$ rural dwellers.
h2. The sane $>$ the insane.
h3. Adults $>$ children.
h4. Older adults $>$ younger adults.

---

[55]*Ibid.*, pp. 75, 77, 86, 99, 105, 114, 129.

[56]*Ibid.*, p. 99.

[57]We are contending that Durkheim's inductive schemata can be viewed most fruitfully as having three levels of increasing generalization. We have designated arbitrarily first-level generalizations as "h_x," second-level generalizations as "H_x," and the one third-level generalization as "H." As one goes from h_x to H, there are fewer generalizations and, conversely, as one goes from H to h_x there are an increasing number of generalizations.

    h5. In March through August people > in September through February.

    h6. In daytime people > in the night.

    h7. Protestants > Catholics > Jews.

    h8. Majority groups > minority groups.

    h9. Upper social classes > lower social classes.

    h10. The learned > the unlearned.

    h11. Males > females.

    h12. The unmarried > the married.

    h13. The married without children > the married with children.

    h14. Those in smaller families > those in larger families.

    h15. Bachelors > widows.

    h16. Those living in time of peace > those living in time of war.

    h17. Soldiers > civilians.

    h18. Elite troops > nonelite troops.

    h19. Those whose society is experiencing an economic crisis > those whose society is not experiencing an economic crisis.

    h20. Those living in a period of rapid social change > those living in a period of slow social change.

    h21. The rich > the poor.

    h22. The morally undisciplined > the morally disciplined.

    h23. Divorcees > nondivorcees.[58]

The enumeration of level-one hypotheses complete, Durkheim turns his attention to synthesizing some higher level generalizations (the second level) from which all previous hypotheses can be deduced. For example, in relation to the first-level hypotheses discussed in Chapters Two and Three of *Suicide*,[59] Durkheim asserts these three second-level generalizations:

    H1. Suicide varies inversely with the degree of integration of religious society.

    H2. Suicide varies inversely with the degree of integration of domestic society.

    H3. Suicide varies inversely with the degree of integration of political society.[60]

---

[58]Durkheim, *Suicide*. The preceding generalizations are found as follows: h1, pp. 70, 253; h2, p. 75; h3, p. 100; h4, p. 101; h5, p. 107; h6, p. 116; h7, Chapter Two; h8, p. 156; h9, p. 165; h10, p. 168; h11, p. 198; h14, p. 199; h15, p. 197; h16, p. 205; h17, pp. 228 ff.; h18, p. 237; h19, p. 241; h20, p. 244; h21, p. 245; h22, p. 256; and h23, p. 261.

[59]*Ibid.*, pp. 152–216. N.B., a hypothesis is a kind of generalization. However, the two terms are used above as if they were roughly equivalent in meaning.

[60]*Ibid.*, p. 208.

Finally, on the third level, Durkheim posits a grand hypothesis intended to subsume all previously mentioned hypotheses. This hypothesis (which is also a grand empirical generalization if we can assume that the previous hypotheses were true and that the determination of the common denominator of them was accurate) states that:

> H. Suicide varies inversely with the degree of integration of the social groups of which the individual forms a part.[61]

In addition to the methodology of determining the causation of suicide, Durkheim devotes a major portion of Book Two of *Suicide,* "Social Causes and Social Types," to constructing an exhaustive typology of suicide.[62] The result of this effort is the claim that all suicides can be fitted into one of four categories or into one of the six permutations of these four categories.[63] Admittedly the categories are primarily for analytical purposes; actual cases of suicide can and in most cases do manifest attributes of more than one category. Since Durkheim's definitions of the four types of suicide are not mutually exclusive, it will be impossible to give pure examples of his types of suicide.

The four basic categories of suicide are the egoistic, the altruistic, the anomic, and the fatalistic. Egoism and altruism are polar types, as are *anomie* and fatalism. Egoistic suicide results from excessive individuation or lack of social integration of the groups of which the individual forms a part. Apathy is the trademark of those who eventually commit egoistic suicide. Protestants are much more prone to commit egoistic suicide than Jews since the Protestant community is less socially integrated than the Jewish community. Egoistic suicide has two subtypes, viz, melancholic languor (in which the potential suicide is depressed and inactive) and epicureanism (in which the apathy manifests itself as a kind of disillusioned matter-of-factness).

Case materials in Chapter 6 provide an illustration of an egoistic suicide (melancholic languor). During the coroner's inquest it

---

[61]*Ibid.,* p. 209.

[62]Giddens, *op. cit.,* p. 5. Giddens contends that Durkheim's types of suicide are really types of social structure producing high rates of suicide. We would say that they are both.

[63]Durkheim, *Suicide,* p. 276. Durkheim denies that fatalism is very common. Because of this denial, Durkheim considers only three mixed types of suicide, viz, ego-anomic, anomic-altruistic, and ego-altruistic (cf. p. 293).

was revealed that T. D. (male, 51 years old, white, never married): ". . . had been telling everybody that he didn't feel good, and, he told various people that he didn't feel like staying around, and he was *tired of living* [italics ours], and so forth."

In another case of egoistic (epicurean) suicide, reported in an Urbana, Illinois, newspaper, an associate professor of engineering at a Mid-Western state university shot himself, leaving this note: "As you know I have a very low opinion of the merits of this world . . . the one thing I have against this world above all else is that it is exceedingly boring."

Altruistic suicide, on the other hand, is characterized by an insufficient individuation. Instead of apathy, we find energy and activity. Whereas the egoistic suicide no longer finds a basis for existence within this life (no reason to live), the altruistic suicide typically finds the basis for existence beyond this life. For example, when a classical Hindu saw his children's children born, it was time for him to retire from the pursuits of this world and to undertake yoga practice in an attempt to achieve *moksha*, or union with Brahman. This classical Eastern asceticism can serve as a paradigm for the altruistic type of suicide. Altruistic suicide (or "heroic suicide" as it sometimes is called) is characteristic of soldiers.[64] Altruistic suicide has three secondary varieties, viz, obligatory, optional, and acute. The first was common among the North American Indians, Polynesians, and lower societies in general.[65] Its primary attribute was duty. A good example of obligatory suicide would be that of the oriental custom known as "suttee" in which the Indian wife was "obligated" to kill herself after her husband died (theoretically the widow chose suicide, but she was expected to make that choice).

The second and third types of altruistic suicide derive from the first. Optional altruistic suicide is marked by a mystical enthusiasm (e.g., that of early Christian martyrs),[66] while in acute altruistic suicide renunciation itself is considered praiseworthy. An example of the latter could be drawn from the asceticism of Theravada Buddhism.[67]

---

[64]*Ibid.*, pp. 228 ff.

[65]*Ibid.*, pp. 222 ff.

[66]*Ibid.*, pp. 224–25.

[67]*Ibid.*, pp. 224–25; and Parsons, *op. cit.*, p. 330. Parsons quite appropriately notices that altruistic suicide and mechanical solidarity are on the same plane because they share the common denominator of obligation.

In both egoistic and altruistic suicide, society influences the act of suicide by virtue of its external and constraining power. In the case of the former, the lack of social integration spawns men who are more or less marginal to society, often in spite of their will to be involved. In the case of the latter, society creates (via the directives of its culture) marginal men who willingly separate themselves from social regulation. (One should remember, however, that the socialization process has an irreducible element of coercion.) One might say that anomic and fatalistic suicide are more the products of a malfunctioning of the normative component of society, whereas egoistic and altruistic suicide result predominantly from a disruption of the structural component of society.[68] This is not to deny that both normative and, especially, structural components are present in all four types of suicide.

Anomic suicide usually results from a temporary but abrupt alteration in the norms of a society. *Anomie* literally means "deregulation" or "normlessness." Durkheim mentions four indices of anomic suicides. First, abrupt social changes seem to be associated with anomic suicide. For example, a major social cataclysm like the Great Depression in the United States in the 1930's is accompanied usually by an increase in the (anomic) suicide rate. The correlation of the suicide rate and economic cycles is discussed at length in Chapters 3 and 7 in reference to Henry and Short's book, *Suicide and Homicide*. Rapid growth in glory or power also seems to be connected with an increased suicide rate. Extreme caution must be exercised in applying this indicator of suicide since not all social changes are in a direct relationship with the suicide rate. A notable exception is international war, in which suicide and social change are related inversely.[69]

Second, on a more general plane, Durkheim suggests that *any* disturbances in the collective order can lead to an increased suicide rate.[70] Under normal conditions social and personal equilibrium prevail, i.e., means are sufficiently proportioned to needs

---

[68]Durkheim fails to make a distinction between society and culture, using "society" to refer both to the structural and the normative components of society. Cf. Anthony Giddens, "A Typology of Suicide," *European Journal of Sociology*, Vol. 7, No. 2 (1966), pp. 276–95.

[69]Louis Dublin, *Suicide: A Sociological and Statistical Study* (New York: The Ronald Press Co., 1963), pp. 63 ff.

[70]Durkheim, *Suicide*, p. 246.

(felt or actual). With *anomie* the relationship between means and ends, between effort and attainment, is upset. The result is confusion, the loss of orientation.[71] Crises often reduce means without a corresponding reduction in needs. With the constraining force of society temporarily disrupted, individuals are thrown back upon themselves and are often unable to regain personal equilibrium.

The man who always looks to the future for satisfaction will have no past (from his perspective). But a past is necessary to endure present crises. Interruptions which prevent pursuit of future goals, especially when permanent, can leave a man in a desperate situation in which he has accomplished nothing—according to *his* definition of the situation. Such a man is unsatisfied and, furthermore, has no prospects of ever reaching his original goals. On the contrary, the man who is able to value limited achievements has some feeling of accomplishment, and thus of satisfaction, when other future needs or goals become unrealizable.

Ruth S. Cavan's case of Marion Blake (pages 198–222) illustrates both the disruption of the means-ends relationship and the resultant dissatisfaction. Cavan writes of this young woman:

> Another characteristic which explains much of her conduct is her lack of conventional moral standards. Stealing of small articles, the abortion, promiscuous relations on her part, even killing another person aroused in her no repulsion or disapproval. Everything was interpreted in relation to her own interests and needs, rather than in relation to the moral norms of the American community where she lived.[72]

Marion displays what Durkheim called "the morbid desire for the infinite," irritation, disgust, and unregulated emotion:

> There is nothing left to me but to read, draw, or strum on the piano of evenings. I am sad and lonely . . . . I am starving. Oh, God, I am ready for the last, last chance. I have taken two already, and they are not right. Life was the first chance, marriage the second, and now I am ready for death, the last chance. It cannot be any worse than it is here.[73]

Third, liberal occupations should serve as an index of anomic suicide.[74] For example, managers of industry should have higher

---

[71]Parsons, *op. cit.*, p. 335.
[72]Ruth Shonle Cavan, *Suicide* (New York: Russell & Russell, Inc., 1965), p. 219.
[73]*Ibid.*, p. 205.
[74]Durkheim, *Suicide*, p. 257.

suicide rates than their employees. In fact, modern, urban industrial societies should have higher suicide rates than traditional, agrarian societies since urban industrial societies display more normlessness than agrarian societies.

Fourth, divorce is a kind of *anomie* (disruption of a domestic means-ends relationship), and thus Durkheim argues that divorced people, especially the ex-husbands, should have higher rates of anomic suicide than the nondivorced.[75]

Anomic suicide can be either general or particular. General anomic suicides are noted for their violent recriminations against life in general, whereas particular anomic suicides often manifest violent recriminations against one specific person in addition to or other than themselves; e.g., in a homicide-suicide (as in the case of Marion Blake, who killed her lover and herself).

Fatalistic suicide, which Durkheim mentions only in a footnote,[76] is a reaction to hyperregulation. When constraint suddenly becomes intense and overpowering (i.e., when someone is sold into slavery or is married very young), suicide occasionally is resorted to, presumably as an escape from unbearable restrictions. Durkheim mentions no subtypes of fatalistic suicide.

From a second diary of a suicide, Cavan cites the case of "a youth who was prematurely tired."[77] This case provides examples of behavior and attitudes characteristic of three of the four types of suicide. Anomic, fatalistic, and egoistic behavior and attitudes such as those in the following excerpts appear frequently in this young man's diary:

Day by day the work at the office becomes more of a burden, a yoke. Come 11:15 or time for lunch, and I feel as if I were leaving a prison. Strive as I may to concentrate my mind on routine work, I look forward to getting away soon after arrival. [Exhibits anomic and fatalistic attributes.]

Life comes first, but by life I mean life with Power. Thus anything that makes for power and for a full life and healthy gratification of the senses is good. . . . Thus, in the future, gratification [of his sex drives] may be quite consistent with my philosophy; in my present weakened state I must hold off if I am to survive. Otherwise it is a case of deliberate suicide, and the only thing to do would be to go ahead and

[75]*Ibid.*, p. 266.
[76]*Ibid.*, p. 276.
[77]Cavan, *op. cit.*, pp. 222 ff.

gratify until disease and weakness made it evident that death would be the only relief. [Exhibits anomic attributes.]

What I might have done had I not been forced to become a victim of our commercial system (so that at twenty-two I am exhausted, my enthusiasm and hope almost killed by deadly routine and no prospect of relief) I do not know. . . . [Exhibits fatalistic attributes.]

I have fled from one refuge to another in the hope of being free, of being able to be myself. . . . [Exhibits fatalistic attributes.]

The continual moving about trying to find a resting place, and consequent disgust and quarrels with relatives, and the feeling that I was indeed alone and without a home . . . [in Chicago, due to his aunt, he was forced to leave his uncle's house and take a room elsewhere]. All this only added to my feeling of loneliness, of homelessness, and I took a small room, after sundry hints from my aunt. [Exhibits egoistic and anomic attributes.][78]

The reader now is referred to Figure 1 for a summary of Durkheim's types of suicide and their attributes.

In the conclusion of Book Two, Durkheim gives a frustratingly brief consideration to possible mixed types of suicide. Figure 2 attempts to schematize Durkheim's typology and to add to it three types that should have been included by Durkheim but were not, elucidating the relationship of fatalistic suicide to egoistic, altruistic, and anomic suicide.

Galley slaves might serve as the appropriate paradigm for the ego-fatalistic suicide type. Such slaves would be characterized by apathy resulting from hyperregulation. The anomic-fatalistic type presents problems. The combination of *anomie* and fatalism produces a nearly self-contradictory type. It is difficult to imagine a suicidal type produced simultaneously by deregulation and over-regulation. On the other hand, so-called juvenile delinquents might serve as a model for anomic-fatalistic suicide. In reference to the juvenile subculture, juveniles are hyperregulated. W. F. Whyte's *Street Corner Society* demonstrates the conformity, the importance of loyalty as a subculture value, and the effect of sub-cultural social position on bowling performances among "Doc's gang."[79] Yet, juveniles are often unable to affirm the general values of a society. In *Delinquent Boys,* Albert Cohen has argued

[78]Cavan, *op. cit.;* the above excerpts are found as follows: pp. 227, 231–32, 232, 234–35, 236, respectively.

[79]W. F. Whyte, *Street Corner Society* (Chicago: University of Chicago Press, 1947).

Figure 1. Durkheim's typology of suicide (pure types)

Basic types	Characteristics	Paradigms	Secondary Types
A. EGOISTIC	Excessive individuation. Apathy. Results from man no longer finding a basis for existence in life.	Within religions, family (domestic society), and politics (wars and revolutions). Protestants vis-à-vis Jews, skid row pariahs.	A1. MELANCHOLIC LANGUOR Depressed and inactive. Reflection is egoistic. A2. EPICUREAN Skeptical, disillusioned matter-of-factness.
B. ALTRUISTIC	Insufficient individuation. Energy of passion or will. Activity. Basis for existence appears situated beyond life. Eastern-like asceticism; try to achieve *moksha* or *nirvana*. "Heroic" suicide.	Lower societies, soldiers, religious martyrs, etc. Hara-kiri, suttee, the kamikaze.	B1. OBLIGATORY Duty. This is clearest type of altruistic suicide. E.g., North American Indians, Polynesians. B2. OPTIONAL Mystical enthusiasm. B3. ACUTE Renunciation itself is praiseworthy; e.g., India. N.B., B2 and B3 derive from B1.
C. ANOMIC	Literally "deregulation," lack of normative restraint. Irritation, disgust. Anger and weariness. Often violence (nonegoistic) and murder (nonaltruistic). Unregulated emotions. Always accompanied by a morbid desire for the infinite. Lack of power controlling individuals gives rise to anomic suicide. Abrupt social change. Poverty restrains it.	Economic crises, sudden social changes, widowhood, divorce, liberal occupations.	C1. GENERAL Violent recriminations against life in general. C2. PARTICULAR Violent recriminations against life in particular, e.g., against one specific person (homicide-suicide).
D. FATALISTIC	Excessive regulation.	Very young husbands. Childless married women. Slaves and prisoners.	

Figure 2.   Durkheim's typology of suicide (mixed types).*

Mixed Types	Characteristics	Paradigms
AB. EGO-ALTRUISTIC	Melancholy tempered with moral fortitude.	Stoic.
AC. EGO-ANOMIC	Mixture of agitation and apathy, of action and reverie.	Upswing of depressive reactions.
AD. EGO-FATALISTIC	Hyperregulation and apathy.	Prisoners, slaves.
BC. ANOMIC-ALTRUISTIC	Exasperated effervescence.	Bankrupt family man.
BD. ALTRUISTIC-FATALISTIC	Forced obligation.	Elite soldiers.
CD. ANOMIC-FATALISTIC	Mixture of normative deregulation and hyperregulation.	Juvenile delinquents.

*Modified by the present author. Cf. fn. 62 in this chapter. Cf. Walter T. Martin, "Theories of Variation in the Suicide Rate," in Jack P. Gibbs (ed.), *Suicide* (New York: Harper & Row, 1968), p. 79.

that the rebellious behavior of delinquents is encouraged structurally by the influence of middle class values which delinquents are forced to live under and be judged by, but which they are unable to adopt.[80] Thus, the delinquent subculture often becomes what Yinger has called a "contraculture" and leads to *anomie* to the degree that delinquents fail to legitimize general social values.[81] It should be noted that delinquents do not commit suicide often. Their aggression usually is directed externally. But anomic-fatalistic suicide is probably rare in any case.

Perhaps the above explains in part why Durkheim fails to give an example of the ego-anomic suicidal type; i.e., it too tends to be self-contradictory. Such a type would include a mixture of apathy and action. It is interesting to consider psychotic suicides as falling in this category since some psychotics experience both profound depression and elation, as in manic-depressive reactions. Finally, altruistic-fatalistic suicide could be suicide resulting from forced obligation, even though on the face of it the phrase "forced

---

[80]Albert Cohen, *Delinquent Boys* (New York: The Free Press, 1955).

[81]J. Milton Yinger, "Subculture and Contraculture," *American Sociological Review,* Vol. 25 (October, 1960), pp. 625–35.

obligation" appears redundant. Could not the "heroic" suicide of the military man fit this category when his heroics were regarded as a learned response to a war situation inculcated by extreme military discipline (i.e., not a voluntary heroic act but a compromised and diluted altruism)?

Finally, what are the relationships between Durkheim's conception of society and his theory of suicide?[82] In general, collectivity and morality are the skeletal concepts upon which explanations of suicide must be fitted. As we have attempted to show above, according to Durkheim the suicide rate is eminently a social (not an individual) phenomenon. It depends upon causes exterior to and dominating individuals.[83] The victim's moral predisposition to commit suicide (i.e., the degree to which he is involved in more or less integrated groups and in the values of those groups) is the crucial variable, not his individual experiences (i.e., his physical and mental health, his financial condition, whether or not he is an alcoholic, etc.).[84] Each people collectively has an inclination to suicide.[85]

The variations in the suicide rates of different nations testify to the "collective inclination to suicide of a people." Table 1 indicates that there are national variations in suicide rates, even though we know that some individual factors, often assumed to be causally linked with suicide, are constant between these nations. Thus, the differences in national suicide rates can be explained only collectively, i.e., in reference to the patterned interaction and norms of a particular nation.

To the degree that the societal groups that the individual is a part of are harmonious, integrated, and regulated, suicide will be less prevalent. The social suicide rate is a better prediction model for the causes of individual suicides than are the motives of individual suicides for the causes of the social suicide rate.[86]

Since suicide represents a weakness in a society's ability to perform its regulatory function, a flaw in the social or moral order, the average number of suicides can be used along with other

---

[82]A task which Durkheim undertakes in Book III of *Suicide*, "The General Nature of Suicide as a Social Phenomenon."

[83]Durkheim, *Suicide*, p. 193.

[84]*Ibid.*, p. 305.

[85]We want to qualify this point later.

[86]Durkheim, *The Division of Labor in Society*, p. 50.

Table 1.   Male and female suicide rates by countries, circa 1954.

Country and Year	Suicide Rate per 100,000 Population		Ratio of Male to Female Rate	Excess of Male Rate
	Male	Female		
Norway, 1954	12.2	2.7	4.5	9.5
Union of South Africa, 1963	19.4	4.4	4.4	15.0
Finland, 1954	31.2	7.6	4.1	23.6
Ireland, 1954	3.2	0.8	4.0	2.4
United States, 1953	16.1	4.3	3.7	11.8
Chile, 1951	7.3	2.1	3.5	5.2
France, 1954	24.7	7.4	3.3	17.3
Canada, 1954	10.9	3.5	3.1	7.4
Spain, 1953	9.1	2.9	3.1	6.2
Sweden, 1953	28.2	9.0	3.1	19.2
New Zealand, 1954	13.4	4.4	3.0	9.0
Portugal, 1951	15.4	5.3	2.9	10.1
Belgium, 1954	20.5	7.3	2.8	13.2
Switzerland, 1954	33.9	12.0	2.8	21.9
Australia, 1953	15.6	6.0	2.6	9.6
Hungary, 1953	27.9	11.8	2.4	16.1
Italy, 1953	9.2	3.9	2.4	5.3
Austria, 1954	33.1	14.4	2.3	18.7
Denmark, 1954	31.4	15.4	3.0	16.0
West Germany, 1955	25.8	12.9	2.0	12.9
Ceylon, 1954	10.2	5.5	1.9	4.7
Netherlands, 1954	8.2	4.3	1.9	3.9
England and Wales, 1954	14.9	8.1	1.8	6.8
Japan, 1954	29.2	17.8	1.6	11.4

Source: United Nations, World Health Organization, *Epidemiological and Vital Statistics Report,* Vol. 9, No. 4 (1956), Table 2. Also United Nations, *Demographic Yearbook,* 1957, Table 17.

crimes as an indicator of the intensity of immorality in a society.[87] Durkheim argues that even though the absolute number of suicides increases, one still could hold that the objective causes of suicide have not increased because higher suicide rates do not result, for example, from economic poverty but from a poverty of morality.[88] That is, the social causes of the suicide rate vary independently of the individual causes of particular suicides. Conversely, a decrease in particular crimes and other social problems would not necessarily be accompanied by a decrease in the suicide rate.

[87]Durkheim, *Suicide,* p. 386.
[88]*Ibid.,* p. 258.

Summary

We have tried to show in this chapter the fundamental *qualitative* difference between individuals and societies in Durkheim's theory of society. This difference is conceived of as a result of the transforming and abstracting function of human association. The product of individuals interacting (i.e., society) is a *collective* representation. Society represents not just the sum of individual thoughts and actions but a synthesis of individual contributions compounded in such a way as to give birth to a new entity which transcends and yet draws from individuals.

Two of the most outstanding attributes of society (to be exact, of social facts) are externality and constraint. Society is both physically external (as in legal canons) and epistemologically external (as in the concept of the social). Society is constraining because social life is *nomic* life. The two means of constraint are the collective conscience (which is manifested in the mechanical solidarity of repressive law) and the mutual interdependence growing out of increasing social differentiation (which is manifested in the organic solidarity of restitutive law).

Durkheim does not distinguish the social from the moral. For him, morality is another aspect of the social. Morality is characterized by obligation and desirability, i.e., to be moral is to substitute (willingly) individual interest to the collective good.

Consistent with his theory of society, Durkheim interprets suicide as a result of social causes. While individual factors do account for some suicides, the social suicide rate cannot be explained by individual causes. Since the social and the individual are different entities, they require a different level of explanation.

Beginning with more particularistic social causes of suicide, Durkheim proceeds via an inductive schema of increasing generalization to the common denominator of all suicides, viz, the lack of social integration of the groups of which the individual forms a part. Durkheim claims that social integration has both structural and normative dimensions.

Finally, Durkheim breaks down suicide into a typology consisting of egoistic, altruistic, anomic, and fatalistic suicide. The similarities and differences of these types of suicide then are discussed at some length.

Suggestions for further reading

Alpert, Harry. *Emile Durkheim and His Sociology*. New York: Russell & Russell, Inc., 1961. In our judgment this is the best general commentary in print on Durkheim's sociology. It is lucidly written, brief, to the point, and thoroughly researched.

Durkheim, Emile. *Suicide*. New York: The Free Press, 1963. The classical sociological statement on suicide. Durkheim's *Suicide* is the point of departure for the Chicago research. See especially Book Two: "Social Causes and Social Types" (pp. 145–294).

Nisbet, Robert A. (ed.). *Émile Durkheim*. Englewood Cliffs, N.J.: Prentice-Hall, Inc., 1965. We found Nisbet's introduction (pp. 9–104) and Hanan's Selvin's essay (pp. 113–36) particularly helpful.

Parsons, Talcott. *The Structure of Social Action*. New York: The Free Press, 1949, pp. 301–472. Important because it treats the development of Durkheim's sociological theory. For example, the evolution of the concept of the Social is considered at length.

Wolff, Kurt H. (ed.). *Essays on Sociology and Philosophy*. New York: Harper & Row, 1960. A good, sound, general commentary on Durkheim's sociology. Contains biographical and historical materials.

CHAPTER 3

The context and consequences of Durkheim's <u>Suicide</u>

In much the same way that Weber's *Protestant Ethic and the Spirit of Capitalism* stimulated other studies on the role of values in the economic development of Western capitalism, Durkheim's *Suicide* became the point of departure for further studies on suicide. In order to understand Durkheim we should know something of the polemics in which he was involved: toward what arguments *Suicide* was directed as a rebuttal. As a bridge between Durkheim's work and our own, we should have at least a superficial grasp of what went between. Accordingly, we have decided to describe briefly the historical context out of which *Suicide* grew and a few representative post-Durkheimian works on suicide.

In examining the immediate context of Durkheim's *Suicide* we will consider the principal theses of Falret, Quetelet, Esquirol, de Fleury, Halbwachs, and Delmas. Some of the more important recent works on suicide include Jack P. Gibbs and Walter T. Martin's *Status Integration and Suicide,* Andrew Henry and James F. Short, Jr.'s *Suicide and Homicide,* Karl Menninger's *Man against Himself,* Louis I. Dublin's *Suicide: A Sociological and Statistical Study,* and Ruth S. Cavan's *Suicide.*[1] These works

---

[1]Jack P. Gibbs and Walter T. Martin, *Status Integration and Suicide* (Eugene, Ore.: The University of Oregon Press, 1964); Andrew Henry and James F. Short,

were selected for exposition because they illustrate (in the order listed) operationalized and empirically tested propositional theory, a social-psychological theory, a psychiatric theory, descriptive statistics necessary for theory construction, and social disorganization theory. Cavan's work was also included because it was a study of Chicago suicides in the late 1920's. Where possible, comparisons will be made with the present study. This chapter focuses upon the theoretical contributions of the works mentioned, although empirical references are included when they are needed to make a theory clear.

The historical context of Durkheim's *Suicide*

Before going forward, let us cast a backward glance at the suicide literature which was at the disposal of Durkheim prior to his writing of *Suicide*. Fortunately a recent issue of the *British Journal of Sociology* contains an excellent historical resume of the European suicide literature (especially the French suicide literature) just before and after Durkheim's publication of *Suicide* in 1897.[2] Anthony Giddens argues that the originality of Durkheim's work did not lie in the empirical "correlations" in *Le Suicide* but in the cogent sociological theory; most of Durkheim's empirical results already had been published in works by other authors:

Suicide was the subject of extended debate even in the eighteenth century. Most eighteenth century works on suicide were concerned with the moral implications of the suicidal act, but toward the end of the century writers began to turn their attention to discussing the significance of the apparently rapidly rising suicide rates in Europe, and out of this a more objective concern with the determinants of suicide began to develop. One of the earliest comprehensive investigations of suicide was made by Falret in his *De l'hypochondrie et du suicide* (1822). Falret examined at some length both the "internal causes" of suicidal tendencies in the

Jr., *Suicide and Homicide* (New York: The Free Press, 1954); Karl Menninger, *Man against Himself* (New York: Harcourt, Brace & World, Inc., 1938); Louis I. Dublin, *Suicide: A Sociological and Statistical Study* (New York: The Ronald Press Co., 1963); and Ruth S. Cavan, *Suicide* (New York: Russell & Russell, Inc., 1965).

[2]Anthony Giddens, "The Suicide Problem in French Sociology," *British Journal of Sociology*, Vol. 16 (March, 1965). We draw heavily on this article for our comments on suicide in French sociology.

individual, which he attributed principally to certain forms of inherited mental disorder, and "external causes" producing variations in the suicide rates between different groups. *De l'hypochondrie et du suicide* was followed by a proliferation of works on suicide by French, German, and Italian writers. Perhaps the most influential of these were those by Guerry (1833), Lisle (1856), and Legoyt (1881) in France, Quetelet (1835) in Belgium, Wagner (1864) and Massaryk (1881) in Germany, and Morselli (1879) and Ferri (1883) in Italy. There were many others. In terms of the sheer bulk of material, suicide was probably one of the most discussed social problems of the nineteenth century. By the time at which Durkheim wrote, a substantial number of empirical correlations had been established linking suicide rates with a range of social factors. Later writers confirmed Falret's contention that suicide rates tend to rise during periods of rapid social change and in times of economic depression; and that rates vary positively with socio-economic position, being highest in professional and liberal occupations, and lowest among the chronically poor. The fact that suicide rates are higher in urban localities was extensively documented. Some writers claimed to have shown that suicide rates covary with crime rates, but are inversely related to rates of homicide. Wagner was perhaps the first to identify clearly a direct relationship between rates of suicide and the religious denominations of Protestantism and Catholicism, but this was quickly substantiated by later investigation. It was widely shown that suicide rates vary by sex, age, and marital status; as well as by time of the year, day of the week, and hour of the day.

Some writers gave prominence to racial and climatic factors in accounting for differential suicide rates. Most, however, questioned this type of explanation, and looked instead to social causes. Quetelet placed great emphasis, as Durkheim later did, on the relative stability of suicide rates from year to year in comparison with other demographic data, attempting to interpret differences between suicide rates in terms of variations in the "moral density" of society. Most writers attributed the general rise in suicide rates to the dissolution of the traditional social order and the transition to industrial civilization, with its concomitants of increasing "rationality" and individualism—an explanation close to that elaborated by Durkheim.

Most of the early nineteenth century investigations of suicide took for granted a close relationship between suicide and mental disorder. The notion that suicide derived from "miserable insanity" was clearly in part a survival of the belief that suicide is of diabolical inspiration, a view which, under the impress of the Church, held sway until some way through the eighteenth century. The theory that suicide is always associated with some form of mental disorder was, however, given its most definitive formulation in Esquirol's classic *Maladies mentales* (1838). "Suicide," asserted Esquirol, "shows all the characteristics of mental disorders of which it is in fact only a symptom." In this view, since suicide is always symptomatic of mental illness, it is to the causes of the latter that the student of suicide must turn in order to explain the phenomenon. The nature and distribution of mental disorder in any population determine the distribution of suicide in that population.

The question of how far, and in what ways, suicide is related to mental disorder became a major problem occupying writers on suicide during the latter half of the nineteenth century and was discussed at some length by Durkheim.[3]

In 1924, M. de Fleury, in *L'Angoisse Humaine*,[4] claimed that the causes of suicide always are derivative of mental disorder; i.e., that they are biopsychological rather than social, as Durkheim claimed. Suicides are found mainly in persons suffering from cyclical depressive disorder (cyclothymia), which depends upon inherited characteristics of temperament. The tendency of states of morbid depression develops largely independently of the objective circumstances of the individual. Thus, it is of little consequence whether the individual is integrated into a group or not. While social and economic changes do affect the suicide rate, they only function to cluster individuals who would have killed themselves anyway.

M. Halbwachs, in *Les Causes du Suicide* (1930),[5] using later statistics (33 years after the publication of Durkheim's *Suicide*), confirmed most of Durkheim's generalizations relating suicide rates to family structure and religious denomination. But he rejected Durkheim's treatment of suicide in relation to isolated variables. For example, Halbwachs argued that religion or the family structure must be considered as a part of a larger whole in order to gain a clear understanding of their relation to the suicide rate. In France the more strongly Catholic groups tend also to be the most conservative and traditional and to have a strongly integrated family structure. The point is that religion and family life are mutually interdependent and thus must be studied together.

---

[3]*Ibid.*, pp. 3–5.

[4]M. de Fleury, *L'Angoisse Humaine* (Paris: Editions de France, 1924) .

[5]Maurice Halbwachs, *Les Causes du Suicide* (Paris: Alcan, 1930) .

Halbwachs thought that the set of factors Durkheim found to be most commonly associated with a high suicide rate was most characteristic of modern urban life. Accordingly, Halbwachs compared suicide rates of urban and rural areas, and he discovered that suicide rates are highest in large cities.

Durkheim had claimed that suicide rates would rise during economic crises. This claim was confirmed by Halbwachs through an examination of the relationship between fluctuations in the business index and suicide in Germany from 1880 to 1914. However, the higher rate of suicide does not just coincide with the trough of the depression but remains high throughout all the levels of the depression. Contrary to Durkheim's contention, Halbwachs found that suicide rates do not rise during periods of economic prosperity but in fact decline (a finding corroborated in a later study of suicide by Andrew Henry and James Short, Jr.).[6] In general, however, Halbwachs' statistical analysis supported Durkheim's results.

Such was not the case with Durkheim's typology of suicide. Halbwachs rejected the tripart division of suicide into egoistic, altruistic, and anomic. He contended that self-sacrifice (altruistic suicide) was so different from "individualized" suicide that it could not be fitted into the same explanatory framework. Halbwachs claimed simply that suicide rates are high in social structures promoting the detachment of individuals from stable relationships with others, e.g., urban communities.

Like Durkheim, Halbwachs attacked the psychiatric thesis advanced by de Fleury and others. He argued that only a minority of suicides are associated with a recognizable form of mental disorder. The "true" cause of suicide is a social *lacuna* which surrounds the individual suicide.

In *Psychologie pathologique du suicide* (1932),[7] F. Archille Delmas defended the views of the psychiatric school against the views of Durkheim and Halbwachs. His main argument was that social factors could not influence suicide since suicide takes

---

[6]In a recent article ("The Economic Cycle and the Social Suicide Rate," *American Sociological Review*, Vol. 32, No. 3 [June, 1967], pp. 457–62) , Albert Pierce argues that suicide rates do rise during periods of prosperity as well as of depression.

[7]F. Archille Delmas, *Psychologie pathologique du suicide* (Paris: Alcan, 1932) . Cf. M. Bonnafous, "Le Suicide: thèse psychiatrique et thèse sociologique," *Revue philosophique*, Vol. 115 (May–June, 1933) , pp. 456–75.

in such a small proportion of any population. While it sounds impressive to say that country A has a suicide rate of 45 but country B has a suicide rate of 5, if you invert these proportions you find 99,955 *did not* commit suicide in country A as compared to 99,995 in country B. Does it not sound ridiculous to say that social factors protected 99,995 in country B but only 99,955 in country A?

Delmas held that the "fundamental cause" of suicide is pathological depression and that depressive states develop largely independent of the external situation of the individual. For example, if suicide rates are higher among the unmarried than the married, it is because depressives tend not to marry.

Status Integration and Suicide

Jack Gibbs and Walter Martin's concept of "status integration" is designed to operationalize Durkheim's concept of "social integration" which is contained in his famous generalization, "suicide varies inversely with the degree of integration of the social groups" (of which the individual forms a part—Gibbs and Martin omit this phrase). They construct the concept of status integration because they believe that Durkheim's theory has never been subjected to a formal test and that it is not testable in Durkheim's formulation. It must be pointed out that the relationship between Durkheim's "social integration" and Gibbs and Martin's "status integration" is unclear. For example, postulate one of the status integration theory attempts to interpret what Durkheim meant by social integration (viz, stable and durable social relationships). Unfortunately postulate one is untestable, too. Thus, Gibbs and Martin are obliged to construct an extended argument consisting of five premises (postulates) and a theorem:

1. The suicide rate of a population varies inversely with the stability and durability of social relationships within that population.
2. The stability and durability of social relationships within a population vary directly with the extent to which individuals within conform to the patterned and socially sanctioned demands and expectations placed upon them by others.
3. The extent to which individuals in a population conform to the patterned and socially sanctioned demands and expectations placed upon

them by others varies inversely with the extent to which individuals in that population are confronted with role conflicts.

4. The extent to which individuals in a population are confronted with role conflicts varies directly with the extent to which individuals occupy incompatible statuses in that population.

5. The extent to which individuals occupy incompatible statuses in a population varies inversely with the degree of status integration in that population.[8]

From these five postulates Gibbs and Martin deduce their major theorem, viz, "the suicide rate of a population varies inversely with the degree of status integration in that population." According to Gibbs and Martin there is considerable empirical support for the major theorem. Unfortunately this tells us nothing of the truth of the five postulates since a valid argument can have a true conclusion and false premises. The definition of a valid argument is that *if* the *premises* are true, then the conclusion must be true. Proving that the theorem is true (which is difficult enough in itself) proves nothing about the truth value of any particular premise.

"Status integration" can be measured in any or all of three ways. For an illustration, let us use Gibbs and Martin's table (Table 2) which deals with the integration of marital statuses.[9] The columns represent status configurations of race, age, religion,

TABLE 2. The integration of marital statuses with selected status configurations in a hypothetical society where marital integration is less than maximum.

Marital Status	All Occupied Status Configurations				
	R1-A1-Re1-O1-S1-P1	R2-A2-Re3-O2-S2-P2	R1-A3-Re3-O3-S1-P1	R1-A4-Re1-O4-S1-P3	R2-A5-Re3-O5-S2-P2
Single	0.15	0.05	0.00	0.35	0.05
Married	0.05	0.75	0.05	0.25	0.90
Widowed	0.60	0.15	0.25	0.20	0.05
Divorced	0.20	0.05	0.70	0.20	0.00
ΣX	1.00	1.00	1.00	1.00	1.00
ΣX^2	0.4250	0.5900	0.5550	0.2650	0.8150
Proportion of population	0.1425	0.3825	0.0870	0.1970	0.1900

Source: Jack P. Gibbs and Walter T. Martin, *Status Integration and Suicide* (Eugene, Ore.: University of Oregon Press, 1964), p. 38.

[8]Gibbs and Martin, *op. cit.,* p. 27.
[9]*Ibid.,* p. 37.

occupation, sex, and parental status. The rows represent marital statuses. In column one, row one, for example, it is shown that 15 percent of the single people in this sample have the status configuration R1, A1, Rel, 01, S1, P1. The first measure of status integration would be simply column proportions. In the case of column one of the present table, the major theorem would predict that married persons would have the highest suicide rate and that widowed persons would have the lowest suicide rate (a peculiar example since it is empirically false). That is, the more occupants of a particular status configuration, the higher the status integration and the lower the suicide rate.

A second measure of status integration would be the sums of squares of the proportions in each column. Once again using the table offered, it would be predicted that people occupying the status configuration represented in the fifth column would have the lowest suicide rate and that the people occupying the status configuration represented by the fourth column would have the highest suicide rate.

A third and final type of status integration measure would be a comparison of the status integration measure of one society (the sum of the sums of squares of the proportions in each column) with the status integration measure of another society or societies. In the table under consideration, this third type of status integration measure would be $0.4250 + 0.5900 + 0.5550 + 0.2650 + 0.8150 = 2.65$.

Having operationalized their major theorem, Gibbs and Martin take up the remainder of their book with tests of the major theorem with regard to the standard variables of age, sex, marital status, race, temporal variations, etc. Cross-cultural comparisons are made in Part Three. The major contribution of Gibbs and Martin is their formal attempt to test Durkheim's generalization about the suicide rate and social integration. It is curious that Gibbs' most recent book provides evidence for an association between the suicide rate and "disruptive social relations" (i.e., postulate one) and makes little or no mention of status integration.[10]

---

[10] Jack P. Gibbs (ed.), *Suicide* (New York: Harper & Row, 1968), pp. 1–2.

Suicide and Homicide

As we will see in Chapter 7, Andrew Henry and James F. Short, Jr.'s *Suicide and Homicide* is primarily an examination of Durkheim's anomic type of suicide since it tests the influence of economic change on the suicide rate. A few of Henry and Short's substantive conclusions have direct bearing on Durkheim's hypotheses. First, troughs of suicide cycles tend to precede in time the peaks of business cycles with which they correspond. Second, suicide does tend to rise during periods of depression and to fall during periods of prosperity, but the increase in suicide during depressions is greater than the decrease in suicide during periods of prosperity. Third, suicide does rise along with the business index during *final* (not during the initial phases of business expansion) speculative phases of business cycles preceding business peaks. Fourth, business cycles are more highly correlated with the suicide of males than with the suicide of females, but the suicide of nonwhite females is more highly correlated with business fluctuations than suicide of nonwhite males. Henry and Short account for this unexpected finding by saying that the nonwhite female's role includes the expectation of more economic responsibility than that of the white female. However, this explanation is not completely satisfactory since another comparison should be made between the economic responsibility of nonwhite females and nonwhite males.

Two of Durkheim's predictions fail to be substantiated by Henry and Short's data. Durkheim suggested that abrupt speculative increases in the business cycle would be accompanied by increases in suicide, and he interpreted this phenomena as a function of the weakening of social controls over behavior at the same time that the "passions" and desires of individuals were increasing. Henry and Short argue that if Durkheim's explanations were correct, then we would expect that years of rapid rates of rise in the business index would be accompanied by rapid rates of rise in suicide, and that the suicide of males (the category engaging in business and financial speculation) would be more subject to the deleterious effects of abrupt rises in business than

the suicide of females (who are less active in business and financial speculation).

However, during years of rapid rise in the business index,
suicide tends to fall.[11] And when it does rise along with the business index during the *final* phases of business expansion, the
increase occurs primarily among females.[12]

Man against Himself

Oddly enough, Karl Menninger does not even mention Emile
Durkheim in *Man against Himself.* Nonetheless, Menninger must
be regarded as one of the chief antagonists of the Durkheimian
theory of suicide because of his nonsocial explanation of suicide.
Menninger writes: "Behavior is never determined only by external
forces; there are impulses from within, the adjustment of which
to external reality necessarily brings about stresses and strains
which may be highly painful, but endurable except to a very
few."[13] Why is it, Menninger asks, that most people adjust to trying external situations? Or, put somewhat differently, why do some
people take their lives and others not, yet all share in the same
external vicissitudes? Clearly, to Menninger, it is not for the
reasons that Cavan gives:

> At first it would seem gratuitous to offer an explanation of suicide. In
> the popular mind suicide is no enigma. Glib explanations are to be read
> with monotonous invariability in the daily newspapers, in life-insurance
> reports, upon death certificates, and in statistical surveys. Suicide, accord-
> ing to these, is the simple and logical consequence of ill-health, discourage-
> ment, financial reverses, humiliation, frustration, or unrequited love. What
> amazes me most is not that these simple explanations are continually
> offered but that they are so readily and unquestioningly accepted in a
> world where science and everyday experience alike confirm the untrust-
> worthiness of the obvious.[14]

The explanation must lie deeper than "personal and social disorganization," because many people experience personal and social
disorganization but refrain from killing themselves. Menninger

11Cf. Pierce, *op. cit.*
12Henry and Short, *op. cit.*, p. 42.
13Menninger, *op. cit.*, p. 17.
14*Ibid.*, p. 16.

wants to argue the causative role of unconscious psychological factors. Personal and social disorganization, at best, give only *necessary conditions* for suicide.

Basically, these "unconscious psychological factors" are variations of what Sigmund Freud called the life-instinct and the death-instinct. Freud's concept of the death-instinct is that from the beginning there exists in all of us strong propensities toward self-destruction and that these come to fruition as actual suicide only in exceptional cases where many circumstances and factors combine to make it possible.

Menninger claims that every true suicidal act must contain three elements: the wish to kill (hate), the wish to be killed (guilt), and the wish to die (hopelessness). If robbed of certain external occasions or objects of gratification, the wish to kill (a form of primitive aggressiveness deriving from frustration)[15] may be turned back upon the person of the "wisher" and carried into effect as suicide. Thus, suicide is regarded as displaced murder, what Menninger calls "murder-in-the-one-hundred-and-eightieth-degree." One might naturally wonder why the aggression was not carried out against the frustrating agent. In some cases, suicide prevails because the would-be murderer was not powerful enough to carry out a murder (e.g., young children who are frustrated by their parents). In other instances, suicide is effected through fear of the object or the consequences of killing the object. Sometimes the conscience intervenes. In a kind of pre-Socratic Greek manner, Menninger argues that love and hate are vying continually for dominance in the unconscious and that murder often is avoided when love triumphs over hate.

Under the heading "the wish to be killed," Menninger explains that the ego must suffer in direct proportion to its externally directed destructiveness. He says that it is as if that part of the destructive instinct which is retained within the ego had to carry on, within the microcosmos of the personality, an activity precisely comparable to that which the ego is directing toward the macrocosmos outside. In *Brothers Karamazov*, for example, Dmitri does not kill his father; but, nevertheless, he seems to demand punishment for himself as if he had committed the mur-

---

[15]See J. Dollard *et al., Frustration and Aggression* (New Haven: Yale, 1939). Cf. Leonard Berkowitz, *Aggression* (New York: McGraw-Hill Book Co., Inc., 1962).

der. Menninger also mentions the case of a prison executioner who killed himself.

Although the wish to kill and wish to be killed are the principal components of the suicidal act, the wish to die must also be present. Paradoxical as it may seem, some people who wish to kill themselves do not wish to die. Menninger recounts several cases of patients pleading with him to save their lives after they themselves had tried to commit suicide.

This internal dialogue just mentioned can have four results, four types of suicide. First, there is suicide in the ordinary sense in which the suicide attempt is successful and thus "whole." Second, there is what Menninger names "chronic suicide," which is "partial" (affects only part of the person physically or psychologically) with a general focus. Included in this category are ascetics and martyrs (reminiscent of Durkheim's altruistic suicide) who suffer but do not die, neurotic invalids, alcoholics, antisocial individuals, and some psychotics.

As an example of "chronic suicide," Menninger records the case of a psychotic patient:

> This woman was a very neat little person who kept her house so immaculate that after fourteen years of married life her furniture still looked brand new. This necessitated a great many prohibitions which she enforced upon her family and upon visitors. Her life moved in rather narrow circles; outside of her home, her only interest was in the church.
>
> A few years after the birth of her second child it was felt necessary to perform a surgical operation from which she seemed to recover but which was followed in turn by recurrent attacks of influenza which would leave her very nervous and upset. She would go in tears to her sisters. It would require several days for them to comfort her. These crying spells became more frequent; it was noted that she left unfinished many things that she started; she felt convinced that she was developing a goiter and that she was going to lose her mind. Finally, she attempted suicide by taking a tablet of poison. A doctor was called who used a stomach pump immediately and she was saved, but from that time on *she insisted that she was dead.*[16]

Third, there is "focal suicide," which is also a partial suicide; but unlike chronic suicide, it has a specific focus rather than a general focus. It may take the form of purposive accidents, impo-

---

[16]Menninger, *op. cit.*, pp. 189–90.

tence, and frigidity, polysurgery, malingering, and self-mutilation. Menninger discusses a case of self-mutilation:

A boy of twenty returned from the war to find that the girl to whom he had been engaged had married another man. This was the precipitating factor in the development of an acute schizophrenic illness with delusions, hallucinations, and queer posturing, which after a few relapses became chronic and necessitated continuous hospitalization. From the standpoint of care he was an exceedingly difficult patient in the hospital because of his persistent efforts to injure himself. He would, for example, tie string tightly about his toes with the evident purpose of producing gangrene. He would slip up behind the heavy doors of the hospital as they were being closed after a physician or nurse and put his fingers into the cracks so as to have them crushed. Upon several occasions he snatched pins from the front of a nurse's uniform and attempted to jab them into his eyes. He would seize and separate the fingers of one hand and by using his leg and his other hand attempt to pull them apart so violently as to tear the webs between them. With his thumb and finger nail he would pinch chunks out of his ear lobes. He frequently dived or plunged from his bed onto the floor, head first, as if attempting to crush his skull. Once he was found nearly asphyxiated as a result of having forced several large stalks of celery deep into his throat.[17]

Finally, Menninger discussed "organic suicide," or the role of the unconscious in affecting the course of a disease. Since blisters, to take one case, have been induced by suggestion,[18] it seems feasible that hostile psychological processes can have a deleterious effect on one's organic condition.

Suicide: A Sociological and Statistical Study

Louis I. Dublin's *Suicide: A Sociological and Statistical Study* brings up-to-date the research done in one of his earlier books, *To Be or Not To Be—A Study of Suicide*.[19] Strictly speaking Dublin has no theory of suicide but rather has materials (especially descriptive, statistical, and historical) for a theory of suicide. Dublin's book serves the very valuable function of providing up-to-date

---

[17]*Ibid.,* p. 230.

[18]*Ibid.,* p. 312.

[19]Louis I. Dublin and Bessie Bunzel, *To Be or Not To Be* (New York: Harrison Smith and Robert Hass, 1933).

information[20] on suicide (the dependent variable) and age, sex, marital status, race, ethnicity, methods of death, seasonal rhythms, rural-urban differences, religion, economics, war, and psychology (independent variables). This book is helpful as an edited source of suicide statistics for the United States. However, Dublin does not present systematic explanations of suicide. There is no bibliography included, and there are very few footnotes in the book.

Suicide

Ruth S. Cavan's *Suicide* is more descriptive than analytical.[21] This conspicuous lack of rigorous logical examination of her data has made Cavan's theory of suicide rather superficial. For example, she writes: "With apparently few exceptions, suicide in contemporary America has one connotation. It is a symptom of complete loss of morale, a result of personal disorganization."[22] But as Durkheim pointed out, personal disorganization in itself does not cause suicide. Menninger has argued that social disorganization affects various people quite differently.

Cavan claims that suicide results from: (1) A "vague craving without an object," e.g., a 25-year-old Chicago woman killed herself simply because she had a strong desire to stop living—she found her life flavorless.[23] (2) A frustration of specific wishes, such as to get into a particular profession, to become someone's wife, to be a member of a particular social class; in general the more specific the unfulfilled wish, the more likely suicide will result. (3) "Long-continued conflict of dominant but incompatible interests." (4) A breakdown of previously satisfactory life-organizations; Cavan states that this type of crisis, e.g., the death of a spouse or economic failure, results in suicide more often than any other single type. (5) Particular kinds of experience, e.g., unemployment, arrest, change of residential location, illness and

---

[20]Most of Dublin's tables are based on the 1960 United States Vital Statistics, records of the National Institute of Mental Health, and records of the Metropolitan Life Insurance Company.

[21]As she told me in a personal conversation: "I had no theory of suicide. We [Louis Wirth, Everett Hughes, Philip Hauser, etc.] had just discovered Chicago and were trying to take it all in." It is difficult to analyze something that you are infatuated with.

[22]Cavan, *op. cit.*, p. 325.

[23]*Ibid.*

disease, alcoholism, insanity, the rupture of intimate relations through quarrels, death, or separation (it seems that this is not a new kind of stimulus of suicide but is merely an extension of type [4]). (6) A personality which makes adjustment to problems difficult. (7) A cessation or dilution of civil sanctions against suicide (this type is similar to Durkheim's anomic suicide); for example, the waning power of the Church's sanctions in modern urban-industrial communities.

In sum, for Cavan suicide is a reaction to a crisis resulting from personal and social disorganization. "Social disorganization" is the loss of control of the mores over the members of the group. The existence of social disorganization makes personal disorganization more likely.

Summary

Post-Durkheimian suicide research can be subsumed under four headings: First, the expansion of the psychological-psychiatric study of suicide. Even though we have been unable to explore the suggestion of this school in our Chicago research (because of the limitations of our data), it poses one of the most serious challenges to the Durkheimian explanation of suicide. Delmas, Esquirol, and de Fleury were among the first to call attention to the role of mental illness in the aetiology of suicide. While many of their arguments appear unjustifiably radical, even ludicrous, in the light of contemporary psychological research, their claim that suicide is caused in part by nonsocial factors (such as organically based depressive psychosis) has become convincing.[24]

The prime contribution of the Menninger school of suicide analysis has been its "biased theories."[25] Menninger's ideas are provocative but not definitive. It is an intriguing suggestion that every aggressive action has an equal and opposite reaction. Furthermore, Menninger's concept of "partial suicides" constitutes a refreshing and rewarding perspective on suicide. Finally, Men-

---

[24]For example, George E. Murphy and Eli Robins ("Social Factors in Suicide," *The Journal of the American Medical Association*, Vol. 199 [January, 1967], pp. 303–8) found that 95 percent of the suicides investigated were psychiatrically ill.

[25]Robert Bierstedt, "Sociology and Humane Learning," *American Sociological Review*, Vol. 25 (February, 1960), p. 309.

ninger played a key role in the application of the frustration-aggression hypothesis to suicide research.

A second post-Durkheimian trend has been the focus on anomic suicide. This is a somewhat puzzling development since egoistic suicide probably occurs more frequently than anomic suicide (see Chapter 8). Halbwachs noticed that the suicide rate was high throughout *all* of an economic depression, not just at the trough, and that suicide does not rise in times of prosperity. Henry and Short concurred in this later finding. They discovered that when there was a rapid rise in the business index, the suicide rate actually fell. Henry and Short's entire book is a refinement and extension of Durkheim's major theses on anomic suicide.

Cavan's work is most correctly viewed as a contribution to the understanding of anomic suicide. She argues that suicide is a result of personal and social disorganization which, in turn, results from crises, especially a breakdown of a previously satisfactory life organization—such as the death of a loved one or economic failure.

Third, we have witnessed a vast proliferation of suicide statistics since Durkheim's *Suicide*. Louis I. Dublin's book provides a representative selection of both governmental and private data which have accumulated over the first six decades of the 20th century. These new statistics have provided raw materials for new theoretical approaches. For example, Dublin's data on suicide in metropolitan areas reveals that the urban suicide rate has fallen precipitously since Durkheim's and Cavan's works. In fact, urban and rural suicide rates are now very nearly the same. These new statistics call for new theories which, unfortunately, have not been forthcoming.

Not only has there been an accumulation of descriptive statistics but we also have seen the early phases of a methodological revolution in Gibbs and Martin's attempt to operationalize Durkheim's concept of social integration.

Fourth, there have been theoretical modifications of Durkheim's theory of suicide. Halbwachs argued that suicide is caused exclusively by the detachment of individuals from stable social relationships, a condition found especially in modern metropolises. He criticized Durkheim for not assessing the *joint* influence of independent variables on suicide. And, finally, he rejected Durkheim's conception of altruistic suicide.

Cavan has no theory of suicide in any rigorous sense of "theory." As we have seen, she attributes suicide to social and personal disorganization. Both Menninger and Henry and Short see suicide as self-directed aggression deriving from frustration. Menninger adds to this the influence of unconscious factors, while Henry and Short add the influence of the concepts of status and external restraint. Dublin has no theory of suicide. Gibbs and Martin associate suicide with a lack of status integration.

In the chapter just concluded we have tried in a small way to update post-Durkheimian suicide research and theory. In Part II we will add our own contribution to the list of empirical examinations of Durkheim's theory of suicide. An original study of 2,153 Cook County, Illinois, suicides will be conducted and supplemented with materials from secondary sources.

Suggestions for further reading

Gibbs, Jack P., and Martin, Walter T. *Status Integration and Suicide.* Eugene, Ore.: University of Oregon Press, 1964. An example of an attempt to operationalize and test Durkheim's concept of social integration. Should be read in conjunction with criticisms by Chambliss and Steele and Hagedorn and Labovitz (see complete bibliography at the end of this book).

Giddens, Anthony. "The Suicide Problem in French Sociology." *British Journal of Sociology,* Vol. 16 (March, 1965), pp. 3–18. Reviews the historical context of Durkheim's *Suicide.* Casts light on the polemics Durkheim was involved in.

Douglas, Jack D. *The Social Meanings of Suicide.* Princeton, N.J.: Princeton University Press, 1967. See Parts I and II for a discussion of pre- and post-Durkheimian sociological theories of suicide.

Menninger, Karl. *Man against Himself.* New York: Harcourt, Brace & World, Inc., 1938. A very readable account of a psychiatric approach to the study of suicide. Stresses the role of "internal causes" (e.g., love, hate, guilt, hopelessness) of suicide. A perspective almost diametrically opposed to that of Durkheim.

PART II

An empirical investigation of suicide in Chicago

CHAPTER 4

Suicide and the social characteristics
of the Chicago area

In 1965 we obtained a grant from the National Science Foundation (GS-793) which allowed us to obtain copies of the death certificates of all the suicides committed in Cook County, Illinois, from 1959 to 1963 (some 2,153 certificates). Our explicit aim was to put Durkheim's hypotheses systematically to empirical test in a non-European, industrialized, urban area. The results of these tests are presented in the following four chapters. Of course, our data allow only partial testing in some cases. The information on a death certificate is limited.[1] Some of the sociological basics are there: age, sex, race, marital status, and occupation. Nevertheless, we were forced to rely heavily on secondary sources to explain many of the patterns that developed from our analysis. For example, coroner's inquest records helped since they included additional information on the sample not recorded on the death certificate. Studies by other researchers of suicide were also used. Because of the limitations of the data, our argument cannot be quite so rigorous as we would like. To be sure, there is no claim that the analysis is definitive. Nevertheless, we found the research exciting, and we believe that the results are important in their

---

[1]See Appendix A.

own right.[2] In the present chapter we outline our sample and methods and make a brief description of the social characteristics of the Chicago area. This is followed by a general statement on suicide in Chicago.

Data and methods

Our sample is made up of 2,153 death certificates. This number constitutes all of the officially recorded suicides, by residence, in Cook County, Illinois, from 1959 through 1963.[3] Cook County was chosen for a number of reasons. It includes the city of Chicago, which increases the likelihood of picking up a significant number of infrequent suicidal types. For example, having Chicago in the sample increased the probability of being able to analyze the influence of race. Furthermore, previous social research in Chicago has made available valuable resource materials. Not only are coding guides readily accessible but the University of Chicago publishes a very helpful community fact book on Chicago.[4] Finally, of no small consideration is the fact that Ruth S. Cavan did a study of suicide in Chicago in the mid-1920's.[5] Her work will serve as a convenient reference. One of the prime functions of Cavan's book will be to permit comparisons for the same metropolitan area after a period of some 40 years. In a small way we hope to be able to say something about metropolitan trends in suicide.

A five-year sample was selected mainly because suicide is a relatively infrequent event. In order to get a large enough number of cases to construct reliable propositions, a five-year span was needed. At the time the data were gathered, 1963 was the last year for which the state's suicide records were complete.

The sample is a total sample. Nevertheless, the representativeness of the Chicago data will be checked against other comparable

---

[2]Our future research on suicidal careers (NIMH Grant No. 14701) should help to complete our present argument since it is based on interview data and has more systematic controls.

[3]See Appendix B for a brief history of our data access problem.

[4]Evelyn M. Kitagawa and Karl E. Taeuber (eds.), Chicago Community Inventory, *Local Community Fact Book, Chicago Metropolitan Area, 1960* (Chicago: University of Chicago, 1963).

[5]Ruth Shonle Cavan, *Suicide* (New York: Russell & Russell, Inc., 1965).

total samples, e.g., suicide in Los Angeles, New York City, Paris, etc. Generally, tests of significance are not necessary in dealing with total samples since you already have the entire universe. But, of course, tests of significance are relevant between universes.

Even though we will test for significant differences between our sample and others, to embark on such a project thoroughly would take us beyond the prescribed limits of this investigation. The variables needed for comparison are not directly or easily accessible. Fortunately, some materials that already are published can help here. Dublin cites 1960 death rates by suicide for United States cities of 100,000 or more population.[6] For example, the range for whites varied from a national high of 30.6 in San Francisco, California, to a low of 2.2 in Knoxville, Tennessee. Thirty-one of the 97 cities listed showed no nonwhite suicides. The high for nonwhites occurred in Worcester, Massachusetts, where the rate of suicide was 43.3 for nonwhites compared with a rate of 7.6 for whites. There seems to be no particular patterning to the distribution of the nonwhite immunity from suicide. Chicago's rates were listed as 11.5 for whites and 3.6 for nonwhites. This means that Chicago's rates are just about at the median point for the cities listed.

Most of our own investigation centers on intrasample contrasts. For example, in Chapter 8 certain areas of the city of Chicago are classified into high and low suicide zones. Data by Durkheim, Cavan, Dublin, and others is interwoven throughout the book in an attempt to check our sample against other samples. A more sophisticated job of controlling might include gathering data on Cook County's attempted suicide rate (which is difficult to determine but is probably six to eight times that of the completed suicide rate),[7] its natural death rate (about which little is known, precisely because it is considered natural; e.g., the coroner conducts no inquests of natural deaths), its homicide rate, its rate of death for chronic and acute illness, and its death rates by accidents. Moreover, it would be necessary to know not just the death rates but also some personal and social attributes of those

---

[6]Louis I. Dublin, *Suicide: A Sociological and Statistical Study* (New York: The Ronald Press Co., 1963), pp. 220–21.

[7]See Erwin Stengel, *Suicide and Attempted Suicide* (Great Britain: Penguin Books, 1964).

dying by various means. We have been unable to do much with these latter controls with the Chicago data. Some of these types of checks are brought in from secondary sources. Chapters 4–8 give a detailed description of the sample. Primary sources of data outside of our data are the Vital Statistics of the United States and the state of Illinois, and the inquest records of the Cook County Coroner's Office (an extension of knowledge about the sample).[8]

The data employed in this study are primarily in the form of suicide rates (unless otherwise qualified, the phrase "suicide rate" always means the crude rate, which is the frequency of suicides per 100,000 population, not controlling for age or sex). This is sound procedure, since we are working with a total sample. The suicide rate is the dependent variable. Major independent variables are sex, age, race, marital status, community area, occupation, time, social class, median family income, education, and quality of housing. The dependent and independent variables are cross-tabulated, with relevant controls being made when possible. When appropriate, tests of significance and measures of association are calculated for our tables.[9]

One of the problems that arose was that the population figures used to determine the suicide rates were available only for the year of 1960 while the sample suicides were for the five-year period from 1959 through 1963. If the 1960 population were multiplied by five, this would allow the computation of rates over the five-year period. Another advantage of this approach is that it would increase the accuracy of the rates in cells where the number of cases otherwise would be dangerously small. That is, as the number of cases increases, the rate is less likely to be biased.

The major disadvantage of this approach is that it ignores possible significant variations in the population in the non-1960 years; e.g., can it be assumed safely that the suicide rates for

[8]U.S. Department of Health, Education and Welfare, "Final Mortality Statistics, 1966," *Monthly Vital Statistics Report,* Vol. 16, No. 12 (March, 1968) ; Illinois Department of Public Health, *Vital Statistics Illinois, 1959–1963,* Illinois Department of Public Health, Springfield, Illinois; and Cook County Coroner's Inquest Records, County Building, Chicago, Illinois.

[9]Since we have a large total sample over a five-year period, most differences are significant. Thus, significance testing is usually unnecessary. We are more interested in the patterning of the differences.

nonwhites would not be biased, given the changes in the proportion of Negroes in Cook County since 1960? One obvious solution to this dilemma is to rely on 1960 data only. A second alternative would be to attempt to specify the amount of error in the various rates by studying trends in population growth comparing population sizes in previous census years (e.g., 1930, 1940, 1950, and 1960). A third check on a general level would be to compute the suicide rates for the total population in Cook County (figures that are known) for all the five years in order to determine the variability of the suicide rates. Unfortunately, this would not guarantee that particular suicide rates which make up the parts of the yearly total rates would be consistent with the general yearly rates.

A fourth procedure would be to avoid rates altogether and to use only percentages of the yearly suicide totals. A fifth alternative would be to use a combination of specific and general frequency counts, percentages, and rates.

We elected to go ahead and multiply the 1960 population figures by five and construct a five-year rate. One reason this was done was that the population figures were so large in comparison with the suicide frequencies that it would take a considerable variation in population size to affect the rate. Furthermore, a study of literature from the Department of City Planning of Chicago suggested that the bias, if any, was likely to be conservative since the population of Chicago had declined about 2 percent from 1950 to 1960.[10] The following section presents a detailed discussion of some of the changes in the Chicago population, especially between 1950 and 1960.

Suicide and social characteristics in the Chicago area

A thorough consideration of suicide and of the social characteristics of Chicago and Cook County in this section is impossible. In writing this chapter we experienced the same frustrations that often come from trying to define "sociology" in the initial lecture of an introductory course. Nonetheless, previews have their part

---

[10]Larry Reich and Thomas P. Melone, *Basic Policies for the Comprehensive Plan of Chicago* (Chicago: Department of City Planning, 1965) .

to play. The reader should regard what follows as a general orientation to a subject. Having been read, it should be considered used up and be discarded.

Table 3 describes the frequency of suicide in Cook County in the context of other selected causes of death. Heart disease, the leading cause of death, accounts for just under half of all the deaths in Cook County. Though deaths by suicide do not approach the astronomical figure of those by heart disease, it is worthy of

Table 3.   Deaths by cause for selected years, Cook County, Illinois.

Year	All Deaths	Suicide	Homicide	Motor Vehicle Accidents	Heart Disease	T.B.*	Ulcer
1950	48,283	474	297	844	21,021	1,530	348
1951	48,827	417	284	820	21,576	1,278	325
1952	49,259	385	310	964	21,732	1,145	306
1953	50,741	431	325	932	22,704	872	346
1954	48,460	431	319	879	21,213	771	324
1955	50,160	415	341	865	22,573	672	342
1956	50,733	435	323	837	22,617	590	315
1957	53,456	430	358	742	23,974	519	378
1958	52,865	482	352	736	23,456	520	390
1959	52,732	481	357	628	23,434	446	402
1960	53,832	444	394	661	23,974	406	435
1961	53,063	438	422	709	23,821	331	438
1962	54,559	482	435	661	24,721	356	441

*Tuberculosis.
Source: Bureau of Statistics, Illinois Department of Public Health, Springfield, Illinois.

note that suicides do exceed deaths by homicide, tuberculosis, and ulcers, and approach those by motor vehicle accidents. It is interesting and somewhat puzzling that suicides have not received the public attention and research funds apparently warranted by their numbers. For example, why are the mass media saturated with murder mysteries but not suicide mysteries? Why does almost every city in the United States over 100,000 population have an organized tuberculosis prevention center but only a few cities have a suicide prevention center? (This situation is changing rapidly. In 1968 there were approximately 75 suicide prevention centers.) Why are peptic ulcers (not duodenal) considered as indicators of occupational success, whereas suicide attempts are looked upon as instances of "temporary insanity"?

The only other remarkable feature of Table 3 is the constancy of the frequency of suicides over the years. In order to determine more exactly the variation in the occurrence of suicides, increments in population must be taken into consideration. Table 4 standardizes suicides by frequency per 100,000 Cook County population for the years 1959 through 1963.

Table 4. Suicide rates per 100,000 population by year for Cook County and Chicago, Illinois, 1959–63.

Year		Cook County	City of Chicago
1959	....	8.2	8.3
1960	....	7.8	8.3
1961	....	8.1	8.9
1962	....	8.5	9.0
1963	....	9.0	9.2
	5-year average	8.3	8.8
		N = 2,153	N = 1,547

Source: Rates computed from death certificates and population of Cook County and Chicago, Illinois, from the records of the Bureau of Statistics, Illinois Department of Public Health, Springfield, Illinois. Unless otherwise specified, the source of data in all subsequent tables is assumed to be our Cook County sample.

With the exception of a slight trough, the suicide rates in Cook County from 1959 to 1963 also have been remarkably stable. When the five-year period is considered as a whole, the suicide rate for Cook County is 8.3. Although Cavan found a rate of 15.3 *in Chicago* from 1919 to 1921, there is evidence that urban rates in general and Chicago rates in particular have declined since Cavan's research.[11] This is true in spite of the fact that both Cook County and Chicago show slightly increased suicide rates over the five-year period being studied.

In every year the suicide rate for the City of Chicago was higher than that of Cook County (which includes the hinterland of Chicago as well as the city). The data show a rate of 7.8 in 1960 for Cook County. Dublin's rate for Chicago in 1960 was 9.4.[12] Some tolerance of difference in rates of independent researchers must be allowed. For example, it was discovered that about 20 death

---

[11]Cavan, *op. cit.*, p. 77.
[12]Dublin, *op. cit.*, p. 223.

certificates each year were mistakenly classified as suicides by the Department of Public Health of the state of Illinois, even though they were marked as "undetermined" in reference to the cause of death.

In the five-year period to be studied, the population of the state of Illinois was about 10 million in any given year, with Cook County making up about half of the state's total. Of the approximately five million people in Cook County, roughly 3.5 million live in the city of Chicago. Table 5 gives the exact popu-

Table 5.   Population of the state of Illinois, Cook County, and Chicago, 1959–63.

Year	Illinois	Cook County	Chicago
1959	9,974,000	5,043,600	3,613,100
1960	10,078,000	5,129,725	3,550,404
1961	10,090,000	5,217,000	3,500,000
1962	10,146,000	5,246,000	3,450,000
1963	10,400,000	5,270,000*	3,534,000*

*Estimate.
    Source: Bureau of Statistics, Illinois Department of Public Health, Springfield, Illinois.

lation distribution. Figure 3 presents a graphic illustration of the boundaries of Chicago and Cook County, with special emphasis on the population distribution of those portions of Cook County that are not within the city limits of Chicago. There is high social density in the near-western municipalities, especially Oak Park and Cicero, and in the near-northern cities of Evanston and Skokie.

One of the striking attributes of Cook County is the virtual nonexistence of a rural population. According to the United States Census criteria for rural areas, less than 1 percent of Cook County's population is rural (see Table 6). Since 99 percent of the Cook County population is classified as urban, in effect our study of suicide is really a study of suicide in an urban area.

Extensive research has been conducted concerning the demographic characteristics of the city of Chicago.[13] In a very cursory manner the salient features of the city population should be accented. Between 1950 and 1960 Chicago's population declined by 70,000 persons, or 1.9 percent. In addition to out-migration,

---

[13]Kitagawa and Taeuber, *op. cit.;* and Reich and Melone, *op. cit.*

Figure 3.   Municipalities of 2,500 or more population, Chicago–Northwestern Indiana standard consolidated area, 1960.

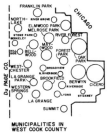

MUNICIPALITIES IN
WEST COOK COUNTY

Table 6.   Area and population of Cook County, Illinois, urban and rural, 1960.

Land area	954 square miles
Number of people	5,120,725
Number of people per square mile	5,377.1
Urban population	5,077,186
Urban population as percentage of county population	99.0*
Rural population	52,539
Rural population as percentage of county population	1.0

*Given that the Cook County population is 99.0 percent urban, it will not be possible to make meaningful rural-urban comparisons in reference to the suicide rate.

decreases in the average household size contributed to the population decline. The number of households actually increased from 1950 to 1960. In general, the population shifts followed the decentralization pattern mentioned by Burgess, with the core ("Central Business District") of the city losing large amounts of its population to the outlying suburban areas.[14]

The city's age groups below 20 and above 64 gained about 19 percent and 26 percent respectively of their 1950 figures while those between the ages of 20 and 64 decreased in numbers. This trend is expected to continue and even to be accelerated in the next 30 years. In general, the changes in the composition of the city population show no significant variation by sex.

Chicago's nonwhite population grew by 323,000, or 64 percent. In 1960 the nonwhite population amounted to 24 percent of the city's total population. Among the 10 largest cities in the United States in 1960, Chicago ranked seventh in nonwhite population (behind Washington, Baltimore, Detroit, Cleveland, St. Louis, and Philadelphia, and ahead of Houston, Los Angeles, and New York). It appears that the majority of nonwhite population growth was due less to migration than to natural increases. It is projected that the city's nonwhite population will number some 1,540,000 by 1980, compared with the 1960 figure of 337,656.

Chicago compares favorably with its suburbs in the middle income brackets ($5,000-$9,000) but suffers by comparison in

---

[14]R. E. Park and E. W. Burgess, *The City* (Chicago: University of Chicago Press, 1925).

lower income and upper income brackets. For example, whereas 30 percent of Chicago families earned less than $5,000 in 1959, only 16 percent of the suburbanites fell in that category. Likewise, while 21 percent of the Chicago families earned over $10,000 in 1959, 32 percent of suburban families did so.

Summary

In Chapter 4 we have said where we are going with our empirical investigation, how we intend to get there, and that we expect to fall somewhat short of the mark given the limitations of our data. Still, our sample is large and covers a five-year period. We are confident that our results will be empirically sound, though limited in the number of variables considered. We begin our empirical analysis in Chapter 5 with a close look at the relationship between the suicide rate and temporal factors.

CHAPTER 5

The deception of plausibility: temporal variations in suicide

It is instructive to see at least in one case how Durkheim treated the relationship of suicide and a nonsocial variable.[1] Remember that Durkheim contended that suicide was a social phenomenon and could only be explained by variation in social variables. Clearly, if there should be a high correlation between seasonal or diurnal variables and suicide, then Durkheim's theory of suicide would be threatened.

When Durkheim discussed the fluctuations of the suicide rate at different times of the year, month, and week, his purpose was to refute theorists who argued that climate and seasonal temperature affected the suicide rate. For example, Morselli had found that there were considerably higher suicide rates in Europe where the climate was temperate.[2] Durkheim countered that the same climatic zone may have a high suicide rate at one time or place and a low suicide rate at another time (in the same place) or at another place (in the same time and zone). In short, when climate is constant, the suicide rate varies (or the converse). Thus, climate cannot explain the variation in the suicide rate.

Cold, foggy, or dark days were considered by Montesquieu to

---

[1]Emile Durkheim, *Suicide* (New York: The Free Press, 1962) , pp. 57–144.
[2]*Ibid.*, p. 105.

be conducive to depression and suicide.[3] Durkheim was also aware of the high suicide rate of the French Army during the retreat from Moscow.[4] Nonetheless, Durkheim's statistics showed that men are more likely to abandon their lives when physical environmental factors are the most conducive to health and comfort, viz, during the daytime, in the summer (see Figure 4.1). This suggested that either temperatures had little to do with suicide or that heat provoked or aggravated suicidal tendencies. For example, Durkheim mentioned that during the Egyptian campaign suicides in the French Army increased and that in the tropics men had been seen to fling themselves into the sea after being in the sun too long.[5] A final possibility was that any extreme temperature provokes suicide.

Durkheim decided that if temperature was the basic cause of suicide, then suicide should vary with temperature.[6] Durkheim's method of determining causation was what John Stuart Mill had called "the Method of Concomitant Variation." Generally, this method states that:

. . . whatever phenomenon varies in any manner whenever another phenomenon varies in some particular manner, is either a cause or an effect of that phenomenon or is connected with it through some fact of causation.[7]

Mill illustrates this method for discovering the relationship between the position of the moon and the tides of the sea:

We cannot try an experiment in the absence of the moon, so as to observe what terrestrial phenomenon her annihilation would put an end to; but when we find that all the variations in the *position* of the moon

---

[3]*Ibid.*, p. 106.

[4]*Ibid.*, p. 110.

[5]*Ibid.*

[6]Furthermore, countries with similar temperatures should have similar suicide rates. Perhaps the most famous refutation of this hypothesis is what Herbert Hendin calls the "Scandinavian suicide phenomenon"; viz, the high suicide rates in Sweden and Denmark and the low suicide rate in Norway (Herbert Hendin, *Suicide and Scandinavia* [Garden City, N.Y.: Anchor Books, 1965]) . Sweden's suicides are a "performance" type; i.e., suicides centered around work and success problems. Denmark's suicides are a "dependency loss" type; i.e., reflect a tendency to passivity and an oversensitivity to abandonment. The Norwegians' demands for success and achievement are far less rigid than those of the Swedish. The Norwegians are less likely than Danes to be hyperdependent as adults. Thus, the Norwegians have a lower suicide rate than either the Swedes or the Danes.

[7]Irving M. Copi, *Introduction to Logic* (2d ed.; New York: The Macmillan Co., 1961) , p. 386.

are followed by corresponding variations in the time and place of high water, the place being always either the part of the earth which is nearest to, or that which is most remote from, the moon, we have ample evidence that the moon is, wholly or partially, the cause which determines the tides.[8]

In order to test Durkheim's hypothesis we constructed Table 7, which portrays the percentage of suicides by month and season. The frequency of suicide was then ranked from high (rank of 1) to low (rank of 12) for each month. This procedure was followed for the Cook County data, Durkheim's data, and for four other control samples. The results are presented in Table 8 and Figure 4.

Table 7.   **Percentage of suicides by month and season in Cook County, Illinois, 1959–63.**

Month		Monthly Percentage	Seasonal Percentage	N
SPRING	March	10 (n = 205)	28	(596)
	April	8 (183)		
	May	10 (208)		
SUMMER	June	9 (186)	25	(543)
	July	8 (185)		
	August	8 (172)		
FALL	September	8 (160)	24	(513)
	October	9 (199)		
	November	7 (154)		
WINTER	December	8 (168)	23	(501)
	January	7 (155)		
	February	8 (178)		
		100 (2,153)	100	(2,153)

Using X^2 as a goodness of fit test on the distribution of suicides by month and by seasons, we find significant differences between the observed and the expected frequencies (i.e., the means for all months and seasons). The probabilities for the actual distribution of suicides for months and seasons are 0.05 ($X^2 = 26$; d.f. = 11) and 0.01 ($X^2 = 13$; d.f. = 3), respectively. Table 7 and Figure 4.2 reveal that suicide is high in March (205 suicides), May (208), and October (199), and low in November (154). Seasonally, most suicides occur in the Spring.

Even though we do discover significant differences in the inci-

---

[8]John S. Mill, *A System of Logic* (1843), Book III, chap. viii, p. 6.

Figure 4. Ranking of suicide frequencies from highest (1) to lowest (12) by months of the year.

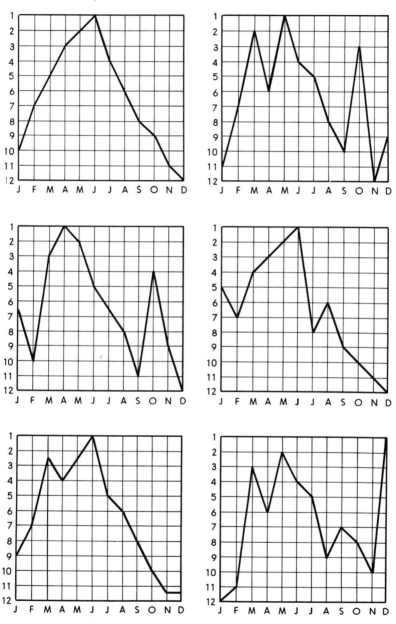

Source: Table 8, p. 81.

dence of suicide by month and season, it is difficult to argue convincingly that these differences are the result of fluctuations in temperature. For example, the incidence of suicide is high in three months with very different temperature. Thus, suicide is relatively constant, while the temperature varies. We shall have to look to other variables than temperature to explain the differences we have uncovered.

When we rank the monthly suicide frequencies from high (1) to low (12) adding controls, there is no evidence that temperature is causally associated with suicide. From Figure 4 and Table 8 we see that the relationship between suicide and temperature is apparently more complex than Durkheim thought.[9] There is, in fact, little correlation between temperature and suicide. Thus, there is nothing to explain.

For example, in the United States in 1960 (Figure 4.3) the incidence of suicide was low in both February (a cold month) and September (a warm month). Cavan found (Figure 4.6) the most suicides in December, not in June, as Durkheim did. In New York City (Figure 4.4) there were a few suicides in February and December (cold months) *and* in July (a warm month). Since suicide and temperature have no consistent relationship, there is no reason for believing them to be causally associated.

Furthermore, there are rapid changes in suicide frequency with no corresponding change in temperature. In New York City, June had the highest incidence of suicide, but July dropped to eighth highest. Cavan's data show November to have the third

---

[9]Durkheim, *op. cit.*, p. 112. The ranks of suicide frequency by month between the six samples are highly correlated. Spearman's rank order correlation* was computed for some of the possible 15 combinations. For example:

$$r_{s12} = +0.71$$
$$r_{s13} = +0.67$$
$$r_{s25} = +0.71$$
$$r_{s26} = +0.57$$
$$r_{s24} = +0.54$$

All correlations were substantial to very strong and were positive, indicating a high amount of agreement on ranks between the six samples.

$$* \, r_s = 1 - \frac{6 \sum\limits_{i=1}^{N} Di^2}{N\,(N^2-1)}$$

Table 8. **Rank of suicide frequency by months for selected places and years.**

Month	1 France, 1866–70	2 Cook County, 1959–63	3 United States, 1960	4 New York, 1958–61	5 U.S. Cities, 1959*	6 Chicago, Illinois 1915–25
January	10	11	6.5	5	9	12
February	7	7	10	7	7	11
March	5	2	3	4	2.5	3
April	3	6	1	3	4	6
May	2	1	2	2	2.5	2
June	1	4	5	1	1	4
July	4	5	6.5	8	5	5
August	6	8	8	6	6	9
September	8	10	11	9	8	7
October	9	3	4	10	10	8
November	11	12	9	11	11.5	10
December	12	9	12	12	11.5	1

*United States cities of 100,000 or more.
Sources: (1) Emile Durkheim, *Suicide* (New York: The Free Press, 1962); (2) Illinois Department of Public Health; (3–5) Louis I. Dublin, *Suicide: A Sociological and Statistical Study* (New York: The Ronald Press Co., 1963); and (6) Ruth S. Cavan, *Suicide* (New York: Russell & Russell, Inc., 1965).

lowest incidence of suicide but December to have the highest incidence of suicide. Such a situation could not exist if suicide and temperature were causally related.

Diurnal variations

If temperature causes suicide, then suicide should be at a maximum at the times of day or night which are the hottest or coldest. According to the United States Weather Bureau, regardless of the time of year the order of decreasing warmth is noon, 6 p.m., midnight, and 6 a.m.[10] Table 9 and Figure 5 give the percentage of suicides by time of day for the Chicago sample. It can be seen that the order of decreasing frequency of suicide is afternoon, late morning, evening, and early morning.[11] There is obviously a significant difference between the percentage of suicides committed in the afternoon and the early morning. Thus, it might appear at first glance that temperature did have some effect on suicide.

[10]U.S. Department of Commerce, Weather Bureau Climatic Guide for Chicago, Illinois, Area, No. 40–11 (Washington, D.C.: U.S. Government Printing Office, June, 1962), p. 38.
[11]$X^2 = 418$; 23 d.f.; $p = 0.001$.

Table 9.   Percentage of suicides by time of day in Cook County, Illinois, 1959–63.

Time of Day		Hourly Percentage		N
EARLY MORNING	12 A.M.	2 (n = 43)		
	1	2	(43)	
	2	2	(36)	
	3	1	(30)	10 (213)
	4	1	(27)	
	5	2	(34)	
LATE MORNING	6	3	(57)	
	7	4	(92)	
	8	4	(84)	
	9	5	(105)	27 (578)
	10	5	(104)	
	11	6	(136)	
AFTERNOON	12 P.M.	5	(105)	
	1	5	(117)	
	2	6	(139)	35 (754)
	3	6	(120)	
	4	6	(127)	
	5	7	(146)	
EVENING	6	7	(142)	
	7	4	(84)	
	8	3	(72)	22 (482)
	9	2	(56)	
	10	3	(67)	
	11	3	(61)	
	UNKNOWN	6	(125)	6 (125)
		100 (2,153)		100 (2,153)

However, Table 10, which relates the frequency of suicide with the time of day, reveals that temperature is certainly not a direct cause of suicides.[12] For example, most suicides are committed not at the hottest or coldest times of the day but in the late afternoon. Note that 6 P.M. had the second highest incidence of suicide (f = 142) but 7 P.M. was ranked 13th in incidence of suicide, even though the temperature was the same for all practical purposes. The reader might also notice that both 8 A.M. and 7 P.M. had 84 suicides, although the former time of day is rather cool and the latter relatively warm. Finally, if extreme tempera-

---

[12] X^2 = 302; 3 d.f.; p = 0.001.

Figure 5.   Frequency of suicides by time of day in Cook County, Illinois, 1959–63.

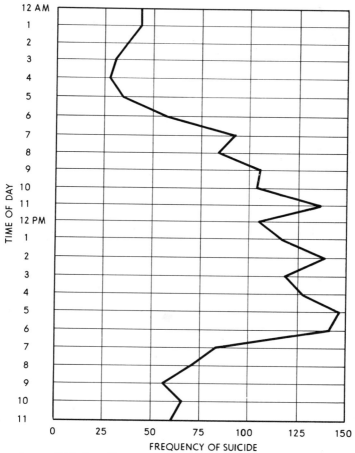

Source: Table 9, p. 82.

tures provoked suicide, then there ought to be more suicides from 11 A.M. to 3 P.M. than from 5 to 7 P.M. Table 10 shows the reverse to be true. Such disparities as the above make it very dubious that there is any causal relationship between temperature and suicide.[13]

---

[13]A final test of suicide and temporal variation was conducted by controlling for day of the week on which the suicide was committed. Since the day of the week has little or no relationship to temperature or climate and since there were no significant differences between the suicide incidences by day of the week, these data are not presented here.

Table 10.   Rank of suicide frequency by time of day in Cook County, Illinois, 1959–63.

	Rank	Time of Day	Frequency
HIGH	1	5 P.M.	146
	2	6 P.M.	142
	3	2 P.M.	139
	4	11 A.M.	136
	5	4 P.M.	127
	6	3 P.M.	120
	7	1 P.M.	117
	8	12 P.M.	105
	9	9 A.M.	105
	10	10 A.M.	104
	11	7 A.M.	92
	12	8 A.M.	84
	13	7 P.M.	84
	14	8 P.M.	72
	15	10 P.M.	67
	16	11 P.M.	61
	17	6 A.M.	57
	18	9 P.M.	56
	19	1 A.M.	43
	20	12 A.M.	43
	21	2 A.M.	36
	22	5 A.M.	34
	23	3 A.M.	30
LOW	24	4 A.M.	27

Discussion

If temperature and climate do not produce temporal variations in the frequency of suicide, what does? For example, why should the incidence of suicide be high in the late afternoon (especially 5 to 7 P.M.) but low in the early morning (2 to 5 A.M.)? Table 11 shows that about 75 percent of the Chicago suicides were committed at home and only 1 percent on the job. Since only about 4 percent of the male suicides were listed as unemployed, it appears that the work situation and fellow employees acted as a kind of constraining force on the would-be suicide. Notice that most suicides were reported immediately after the end of the workday when the individual was suddenly on his own. Thus, it is a reasonable hypothesis that the 5 to 7 P.M. suicides were in part a response to occupational *anomie* and egoism.

Such an interpretation of the data is consistent with Durkheim's remarks in the Preface to the second edition of *The Division of*

Table 11.   Suicides by place of injury and sex, Cook County, Illinois, 1959–63.

Place of Injury	Male		Female		Total	
	%	N	%	N	%	N
Home	72	1,116	80	481	74	1,597
Job	2	24	—	2	1	26
Confined	3	41	2	11	2	52
Hospital	4	44	3	17	3	61
Public lodging	4	61	4	23	4	84
Outside	8	133	6	38	8	171
Other	7	114	5	31	7	145
Unknown	1	16	—	1	1	17
Total: %	100		100		100	
N		1,549		604		2,153

$$X^2 = 200; \text{d.f.} = 7;$$
$$p = 0.002$$

Labor in Society.[14] He argues that economic, administrative, military, religious, and familial institutions have lost much of their power to regulate in modern society.[15] Since many persons live almost entirely within the commercial and industrial world,

. . . what we especially see in the occupational group is a moral power capable of constraining individual egos, of maintaining a spirited sentiment of common solidarity in the consciousness of all the workers. . . .[16]

In another passage which reminds one of S. M. Lipset's *et al.*, *Union Democracy*,[17] Durkheim writes that:

A nation can be maintained only if, between the State and the individual, there is intercalculated a whole series of secondary groups near enough to the individuals to attract them strongly in their sphere of action and drag them in this way, into the general torrent of social life. We have shown how occupational groups are suited to fill this role. . . . Occupations today absorb the major part of our collective forces. . . . Perhaps now we shall be better able to explain the conclusions we reached at the end of our book, *Le Suicide*.[18]

---

[14]Emile Durkheim, *The Division of Labor in Society* (New York: The Free Press, 1960), pp. 1–31.

[15]*Ibid.*, p. 3.

[16]*Ibid.*, p. 10.

[17]Seymour M. Lipset *et al.*, *Union Democracy* (New York: The Free Press, 1956), *passim*.

[18]Durkheim, *The Division of Labor in Society*, pp. 28–29.

If occupational *anomie* and occupational egoism are causes of suicide, then during the 5 to 7 P.M. period suicides should be lower on Saturdays and Sundays (nonwork days) than during the workweek (i.e., Monday through Friday). The relative *anomie* and isolation should be greater after a workday. Table 12 con-

Table 12.   Suicides by day, time, and sex, Cook County, Illinois, 1959–63.

Day of Week	5–7 P.M.	
	Males	Females
Sunday	25	20
Monday	40	19
Tuesday	26	23
Wednesday	28	16
Thursday	29	22
Friday	28	23
Saturday	24	19
Total	200	142

X^2 for Sunday and Monday only has a probability of 0.19, which approaches statistical significance.

firms this prediction and thus lends support to Durkheim's contention that work is a suicidal prophylactic. Note particularly that male suicides skyrocket after their first day back at work. Since most females in the sample were housewives (61 percent), their suicides show no significant weekend-workweek variation.

Furthermore, if the work situation were the main causal variable, we would expect more males than females to suicide between 4 and 6 P.M. since more males in the sample were employed (96 percent versus 36 percent). Table 13 confirms this prediction.

Table 13.   Suicides by time and sex, Cook County, Illinois, 1959–63.

Time of Day	Males	Females	Ratio of Males to Females
3–4 P.M.	85	35	2.42
4–5 P.M.	92	35	2.63
5–6 P.M.	106	40	2.65
6–7 P.M.	94	48	1.96
Total	377	158	

However, as we shall see in the following chapter, this finding is far from conclusive since the ratio of all male-female suicides is 2.5:1. If the work situation is the primary determinant in the male suicide, we would expect even larger differences in the male-female suicide ratio at after-work hours than we actually find. The dilemma is that 96 percent of the males in the sample work (do not commit suicide at work) and yet do not show a particularly striking rise in suicide during normal after-work hours. There are several possible solutions to this dilemma. At this point in our study we can only suggest what they are since a full discussion of the dilemma would force us to introduce data prematurely and out of context. First, we may have to reject partially the first horn of the dilemma. It is highly dubious that 96 percent of the males were working when they suicided. For one thing the death certificate calls for "usual occupation," not present occupation. In addition there is evidence that unemployment is understated on the death certificate.[19] If either of these two possibilities are fact, then while suicidal males still have a work problem, it would not be so likely to manifest itself at the end of the workday. For example, they may have been fired or retired just prior to their suicide. Second, occupational *anomie* and egoism can manifest itself at other nonwork times. For example, during the lunch hour the male-female suicide ratio is 2.8:1; everyday between 7 P.M. and 8 A.M., the ratio is 2.6:1; and on weekends, the ratio is 2.6:1. Third, the day of the suicide may be vocationally unique. A man who usually works could quite conceivably depart from his regular work pattern in order to commit suicide and yet not have this "truancy" reported on the death certificate. Finally, the female suicide incidence for 3 to 7 P.M. could be overestimated on the death certificates (for the reasons considered below).

Given the limitations of our data, we can only speculate on the relationship between time and female suicides. Most previous research has shown marital discord to be the functional equivalent of male work problems in causing female suicide.[20] For example, data in the following chapter will reveal that the suicide rate for females plateaus between ages 35 to 45, whereas male suicides

---

[19]Warren Breed, "Occupational Mobility and Suicide among White Males," *American Sociological Review,* Vol. 28, No. 2 (April, 1963), pp. 182 ff.

[20]See Chapter 6 of this book.

continue to increase with age. The suicide rate for married females is constant or declining at retirement age but is rising sharply for males. Our data (see Table 14) demonstrate that marriage protects the female less than the male (the female has what Durkheim called a lower "coefficient of preservation").

Table 14.   Suicide rates per 100,000 population by age, sex, and marital status, Cook County, Illinois, 1959–63.

Age Group	Males			Females		
	Single	Married	Ratio of Single to Married	Single	Married	Ratio of Single to Married
35–44	29.8	16.7	1.8	9.4	5.9	1.6
45–54	39.0	25.6	1.5	8.8	7.5	1.2
55–64	58.3	32.4	1.8	12.3	7.0	1.7

If marital discord was an important factor in the suicidal deaths of females, then we would expect a high incidence of female suicides when the husbands and children come home and are available for interaction; i.e., 5 to 7 P.M. Furthermore, it seems plausible that female suicides increase as the day wears on not necessarily because they are more likely to suicide then, but because they are more likely to be discovered then by their husbands and children. The time of death on the death certificate is often the time the body was found, not when the death actually occurred. Thus, many females classified as late afternoon suicides probably in fact suicide earlier in the day. As Table 15 suggests, most females are discovered by their spouses—a high percentage of whom work. Further discussion of the aetiology of female suicides will have to be deferred until the next chapter.

There is less consistency in seasonal variations in suicide. Thus, it is less clear what needs to be explained. Generally, suicide is low in the winter, increases in the spring and early summer, and declines in early fall. Sometimes suicide rises again in October. Consistent with our earlier interpretations, early summer increases might be explained in part by holidays. That is, the summer is a time when people are suddenly freed for a few weeks from their jobs. The result is temporary *anomie*. Furthermore, isolation should be felt more keenly in the summer since perceived inter-

Table 15. Suicides by relation of informant to decedent and sex, Cook County, Illinois, 1959–63.

Relation of Informant	Male		Female		Total	
	%	N	%	N	%	N
Husband	0	0	40	239	11	239
Wife	26	408	0	0	19	408
Daughter	5	79	8	47	6	126
Son	15	234	8	50	13	284
Mother	3	38	4	22	3	60
Father	5	84	5	27	5	111
Sister	7	104	9	54	7	158
Brother	12	185	7	45	11	230
Step-child	1	16	—	2	1	18
Other relative	13	199	10	58	12	257
Friend	8	119	6	37	7	156
Custodian	—	1	—	0	—	1
Coroner	2	33	1	8	2	41
Other	3	49	2	15	3	64
Total: %	100		100		100	
N		1,549		604		2,153

action of others increases sharply. In the winter there is less leisure and less *anomie*. Isolation is a common phenomenon. Since everyone is more isolated, there is less differential egoism. Durkheim contended that:

If voluntary deaths increase from January to July, it is not because heat disturbs the organism but because social life is more intense. To be sure, this greater intensity derives from the greater ease of development of social life in the summer than in the winter, owing to the sun's position on the ecliptic, the state of the atmosphere, etc. But the physical environment does not stimulate it directly; above all, it has no effect on the progression of suicide. The latter depends on social conditions. Of course, we are yet uncertain how collective life can have this effect.[21]

Conclusion

This chapter is intended to serve as an illustration of Durkheim's elimination from causative contention of what he labels "extra-social factors." Our main conclusion is that suicide is not caused directly by temperature or climate. The chapter is a

---

[21]Durkheim, *Suicide,* pp. 121–22.

prototype of Durkheim's negative analysis. No serious attempt has been made to establish causal connections. Furthermore, we have evaded the question of indirect or multiple causation, although it was suggested that certain times were conducive to particular human activities, which in turn had a causal influence on suicide.

In spite of inconclusive evidence, we have argued that the failure of social constraint is a better predictor of temporal variations in suicide than temperature or climate. More specifically, we claimed that occupational *anomie* and egoism and marital discord were in large part responsible for the variation in suicide over time. Other factors were discovery of female suicides late in the day due to interaction patterns, greater perceived isolation during the summer months deriving from increasingly visible interaction of others, and interaction-pattern change during holidays. Nonetheless, social variables were only implicit in the present analysis. We have yet to consider sociological variables explicitly, making a serious attempt to establish probable causal relationships. It is to this task that we turn now.

Suggestions for further reading

Borman, Leonard D.   "Chicago Call for Help Clinic: Summary Report and Comparison of Some Findings." Paper read at the First Annual National Conference on Suicidology, Chicago, Illinois, March 20, 1968. Illustrates basic differences in the temporal patterns of suicide prevention center clients and completed suicides.

Dublin, Louis I. *Suicide: A Sociological and Statistical Study,* chap. vii, "Seasonal Rhythms in Suicide." New York: The Ronald Press Co., 1963. United States and English data compared with Durkheim's French sample.

Durkheim, Emile.   *Suicide,* chap. iii, "Suicide and Cosmic Factors." New York: The Free Press, 1962. Durkheim argues that climate or temperature are extrasocial factors and do not cause suicide.

Hendin, Herbert.   *Suicide and Scandinavia.* Garden City, N.Y.: Anchor Books, 1965. Demonstrates that while there is little temporal variation among Sweden, Denmark, and Norway, the suicide rates vary considerably. Psychiatric explanations for the variation in suicide are offered.

Morselli, Henry.   *Suicide: An Essay in Comparative Moral Statistics.* New York: D. Appleton, 1903.

CHAPTER 6

Some core sociological variables:
sex, age, race, and marital status

Sex, age, race, and marital status are "core" variables in that they indicate fundamental, and in most cases highly visible, human differentiation. Some of the most undeniable truisms concerning human beings are that they are divided into male and female, young and old, black and white, married and unmarried. Furthermore, these variables are core variables because they almost always are highly associated with pronounced variation in human behavior and attitudes. Suicide rates are no exception. Durkheim discovered significant differences in suicide rates by sex, age, and marital status. As we will see, Durkheim did not consider race a social factor.

Table 16 represents Durkheim's findings (converted from rates per million to rates per 100,000 for purposes of facilitating comparison) on the variation of suicide rates by age and sex in France from 1835 to 1844. From this table Durkheim concludes that suicide is very rare during childhood and reaches its peak only in old age.[1] A second important observation is that suicide is essentially a male phenomenon.[2]

The Chicago data (Table 17) substantiate Durkheim's hy-

---

[1] Emile Durkheim, *Suicide* (New York: The Free Press, 1962), p. 101.
[2] *Ibid.*, p. 72. Cf. p. 166.

Table 16. Suicide rates per 100,000 population by age and sex, France, 1835–44.

Age Group	Males	Females
Below 16	0.2	0.1
16–20	5.7	3.2
20–30	13.1	4.5
30–40	15.6	4.4
40–50	20.5	6.5
50–60	21.8	7.5
60–70	27.4	8.4
70–80	31.7	9.2
80 and above	34.5	8.1

Source: Emile Durkheim, *Suicide* (New York: The Free Press, 1962).

pothesis that suicide is extremely uncommon among both males and females age 14 and under but not that suicide reaches its peak only in old age. The latter hypothesis is true for males (indeed, the Chicago sample shows even higher rates than does Durkheim's) but not for females. The Chicago female suicide rate peaks at around age 50 and remains on more or less of a plateau until the age 85 and over, then it drops. This exception to Durkheim's hypothesis is supported by Dublin who discovered the same female plateau using 1959 United States Vital Statistics and Census data (see Table 18).

Table 17. Suicide rates per 100,000 population by age and sex, Cook County, Illinois, 1959–63.

Age Group	Males*	Females†	N
0–14	—‡	—‡	2
15–24	6.2	2.5	131
25–34	11.0	5.3	276
35–44	14.2	6.9	385
45–54	20.5	8.0	456
55–64	24.4	8.5	406
65–74	34.9	8.1	329
75–84	48.9	8.6	145
85 and over	54.3	4.7	22
Unknown	—	—	1
N	1,549	804	2,153

*Pearson product-moment correlation between Cook County male suicide rates and United States male suicide rates (1959) = + 0.96.

†Pearson product-moment correlation between Cook County female suicide rates and United States female suicide rates (1959) = + 0.94.

‡Blank cells indicate that there were too few cases to permit computation of accurate rates.

Figure 6.   Suicide rates per 100,000 population by age and sex, Cook County, Illinois, 1959-63, and France, 1835-44.

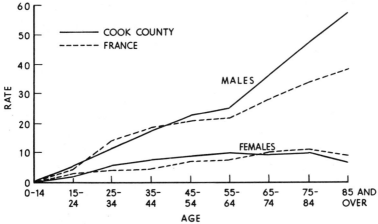

Source: Tables 16 and 17, p. 92; and Emile Durkheim's *Suicide* (New York: The Free Press, 1962).

Age and the suicide rate

These being the facts, what is their explanation? To begin with the older a person is, the greater is his wish to die. As noted in Chapter 3, Menninger theorized from clinical experiences that

Table 18.   Mortality from suicide by marital status and age groups among men and women 15 years and over in the United States, 1959 (rates per 100,000 population).

Age Group	Total	Single	Married Males	Widowed	Divorced
15-24	7.4	6.8	8.4	—	19.7
25-34	14.5	23.2	11.1	95.8	66.7
35-44	20.5	29.8	16.7	81.7	112.6
45-54	30.3	39.0	25.6	58.3	111.7
55-64	39.1	58.3	32.4	65.0	80.4
65-74	45.5	82.0	33.6	79.6	152.5
75 and over	54.6	85.3	34.5	79.2	140.0
			Females		
15-24	2.1	1.7	2.4	—	12.4
25-34	5.5	9.2	4.7	7.2	17.8
35-44	6.9	9.4	5.9	10.2	24.4
45-54	8.5	8.8	7.5	12.0	17.4
55-64	9.8	12.3	8.0	12.4	19.6
65-74	9.7	9.6	7.5	11.3	25.8
75 and over	6.4	4.0	4.6	6.9	18.4

Source: National Office of Vital Statistics, unpublished data.

every suicidal act had at least three components: the wish to kill, the wish to be killed, and the wish to die.[3] These three components are reflected in conscious hate, guilt, and hopelessness, respectively. In an imaginative piece of work Shneidman and Farberow analyzed suicide notes by age in terms of the predominant component expressed in the note. Generally, they found that the wish to kill and the wish to be killed decreased with age while the wish to die increased.[4] One of the sources of hopelessness among the old is their failing health. Failing health is associated positively with both age and the suicide rate.[5] The older one is, the more likely he is to be ill. The more ill a person is the more likely he is to kill himself. The truth of this generalization was particularly evident in the African suicides studied by Paul Bohannan.[6]

On the other hand, hopelessness among the old is not simply the result of physical and mental illness.[7] The responses to the tribulations of old age are conditioned by social factors. For example, the more socially isolated a person is, the less is his will to live.[8] Most persons as they become older also become more socially isolated. Their friends and relatives die, their children grow up and move away, the associations which were important to them tend to dissolve. In short, they become more excessively individuated (what Durkheim would have called more "egoistic").

Furthermore, poor health often contributes to the loss or modi-

---

[3]Karl Menninger, *Man against Himself* (New York: Harcourt, Brace & World, Inc., 1938), pp. 24–71. The "wish to die" is more highly associated with completed suicide than either the "wish to kill" or the "wish to be killed."

[4]Norman L. Farberow and Edwin S. Shneidman, "Suicide and Age," in Edwin S. Shneidman and Norman L. Farberow (eds.), *Clues to Suicide* (New York: McGraw-Hill Book Co., Inc., 1957), pp. 41–49. Cf. I. R. C. Batchelor, "Suicide in Old Age," *ibid.*, p. 148. "Violent methods are more commonly employed (by older people) than they are by younger people."

[5]Batchelor, *ibid.*, p. 145, ". . . in old age the great majority of suicidal people are suffering from psychoses, usually depressive and organic dementias."

[6]Paul Bohannan (ed.), *African Homicide and Suicide* (Princeton, N.J.: Princeton University Press, 1960). Cf. Ronald Maris, "The Sociology of Suicide Prevention: Policy Implications of Differences between Suicidal Patients and Completed Suicides," paper presented in Boston at the 1968 Annual Meeting of the American Sociological Association.

[7]Erwin Stengel, *Suicide and Attempted Suicide* (Great Britain: Penguin Books, 1964), p. 39. Cf. Batchelor, *op. cit.*, p. 146.

[8]Batchelor, *op. cit.*, p. 150. Among the attempted suicides investigated in Scotland, feelings of loneliness, of being a burden on others, or of being unwanted were found in about 60 percent of the cases.

fication of a previous self-conception, especially for males. Nobel prize winner in physics, Percy Bridgman, left this suicide note: "Why wait, my work is done?" Older males often experience problems of adjustment upon withdrawal of previously held vocational rights and privileges.[9] Occupational retirement signifies not only a change in one's job status but also a change in the material basis for one's self-conception and in the external sources of order and discipline. Thus, among males, the older one is, the more *anomie* (normlessness) and self-image problems experienced, the higher the suicide rate. The majority of women never experience occupational deprivation. Accordingly, their suicide pattern shows little correlation with work.

Shneidman and Farbérow have shown that the younger a person is, the greater his wish to kill.[10] Suicide among the young occurs primarily because aggression cannot be vented on external, frustrating objects. Thus, youthful suicides are a good example of what Karl Menninger has called "murder-in-the-one-hundred-and-eightieth-degree."[11] Marshall Schechter has described the psychodynamics of self destruction in children:

In general, in adults . . . when an individual's hostility cannot be expressed outwardly, it is turned against the introjected objects, which—because they are a part of the self—results in the attempted or actual destruction of the self . . . these descriptions have also stressed the factor of the extreme dependence of the child on the parent, his love object. Thus, whenever children feel the threat of the loss of a love object, they not only develop feelings of rage, but feelings of helplessness and worthlessness as well . . . the child's size and ego-status also militate against the use of specific instruments of destruction. Thus, children rarely commit suicide or even make overt suicidal attempts or threats, but rather express their self-destruction feelings in other ways. These may be called "suicidal equivalents," that is, attenuated attacks on the introjected object which result in depressions, "accidental" injuries, antisocial acts, and the like—all of which have the potentiality of ending in the destruction of the individual.[12]

The interesting question about children is why so few of them

[9]*Ibid.*, p. 149.

[10]Shneidman and Farberow, *Clues to Suicide*, p. 45.

[11]Menninger, *op. cit.*, pp. 23–45. Cf. Marshall D. Schechter, "The Recognition and Treatment of Suicide in Children," *Clues to Suicide*, p. 131.

[12]Schechter, *op. cit.*, pp. 131–32.

suicide. Schechter has described the psychodynamic restraints. Sociologically we would argue that parents are to children what American whites are to American Negroes and what men are to women, viz, targets for aggression and sources of external constraint. On the one hand, parents provide children with alternative outlets for aggression, a perceived source of frustration outside of the child. On the other hand, children are subjected to greater external constraint than adults; e.g., to more parental regulation and familial involvement. Almost all children have families, not nearly all adults have spouses or children of their own. Furthermore, adulthood confers freedom largely absent in adolescence and childhood. The net result is a clear differential in social constraint for children and adults. It might be remarked that the suicide rate for the very old drops sharply and that old age almost always marks a return to a childlike dependency and constraint.

Finally, children have fewer objective circumstances conducive to the generation of feelings of hopelessness. Among the young there is less physical and severe mental illness, more opportunity for situational change, less time to have developed grave disenchantments with the world. Thus, the younger a person is, the more dependent, regulated, and involved the person is with other persons, the greater the number of targets for external aggression, the greater the wish to kill, the less hopelessness felt, and the lower the suicide rate.

Sex and the suicide rate

Durkheim found roughly three times as many male suicides as female suicides in all age brackets. Our sample shows rapidly increasing disparities between the male and female rates, starting with a male-female ratio of about 2:1 in the younger ages, rising to 3:1 in the middle ages, and culminating with the male rates far outstripping the female rates in the last two age brackets. Dublin's data correspond to Durkheim's from ages 15 to 65 but confirm our findings on the suicide rates of males and females ages 65 and over. There is agreement among all researchers that male suicides exceed female suicides at all ages.

Why should males be more likely to suicide than females? The answer may be simply that females choose less lethal methods for their attempts. Table 19 shows that while men prefer the

Table 19. Suicide rates per 100,000 population by method of death and sex, Cook County, Illinois, 1959–63.

Method	Males	Females	N
Firearms	4.8	0.8	703
Hanging	3.6	0.9	578
Gases	1.2	0.5	206
Poisons	1.0	1.2	282
Cutting or piercing instruments	0.5	0.1	75
Jumping from heights	0.9	0.5	169
Drowning	0.4	0.2	68
Crushing	0.1	0.08	25
Other methods	0.09	0.3	47
N	1,549	604	2,153

highly lethal methods of firearms, women prefer the far less lethal method of poisons. The lethality of the method used becomes especially pertinent to the question of the male-female suicide rate differential when it is known that the ratio of the *attempted* suicide rate is three females for every male, i.e., exactly the opposite of the completed suicide rate sex ratio.[13] If the lethality of the suicide attempt were held constant, we would expect the male and female suicide rates to be approximately equal.

But why do females choose less lethal methods for their suicide attempts? Although it could be argued that women are less familiar with the use of firearms, that they are more concerned with their appearance after death, etc., we contend that the methods chosen by females and males reflect the differential nature of their motivation to suicide.[14] Female suicides are usually responses to marital problems that manifest themselves relatively early in the female's life. The female suicide is more of a sign of a wish to kill her spouse or children—a retroflexed anger or "cry for help" in a domestic crisis—than it is a sincere wish to die. The female suicide is relatively young and still has hope for a resolution of her problems before her death. Often a suicide attempt is a prob-

---

[13]Stengel, *op. cit.*, p. 76; and Norman L. Farberow and Edwin S. Shneidman (eds.), *The Cry for Help* (New York: McGraw-Hill Book Co., Inc., 1961), p. 28.

[14]Peter Sainsbury, *Suicide in London* (London: Chapman & Hall, Ltd., 1955), p. 80.

lem-solving act. Finally, since the female suicide attempter is usually married, has children, and is not exposed to job failure, she is more regulated and less isolated than the male. Jack Gibbs and Walter Martin contend that female status-configurations are more integrated and that they experience less role conflict than males.[15] Since status integration and the suicide rate are inversely related, females have lower suicide rates than males.

Male suicides are usually responses to work problems (such as retirement, unemployment, and downward occupational mobility) which occur relatively late.[16] For example, Andrew Henry and James Short, Jr., have shown that male suicide rates are more highly correlated with fluctuations in the business cycle than female suicide rates are.[17] The male suicide has less hope than the female; he wants primarily to die, not to kill. His vocational aspirations and achievement have made him more vulnerable to work failure, retirement problems, and the resultant personal and social *anomie* and isolation. The highest rates of male suicides occur among those who live alone, are unmarried or divorced, and have no children.

In order to explore the dynamics of older male suicides, a systematic random sample of white males, age 50 or more, who were unmarried or- separate, was drawn from the total sample. The cases of each of the suicides selected were then studied in some depth by analyzing their coroner's inquest records. One of the striking characteristics of the cases was the isolation of the suicides, what Durkheim would have called their "egoism." These men were highly isolated in a number of ways. For example, consider the factor of residence. Some lived alone in attics; others lived in skid row hotels; still others lived by themselves in apartments. About half of the men lived alone. The attribute of physical isolation is worth noting because often it is a symptom of social isolation.

More prominent than the physical isolation of the cases was

---

[15] Jack P. Gibbs and Walter T. Martin, *Status Integration and Suicide* (Eugene, Ore.: The University of Oregon Press, 1964), pp. 26, 61–62.

[16] Warren Breed, "Occupational Mobility and Suicide among White Males," *American Sociological Review*, Vol. 28, No. 2 (April, 1963), pp. 179–88.

[17] Andrew Henry and James F. Short, Jr., *Suicide and Homicide* (New York: The Free Press, 1954), p. 31.

their social isolation. When one man's landlady found him hanging, she exclaimed, "This isn't for me," and fled the attic. In another case a man's sister-in-law did not try to cut him down when she found him hanging. Many of those testifying at the various inquests commented upon their surprise that so-and-so would kill himself. One can only wonder how close these "friends" and relatives were to the decedents. One man's son-in-law claimed that he knew "nothing at all" about the suicide of his father-in-law, even though they lived in the same house. In the case of the skid row pariahs it is rather unlikely that they had many good friends since their known contacts were primarily exploitive (such as trying to sell articles to each other for money to buy alcohol).

Most of the men studied had no dependents. It was not uncommon for there to be no relatives present at the inquest or for the relatives who were present to have had no contact with the decedent for quite some time. Many of those testifying at the inquest had only a contractual relationship with the deceased. For example, several of the cases were best known by their landlords.

In these studies it would appear that the will to live often was negated by poor physical health and concomitant mild neuroses. It was not uncommon for those suffering from the infirmities of old age to say that they wished to die. One man gave up hope of being cured of his asthma attacks. Another was "tired of living." The extreme poverty of some made subsistence itself a chore. One suicide note indicated that the suicide felt "there was no other way out" of his imagined serious illness. Another claimed that he "couldn't take 'it' [*sic*] any longer."

The social isolation and apathy of these cases rather clearly classify them as Durkheim's egoistic suicide type. But why should older, white males who are single tend to be excessively individuated? By definition, being single is to be relatively isolated and so requires little explanation. Becoming older usually entails progressive dependence upon others in order to meet your basic needs. Many people, including friends and relatives of aging individuals, refuse or are unable to assume the burden of caring for the dependent aged. Consequently, more often than not older people are left to fend for themselves or are cared for by professional "sitters." Not only are the dependent aged a nuisance but they can also be depressing to be around. They can serve as a mirror which reflects the ultimate situation of the viewer.

Recently some attention has been focused on the consequences of treatment of suicide attempts for accomplishing suicide.[18] Although the overall effect on the suicide rate is probably minor, it is interesting to speculate that females receive more efficient treatment when they attempt suicide than males do and that as a result of this better treatment more females than males survive.

We conclude that the higher male suicide rate and his use of more lethal methods of attempting suicide are both indicators of his differential motivation to suicide *vis-à-vis* the female.

Race and the suicide rate

Having discussed suicide in relation to sex and age, it would seem natural, or at least conventional, to consider differentials in suicide rates by race. Durkheim, however, treats race as an "extra-social factor" or nonsocial factor. It is extrasocial because races are differentiated by organic characteristics, i.e., resemblance and filiation of groups of people based on heredity.[19] The implication is that the social is nonorganic and that it cannot be transmitted from generation to generation by some genetic process but must be learned by being raised in a particular group context.

In retrospect it becomes fairly clear that to the degree that sex and age are regarded as biological phenomena, they, too, fall outside the realm of the social. Of the core variables, only marital status is a purely social factor. If the criterion for a factor being social is whether or not the factor is discussed in Book One or in Book Two of Durkheim's *Suicide* (entitled "Extra-Social Factors" and "Social Causes and Social Types" respectively), then race is nonsocial, marital status is social, and sex and age are marginal variables which have both social and nonsocial aspects. It would have been heuristic to treat all four of the core variables in the manner that sex and age are treated; i.e., to the degree that

---

[18]James L. Wilkins and Irwin Goffman, "Accomplishing Suicide," paper presented in Miami at the 1966 Annual Meeting of the American Sociological Association.

[19]Durkheim, *op. cit.*, pp. 82 ff.

a variable is organic or physical, it should be regarded as nonsocial and, conversely, to the degree that a variable is not physically given (i.e., to the degree that it is a product of human interaction), it should be designated social.

In Durkheim's discussion of race he ignores the possibility that nonsocial phenomena can have far-reaching social ramifications by virtue of being defined as social. Ethnocentrism is a striking example of the reification of this possibility.

It would appear that Durkheim is being reductionistic and inconsistent when he claims that race is nonsocial. Furthermore, Durkheim's arguments do not refute the *possibility* that suicidal types or tendencies may be inherited (an argument used to discredit the causal role of race in suicide). For example, Durkheim writes:

For as suicide by itself is in no sense sexual, there is no reason why inheritance should afflict men rather than women. Now, actually, the suicides of females are known to be very few, only a slight fraction of those of males. This would not be so if heredity had the influence attributed to it.[20]

Where is the evidence that suicide "is in no sense sexual"? How does the variation of suicide with age show that no organic-psychic state can possibly be its determining cause?[21] Baldness seems to be inherited, and yet it appears late in life and primarily among males.

It has become common in post-Durkheimian suicide literature to regard race as a social phenomenon (in the sense that physical givens have social consequences) and thus to present suicide rates in which race is controlled for.

Table 20 presents the Chicago sex and age data controlled for race. The suicide rate decreased from white males to nonwhite males, white females, and nonwhite females, regardless of age. The ratio of white to nonwhite suicides in the Chicago data was 2.2 for both males and females (see Table 21). Dublin found ratios of 2.4 for males and 2.7 for females in 1960.[22] Suicide is virtually absent among the 0–14 age group for all races. Only in

---

[20]*Ibid.*, p. 99.

[21]*Ibid.*, p. 102.

[22]Louis I. Dublin, *Suicide: A Sociological and Statistical Study* (New York: The Ronald Press Co., 1963), p. 34.

Table 20. Suicide rates per 100,000 population by sex, age, and race, Cook County, Illinois, 1959–63.

Age Group	Males			Females			N
	White	Nonwhite Cook County	Nonwhite U.S. 1960*	White	Nonwhite Cook County	Nonwhite U.S. 1960*	
0-14	—	—	—	—	—	—	2
15-24	6.4	5.1	5.3	2.2	3.7	1.5	131
25-34	10.9	11.7	12.9	6.2	—	3.5	276
35-44	14.8	11.0	13.5	7.4	4.4	3.7	385
45-54	22.5	—	12.8	8.6	3.6	3.2	456
55-64	28.2	—	16.9	7.9	—	3.4	406
65-74	36.7	—	12.6	8.6	—	3.8	329
75-84	52.0	—	11.3	9.4	—	4.2	145
85 and over	61.6	—	15.9	—	—	5.0	22
Unknown	—	—	—	—	—	—	1
N	1,417	132		552	52		2,153

*Source: National Office of Vital Statistics, unpublished data.

Table 21. Suicide rates per 100,000 population by sex and race, Cook County, Illinois, 1959–1963*.

	Males	Females	N	Ratio of Males to Females
White	13.7	5.1	1,971	2.7
Nonwhite	6.3	2.3	182	2.7
N	1,549	604	2,153	
Ratio of white to nonwhite	2.2	2.2		

*It is customary to include distributions of homicides and accidents as controls on the suicide rate distribution. We could not obtain these controls for Cook County, but we do have data on them nationally (remember the high positive correlation between Cook County and national suicide rates):

	Homicide Rates per 100,000			Accident Rates per 100,000		
	Male	Female	Ratio of M to F	Male	Female	Ratio of M to F
White	3.9	1.5	2.6	72.2	33.0	2.2
Nonwhite	35.7	9.1	4.0	94.0	38.1	2.5
Ratio of W to NW	0.1	0.2		0.8	0.9	

Notice especially the nonwhite, white ratio reversals with homicide and accident rates and the nonwhite male homicide rate excess.

one cell does the suicidal frequency hierarchy reverse itself. Suicides of nonwhite females outnumber those of white females in the 15–24 age bracket. Furthermore, nonwhite suicides peak early and remain on a plateau, except for a slight increase among the very old. Contrary to the pattern of white suicides, nonwhite suicides are concentrated in the 15–45 age group (in the Chicago data). Thus, three patterns in the Chicago data call for an explanation: the low Negro suicide rate, the concentration of Negro suicides in the 15–45 age category, and the high suicide rate among young Negro females.[23]

Why should the Negro suicide rate generally be lower than that of whites? Negroes tend to experience more frustration than do whites, particularly in their efforts to realize vocational aspirations. Negro aggression is more likely to be other-directed rather than self-directed, primarily because they undergo a *status* deprivation relative to most whites and because they have a higher degree of relational involvement than do most whites.[24] In other words,

---

[23]Ninety-seven percent of Chicago's nonwhite population were Negroes (1960).

[24]The South Side of Chicago is a huge Negro ghetto with a high degree of what Henry and Short call "relational involvement." For example, the Negro community has a very high population per household (see our Chapter 8).

Figure 7.   Suicide rates per 100,000 population by sex, age, and race, Cook County, Illinois, 1959–63.

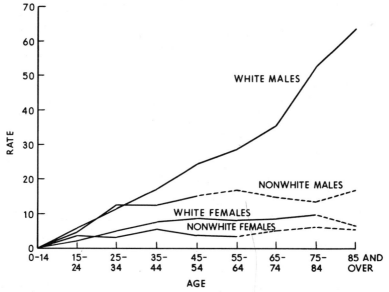

Source: Nonwhite rates in part approximated from National Vital Statistics data (dotted lines indicate approximations).

Negroes as a group are externally constrained more than whites as a group. Earlier researchers have demonstrated that the suicide rate varies inversely with the strength of the relational system.[25] When people are subjected to strong external constraint, by virtue either of subordinate status or intense involvement in social relationships with other persons, it is easier to blame others when frustration occurs. But when the external constraints are weak, the self must bear a greater burden of responsibility for frustration. Thus, it has been hypothesized that Negroes are more likely than whites to commit homicide and less likely than whites to commit suicide.[26] The Chicago research adds further confirmation of this hypothesis.

It is important for our general theory of suicide to note that among Negroes strong external constraint is associated with a *low* suicide rate. However, having emphasized this association, we

[25]Henry and Short, *op. cit.*
[26]*Ibid., passim.*

must ask the further question, "What *does* cause Negro suicides?" Once again it was necessary to turn to case histories from the Cook County coroner's files to attempt to answer the question. This time we made a systematic random sample of Negro suicides, ages 15–45. From inquest records several salient characteristics emerged.

First, physical health did not play a very large role in the aetiology of Negro suicides, but neurotic behavior apparently did play a major role. Undoubtedly the youth of the Negro suicides diminishes the relevance of the physical factor. In any case, mental health, not physical health, was the keynote in the type of suicide illustrated in the cases studied.

In all cases the decedents' physical health was recorded officially as good. Furthermore, the decedents' mental condition was conspicuously poor. For example, one young woman suffered from a "pregnancy psychosis." Another young woman was a chronic depressive whose condition probably was associated with the deprivation of her son's attention and her husband's refusal to let her behave religiously or to smoke. Still another woman manifested a stoical depression. A 27-year-old male was distraught "because his girlfriend left him." A 26-year-old male was upset because he was separated from his wife and children.

A mildly striking difference between the young Negro cases and the previous cases of older white males is the former's lack of social isolation. Suicide does not seem to be a product of excessive individuation but rather of a malfunctioning of social interaction. Isolation was more difficult, if for no other reason than because the Negro decedents had more dependents than the subjects of the first cases.

The Negro subculture puts a high premium on gregariousness.[27] Thus, when a young woman was estranged from her son and her husband, when a young man's love-life became unhappy, and when another young man was unable to visit his children, they were very likely to be profoundly disturbed. Their objective situations were intensified perhaps because satisfying social rela-

---

[27]Daniel P. Moynihan, "Employment, Income, and the Ordeal of the Negro Family," in Talcott Parsons and Kenneth B. Clark (eds.), *The Negro American* (Cambridge: Houghton Mifflin Co., 1966), p. 147; and Thomas F. Pettigrew, *A Profile of the Negro American* (Princeton, N.J.: D. Van Nostrand Co., Inc., 1964), pp. 18–19.

tionships were more highly valued in the Negro subculture than in the white.

The Negro cases present dramatic illustrations of what Edwin Shneidman calls "the cry for help."[28] As we have seen, often young people in an estranged domestic situation (especially females) do not really want to kill themselves but rather some frustrating external object. Nevertheless, they attempt suicide in an effort to draw attention to their profound dissatisfaction with their present circumstances. For example, one young male in the cases studied shot four others but *poisoned* himself. If he really wanted to die, shooting himself would have been much more certain. It has been noted earlier that women prefer poisoning to all other suicide methods and that although women are more likely than men to attempt suicide, they are far less successful.

Another interesting aspect of the Negro suicides is their *ad hoc* character. It often seems that if the particular crisis could have been weathered, suicide often could have been avoided. In the cases of the older white males the circumstances giving rise to the suicides were more pervasive and less likely to pass with time.

What tentative conclusions can we draw from the depth study of cases of Negro suicides? For one thing the Negro's high degree of social regulation and involvement with others probably is a major factor in the low Negro suicide rate. However, it is possible that hyperregulation is also a cause of Negro suicides; external constraint may be like a two-edged sword. In an unpublished paper on Negro suicides in New Orleans, Warren Breed observed many of the same contrasts between white and Negro suicides as we did in Chicago.[29] Not only were the New Orleans' Negroes more sociable (i.e., more frequent in church attendance, visited friends and neighbors more often, etc.) than whites, had fewer work problems than whites, were younger than the whites, but also the Negroes had more difficulty with authority, especially the police. The Negro's suicide in response to hyperregulation by the police suggests that extreme external constraint *in some limited circumstances* can actually cause, not prevent, suicide. Such

---

28Cf. Carl I. Wold, "The Cry for Help," unpublished manuscript from Los Angeles Suicide Prevention Center, Los Angeles, California, 1965.

29Warren Breed, "The Negro and Fatalistic Suicide," unpublished manuscript (New Orleans, La.: Tulane University, 1967).

suicides were called "fatalistic" by Durkheim.[30] We must return to this apparent anomaly in our findings when we construct our formal theory of suicide. The theory will not be adequate if mutually contradictory theorems can be derived from the postulate.

A second major finding from the case materials is that Negro suicides are often generated from transient domestic crises. Most Negro suicides are the consequence of retroflexed anger rather than of the wish to die. Since the Negroes are young and the crises acute rather than chronic, if the "cry for help" is heeded and professional treatment administered, there is an excellent chance of preventing Negro suicides.[31]

We are left with the question as to why young Negro females should have a particularly high suicide rate. It is well known that young Negro women are more often expected to manage and support their family than are young white women.[32] This fact suggests that the nonwhite female's role is similar to the white male's role. For example, Henry and Short found that nonwhite female suicide was more highly correlated with fluctuations in the business cycle than was nonwhite male suicide.[33] It follows that the nonwhite female is subjected to both domestic conflicts and to work problems associated with playing the role of the breadwinner. This double stress could easily account for the young Negro female having a higher suicide rate than the young white female. Apparently the more women who enter into the work world, the greater is their proneness to suicide. In Japan since the industrialization following World War II, the suicide rate of young women has risen rapidly.[34]

Marital status and the suicide rate

In his discussion of marital status and suicide, Durkheim claimed that from about 20 years on, married persons of both sexes enjoy a "coefficient of preservation" (i.e., married persons

---

[30]Durkheim, *op. cit.*, p. 276.

[31]Cf. Lee N. Robins, "Suicide and Violence: Explaining the Low Negro Suicide Rate," paper read at the Annual Meeting of the American Sociological Association, San Francisco, California, 1967.

[32]Pettigrew, *op. cit.*, pp. 15 ff.; and Moynihan, *op. cit.*, pp. 147 ff.

[33]Henry and Short, *op. cit.*, p. 87.

[34]Dublin, *op. cit.*, p. 24.

are so many times *less* likely to suicide) in comparison with un-married persons, that the coefficient of preservation of married people varies with the sexes, and that too early marriages have an aggravating influence on suicide, especially for men.

The Chicago data (see Table 23) and the 1959 United States Vital Statistics confirm Durkheim's hypothesis that from age 25 on marriage protects against suicide, although the protection is less for females than for males.[35] Actually, married females have a higher coefficient of preservation than married males. For ex-ample, married females 25 to 54 years old are about twice as immune to suicide as 25- to 54-year-old married males. *But* it is doubtful that their marriage is offering much immunity since marriage protects females less than males, especially in the 45- to 54-year-old age group. Over age 65 married females are three times as immune to suicide as married males; however, once again, little of this immunity derives from their marriages.

The data also show that married males and females have a higher coefficient of preservation than nonmarried males and females, although, again, the protection is less for females than males. For example, the coefficient of preservation of married males versus divorced males 35 to 44 years old is 6, but for married females versus divorced females, the coefficient is 5. The coefficient of preservation increases for married males as we compare them successively with never-married, widowed, and divorced males.

Table 22.   Ratio of suicide rates of the never-married to the married by sex and age, Cook County, Illinois, 1959–63.

Age Group	Males	Females
0–14	—	—
15–24	1.0	0.74
25–34	3.3	2.5
35–44	2.2	2.1
45–54	1.6	0.91
55–64	1.5	1.5
65–74	1.7	—
75 +	1.9	—

Source: Table 23, p. 109.

[35]Pow Meng Yap, *Suicide in Hong Kong* (Hong Kong: Hong Kong University Press, 1958), pp. 28 ff.; and Calvin F. Schmid, *Suicides in Seattle, 1914 to 1925* (Seattle, Wash.: University of Washington Press, 1928), pp. 39 ff.

Table 23. Suicide rates per 100,000 population by marital status, sex, and age, Cook County, Illinois, 1959–63.

Age Group	Males				Females					N
	Married	Never Married	Widowed	Divorced	Married	Never Married	Widowed	Divorced	Unknown	
0-14	—	—	—	—	—	—	—	—	—	2
15-24	6.0	6.1	—	—	2.7	2.0	—	—	—	131
25-34	7.0	22.8	—	32.3	3.7	9.3	—	19.0	—	276
35-44	10.5	23.2	—	60.0	5.2	10.8	—	24.0	—	385
45-54	16.9	26.6	33.3	69.5	7.8	7.1	6.8	—	—	456
55-64	19.3	29.0	34.1	61.0	6.3	9.4	10.1	—	—	406
65-74	16.3	43.5	59.8	—	8.3	—	7.0	—	—	329
75 and over	36.2	67.3	63.5	—	—	—	8.1	—	—	167
Unknown	—	—	—	—	—	—	—	—	50	1
N	372	328	174	133	342	86	104	64	50	
		1,507				596				2,153

The younger the married male is, the stronger this trend is; i.e., the more marriage protects against suicide (with the exception of very young married males and old, single males). The same pattern of immunity holds for married females, but the coefficient of preservation is generally less. Being younger is not as aggravating for married females as it is for married males. For example, early widowhood or divorce is much less likely to culminate in suicide for females than for males.

These being the facts, how do we explain them? First, why should marriage protect against suicide? We argue that the external constraint of the married is greater than that of the unmarried. Henry and Short write:

> We assume that the relational system of the married is stronger, on the average, than the relational system of the unmarried. . . . With (this) assumption the data support the hypothesis that suicide varies inversely with the strength of the relational system (because persons with strong relational systems are subjected to greater external restraints than persons with weak relational systems).[36]

All married persons have at least one significant human being besides themselves to contend with. Marriage is a source of regulation. It requires that one take into account the desires, needs, and rights of at least one other person. Thus, the decision to suicide must involve a consideration of the consequences of the act for the spouse as well as for the suicide. For example, "What would she think of me?" "Would she still receive my full insurance benefits?" "How would the children be treated at school?" "Will he discover me before I die and try to save me?"

Durkheim concluded that the family was the essential factor in the immunity of married persons.[37] The larger the family the less the chance of suicide. Data show that when marriage produces children, the coefficient of preservation is almost doubled.[38] The assumption is that larger families mean more regulation of individual activity and less social isolation. In Chapter 8 we check the population per household in Negro communities (which have a very low suicide rate) and find them to have a significantly

---

[36]Henry and Short, *op. cit.*, pp. 16 and 75.
[37]Durkheim, *op. cit.*, p. 198.
[38]*Ibid.*, p. 186.

higher population per household than communities with very high suicide rates. This finding lends additional support to the constraining force of significant others.

There have been other explanations of the low suicide rate of the married. One of the most common is that superior human beings are selected for marriage. Conversely, physical, social, and psychological misfits are rejected for marriage. Consequently, the unmarried population is inferior in ways that increase their tendency to suicide. Durkheim describes this hypothesis of "matrimonial selection":

> Marriage in fact does make for some sort of selection among the population at large. Not everyone who wants to, gets married; one has little chance of founding a family successfully without certain qualities of health, fortune and morality. People without them, unless through a conjunction of exceptionally favorable circumstances, are thus involuntarily relegated to the unmarried class which consequently includes the dregs of the country. The sick, the incurable, the people of too little means or known weaknesses are found here. Hence, if this part of the population is so far inferior to the other, it naturally proves this inferiority by . . . a stronger suicidal tendency.[39]

There are at least two reasons why the selection hypothesis is not convincing. First, if it were true, then the suicide rate among young married persons ought to be less than that among young unmarried persons. There is in fact a coefficient of aggravation at ages 15 to 25 among married persons. Second, there is in modern industrial society a tendency for professionals and students to defer marriage longer than the less talented and less ambitious. Only the grossly inferior are disqualified from marriage; and their numbers are not sufficient to account for the different suicide rates of the married and unmarried.

A second major finding to be explained is the lower level of protection which marriage offers females. Why should marriage protect females less than males? The answer to this question is contained in our earlier discussion of the aetiology of female suicides. It is primarily that marital problems are the major cause of suicide and suicide attempts among females, while for males work problems, not marriage, are especially associated with sui-

---

[39]*Ibid.*, p. 180.

cide. In a study of changes leading to recovery of patients who
had attempted suicide, Leonard Moss and Donald Hamilton discovered that: "Recovery requires a major change in the life
situation. . . . The most common changes, in the order of frequency, were (1) changes in occupation or retirement, and (2)
significant improvement in the marital relationship."[40]

Our solution is somewhat evasive. For example, we have not
considered adequately why marital problems provoke female suicides more than male suicides. It is clear why occupational problems do not provoke female suicides. Most of them do not have
an occupation. Perhaps it follows that for females their marriage
is their profession, their life's work. Consequently, to have a
marriage fail is more profoundly disturbing to females since
their identity, their sense of self-worth, is inextricably bound up
with having children, a congenial relationship with their spouses,
an attractive home, etc. The male, on the other hand, always has
his work. But these are only speculations. Someone needs to gather
data which bear on the problem.

Table 23 also shows that marriage protects the young less than
the old. Among males and females age 15–24, suicide rates for
the married are higher or about the same as those of the single.
The rate for married males is 6.0 as compared to 6.1 for single
males. This is in marked contrast with all following age brackets
in which married males have far smaller suicide rates than do
never-married males. Married females have a rate of 2.7, while
never-married females have a rate of 2.0. Dublin's work gives
further support to Durkheim's contention. The rates for the
married versus the never-married males and females (ages 15–24)
are 8.4 versus 6.8 and 2.4 versus 1.7, respectively.[41]

Why should marriage protect the young less than the old? To
begin with, remember that the young in all marital categories are
relatively unlikely to suicide. Being single does not keep the
suicide rate low; age does. What we are trying to account for is
the small but consistent difference between groups with low
suicide rates. Having said this, we may go on to point out that
young married couples are more likely to be mismatches than

---

[40]Leonard M. Moss and Donald M. Hamilton, "Psychotherapy of the Suicidal
Patient," *Clues to Suicide*, p. 107.

[41]Dublin, *op. cit.*, p. 27.

older married couples. Young husbands and wives are less likely to be fully developed emotionally and professionally; their self-images and aspirations are still in flux. Marital conflict is more likely among the young. Notice that the 15–25 age category would be expected to have more than its share of marital conflicts. Beginning with age 25 many of these mismatches have been resolved in one way or another. Consequently, older marriages are less stressful, at least in terms of preliminary adjustment difficulties.

Furthermore, early marriages result in a more sudden and dramatic change in the life styles of marriage partners. It is a rather abrupt shift to move from a relatively dependent and protected environment to one of major responsibility. Undoubtedly some *anomie* is generated. Notice also that young married persons have fewer children. It has been demonstrated earlier that expanding the nuclear family adds additional regulation and is associated with a lower suicide rate.

Finally, Durkheim mentions the possibility that after the initial charm of the young marriage has worn off, a kind of fatalism sets in, especially for males.[42] It is possible that young males find the discipline of marriage oppressive, especially if their reference group is other young married male acquaintances whose style of life stands in marked contrast to that of married males.

In conclusion, we must ask if widows have a higher coefficient of preservation than the unmarried. Put in other words, does having been married offer more protection against suicide than being single or divorced? The Chicago and United States Vital Statistics data confirm the hypothesis for widows versus divorcees (although the coefficient of preservation is less for females than for males). However, for widows versus the never-married, the hypothesis only holds for males and females age 65 and older and for single females, ages 25–34.

The sociological explanation for these data is rather straightforward. First, divorce is very disorganizing and stressful. The divorcee experiences considerably more *anomie* and isolation than the widow. The break is symbolic of deep-running problems of adjustment rather than of a simple, natural disaster. Second, the widow is *unavoidably* separated from the spouse. The divorcee

---

[42]Durkheim, *op. cit.*, pp. 275–76.

probably suffers from more guilt than the widow. Third, the divorcee may be denied the custody of any children, whereas the children are often brought closer to the widow. Fourth, the widow has more viable, consanguinal, familial relationships than either the divorcee or the never-married person. Finally, the 25–65-year-old widow has experienced the loss of a significant other compared with the single person of the same age. In addition, the young to middle-aged single person still has his job, his friends, and the possibility of marriage.

Conclusion

In general, the Chicago data confirm all of Durkheim's hypotheses on age, sex, race, and marital status. Older persons are more likely to suicide than younger persons. However, our data force us to qualify Durkheim's hypothesis for females. Female suicides peak at about age 35 and show no significant increases thereafter. Males are more likely to suicide than females at all ages. Whereas Durkheim found the male-female differential to be about the same at all ages, the Chicago data reveal that as age increases the male suicide rate exceeds the female suicide rate more and more. In short, the ratio of the male suicide rate to the female suicide rate increases with age.

By way of explanation we argued that the older males are, the more illness, the fewer significant others, the more occupational problems, *anomie,* and social isolation, the greater the wish to die, and the higher the suicide rate. Young females have more marital problems, more familial constraints, a greater wish to kill, use less lethal methods, and have a lower suicide rate than males.

Since Durkheim considered race a nonsocial fact, he presented no data nor offered any explanation of racial variation in the suicide rate. Nevertheless, social forces do vary by race. Our data show that whites are more likely to suicide than Negroes, with the exception that young Negro women have a higher suicide rate than young white women. Negro suicides are concentrated in the 15–45 age group. Negroes are highly constrained by their minority status, large families, and intimate associations with friends and neighbors. Furthermore, while they are frustrated by this hyperregulation, aggression is usually directed against external targets. Thus, their suicide rate is low. When suicide does occur, it often appears to be the consequence of retroflexed anger arising out of domestic crises.

We found general support for Durkheim's contention that the unmarried, married males, and those who married early were more likely to suicide than the married, married females, and those who married late. Although our data confirm that the divorced have a higher suicide rate than widows and widowers, only single males 65 and older exceeded the suicide rate of the widowed. The low suicide rate of the married can be explained in part by the large number of significant others a married person has. Spouses, children, and relatives function to minimize *anomie* and egoism. Likewise, the widowed have more significant others than the divorced. For example, widows have more consanguinal familial *restraints*. Furthermore, the divorced are separated from the spouse, children, and relatives. Although widowhood and divorce are both stressful experiences, it is likely that the divorcee feels more guilt for the rupture than the widow and thus has a greater wish to be killed.

Overall the findings of this chapter provide support for our major generalization; the more external constraint, the lower the suicide rate. Possible exceptions were uncovered in the discussion of Negro suicides and the suicides of young married couples. However, these possible exceptions are not disturbing since the suicide rates of both groups are very low.

Suggestions for further reading

Bohannan, Paul (ed.). *African Homicide and Suicide.* Princeton, N.J.: Princeton University Press, 1960. A pioneering research effort to explore suicide among African blacks. Recently published in paperback (New York: Atheneum, 1967).

Dublin, Louis I. *Suicide: A Sociological and Statistical Study,* chaps. iii, iv. New York: The Ronald Press Co., 1963. United States descriptive statistics on suicide, controlling for age, sex, marital status, and race.

Durkheim, Emile. *Suicide,* pp. 171–216, 259–76. New York: The Free Press, 1962. The classic statement of the relationship of suicide and marital status.

Henry, Andrew F., and Short, James F., Jr. *Suicide and Homicide,* chap. ii. New York: The Free Press, 1954. Considers the influence of business cycles and frustration-aggression on suicide by sex, race, age, and marital status.

Robins, Lee N. "Suicide and Violence: Explaining the Low Negro Suicide Rate." Paper read at the Annual Meeting of the American Sociological Association, San Francisco, California, 1967. Doubts that violence (e.g., homicide) substitutes for suicide among nonwhites.

Shneidman, Edwin S., and Farberow, Norman L. (eds.). *Clues to Suicide,* chaps. v, xiii, xiv. New York: McGraw-Hill Book Co., Inc., 1957. Three excellent essays on suicide and age.

Yap, Pow Meng. *Suicide in Hong Kong.* Hong Kong: Hong Kong University Press, 1958. A statistical survey of Hong Kong suicides by a psychiatrist.

CHAPTER 7

Suicide, status, and mobility

In every society that we know of there exist organized inequalities: people are different. They have varying amounts of money and sources of money. Some are doctors; others are laborers. A few have attended college; most have not. More importantly these differences are patterned. To say that patterned inequalities of wealth, power, and prestige exist is to argue that societies are "stratified." Differential and relatively consistent amounts of wealth, power, and prestige in society give rise to social classes. The concept of social stratification implies that social classes may be considered as arranged roughly in a hierarchical order, with those groups on the very top having a disproportionate share of wealth, power, and prestige and the groups at the bottom of the hierarchy being similarly disprivileged. In this chapter we shall be concerned with the relationship of social class or socioeconomic status ("SES") to the suicide rate.

Durkheim and Henry and Short have argued that the suicide rate has a direct relationship with social class: the higher the socioeconomic status, the higher the suicide rate. The analysis of the Chicago data reveals an inverse relationship. Clearly, this is a serendipitous finding; one which poses a serious challenge to Durkheim's and Henry and Short's explanations of suicide.

117

Somehow our unanticipated, anomalous, and strategic datum must be reconciled with Durkheim's results. We choose to proceed by an analysis and critique of Henry and Short's *Suicide and Homicide* since it incorporates and develops Durkheim's argument in a systematic social-psychological theory of suicide. In effect we hope to eliminate two rival explanations of suicide with the exegesis of one serendipitous result.

Henry and Short's *Suicide and Homicide*

Since 1954 Andrew Henry and James F. Short, Jr.'s *Suicide and Homicide* has had a marked influence on suicide research.[1] This work is primarily an examination of Durkheim's anomic type of suicide since it tests the influence of economic change on the suicide rate. Henry and Short use the so-called "Burns and Mitchell technique" for measuring the business cycles in the United States (especially from about 1940 to 1950) and the Ayres' Index of Industrial Activity.[2] Business cycles are then compared with various levels of suicide frequency.

The key concepts in Henry and Short's work are: (1) the frustration-aggression hypothesis, (2) social status, and (3) external and internal restraint. They assume that aggression is often a consequence of frustration, that business cycles produce variation in the hierarchical ranking of persons and groups, and that frustrations are generated by interference with the "goal response" of maintaining a constant or rising position in a status hierarchy relative to the status position of others in the same system.

"External restraint" includes the notions of "vertical restraint" (restraint deriving from one's subordinate position in a status

---

[1]Andrew F. Henry and James F. Short, Jr., *Suicide and Homicide* (New York: The Free Press, 1954), is a provocative and closely argued book. What follows is by no means an attempt to discredit its merits. In fact Henry and Short themselves have provided the impetus for our investigations. They write in a chapter entitled "Some Research Suggestions" that they "used the general positive association between suicide and status . . . as the basis of an assumption that persons committing suicide within each gross ascriptive category are recruited from the upper classes of the category. This assumption should be tested by examination of certificates of death by suicide." Our work is designed to test this assumption by the means suggested.

[2]*Ibid.*, Appendix II, pp. 133, n. 5; 141–54.

hierarchy) and "horizontal restraint" (restraint deriving from the degree of relational involvement with others). For example, it is argued that Negroes are more vertically restrained than whites and that the married are more horizontally restrained than the divorced. It was found that status was associated with fluctuations in the suicide rate in five out of six of the tests which Henry and Short performed and that suicide does vary inversely with the strength of the relational system.[3]

Strong internal restraint is associated with self-oriented aggression. The stricter the superego restraint, the greater the internal restraint.[4] Henry and Short argue that:

. . . the psychological legitimization of other-directed aggression consequent to frustration varies inversely with the degree to which other-oriented aggression threatens or has threatened the flow of nurturance and love.[5]

For example, if children are subjected to high parental severity, then rather than jeopardize the nurturance provided by their parents, the children will tend to vent their frustration upon themselves, both during childhood and later when frustrated as adults.

Henry and Short claim that the reactions of both suicide and homicide to the business cycle can be interpreted consistently as aggressive reactions to frustrations generated by the flow of economic forces. They suggest that when people are subjected to strong external restraint (and weak internal restraint) by virtue either of subordinate status or intense involvement in social relationships with other persons, it is easy to blame others when frustration occurs (i.e., structural circumstances favor externally directed aggression). But when the external restraints are weak (and internal restraints are strong), the self must bear the responsibility for frustration (i.e., structural circumstances favor internally directed aggression). Their major hypothesis is that suicide of higher status categories is more sensitive to frustrations produced by the business cycle than suicide of lower status categories

---

[3]*Ibid.*, p. 15.
[4]*Ibid.*, p. 104.
[5]*Ibid.*, p. 115.

subordinated in the social system.[6] It was substantiated in four separate tests.[7]

The Henry and Short hypothesis that "high status categories will have higher suicide rates than low status categories" has received much support in the suicide literature. Emile Durkheim wrote that suicide "is exceptionally frequent in the highest classes of society."[8] Ruth S. Cavan's 1929 study of suicide in Chicago revealed high suicide rates for professionals and highly educated classes.[9] As late as 1958 Elwin Powell wrote that:

> The central thesis of the sociological approach to the study of suicide can be stated as follows: the nature and incidence of suicide varies with social status. Status is defined as any position in any social system. . . . Schmid and van Arsdol suggest the possibility that blue-collar workers have a higher suicide rate than white-collar. Our findings, however, do not support this contention. For the combined professional-managerial and sales-clerical population the average annual rate was 24.6 as opposed to 19.6 for manual workers.[10]

Finally, on the basis of their major theorem concerning status integration and suicide potential, Jack Gibbs and Walter Martin predicted that members of lower status occupations (operatives, craftsmen, and nonfarm laborers) would have some of the *lowest* suicide rates of any of the occupational groups.[11]

---

[6]*Ibid.*, p. 70, "high status categories will have higher suicide rates than low status categories"; p. 15, "the degree of increase (of suicide during depressions) is greatest for high status categories"; p. 27, "suicide of high status categories will be more highly correlated with the business cycle than suicide of lower status categories"; p. 55, ". . . suicide is concentrated in the high status categories of American society. . . ." Note that Henry and Short consider whites, males, persons with high incomes, young and middle-aged persons, and military officers to be in high status categories while Negroes, females, persons with low incomes, old persons, and enlisted men are in low status categories (p. 70).

[7]*Ibid.*, p. 43.

[8]Emile Durkheim, *Suicide* (New York: The Free Press, 1962), p. 165. Cf. Austin L. Porterfield and Jack P. Gibbs, "Occupational Prestige and Social Mobility in Suicides in New Zealand," *American Journal of Sociology*, Vol. 66 (September, 1960), pp. 147–52.

[9]Ruth Shonle Cavan, *Suicide* (New York: Russell & Russell, Inc., 1965), p. 324.

[10]Elwin Powell, "Occupations, Status, and Suicide," *American Sociological Review*, Vol. 23, No. 2 (April, 1958), pp. 131 and 134.

[11]Jack P. Gibbs and Walter T. Martin, *Status Integration and Suicide* (Eugene, Ore.: The University of Oregon Press, 1964), p. 62.

Proposed inadequacies of the Henry and Short hypothesis

In this chapter three major criticisms of the Henry and Short hypothesis will be offered: (1) members of high status categories or persons who are relatively unrestrained do *not* have the highest suicide rates; (2) distinguishing status data (such as occupation or social class) into simply high and low categories obscures important relationships between social status and suicide rates; and (3) status change is more highly related to suicide rates than is status position.

Data and methods

Three tables from the Cook County study are employed here.[12] One table presents the suicide rates per 100,000 population by occupation. Since occupation is obviously not the only indicator of social status, a second table was constructed by giving each occupation listed on the death certificates a socioeconomic status score based on a United States Census Bureau Index.[13] The Census Bureau Index combines occupation, income, and educational levels into one scale. The SES scores are trichotomized to correspond to the social status categories by occupation. A third table shows the effect of race on the suicide rates of males of various social statuses.

In order to support the third criticism of the Henry and Short hypothesis, it is necessary to supplement the present Cook County data with other recent studies of suicide and social mobility. Foremost among these is the work of Warren Breed in New Orleans.[14] Additional support is drawn from Peter Sainsbury's work in London, Pow Meng Yap's analysis of suicide in Hong Kong,

---

[12] It was decided to restrict the present investigation to males since the occupational data for females were incomplete and unreliable.

[13] U.S. Bureau of the Census, *Methodology and Scores of Socioeconomic Status* (Working Paper No. 15) (Washington, D.C., 1963).

[14] Warren Breed, "Occupational Mobility and Suicide among White Males," *American Sociological Review*, Vol. 28, No. 2 (April, 1963), pp. 179–88. Cf. Warren Breed, "Suicide, Migration, and Race: A Study of Cases in New Orleans," *The Journal of Social Issues*, Vol. 22, No. 1, pp. 30–43.

and Louis I. Dublin's recent descriptive statistics of suicide.[15]

Development of the criticisms

1. From Tables 24 and 25 we can see that the social status hierarchy is *inversely* related to the suicide rate. Nonmanual laborers tend to be more immune to suicide than manual workers.[16] Cer-

Table 24.   Suicide rates per 100,000 population by social status and occupation among males in Cook County, Illinois, 1959–63.

	Occupations	Suicide Rates	N
UPPER SOCIAL STATUS	Professional, technical, and kindred workers	14.8	111
	Farmers and farm managers	—	6
	Managers, proprietors, and officials	15.8	110
MIDDLE SOCIAL STATUS	Clerical and kindred workers	13.0	88
	Sales workers	19.8	102
	Craftsmen, foremen, and kindred workers	20.9	293
LOWER SOCIAL STATUS	Operatives and kindred workers	23.3	325
	Private household workers	—	1
	Service workers	46.4	236
	Farm laborers and foremen	—	0
	Laborers	50.6	209
	Occupation unknown*	12.5	67
	N		1,549

*Includes unemployed.

tainly, if high income and relative youth are taken as indicators of high status in 20th century America (as Henry and Short do; see footnote 6 of this chapter), then the present data from Cook

---

[15]Peter Sainsbury, *Suicide in London* (London: Chapman & Hall, Ltd., 1955); Pow Meng Yap, *Suicide in Hong Kong* (Hong Kong: Hong Kong University Press, 1958); and Louis I. Dublin, *Suicide: A Sociological and Statistical Study* (New York: The Ronald Press Co., 1963).

[16]We admit that our criticisms depend heavily upon the reliability of the official death certificates. Some sociologists have argued that any research resting on such "official statistics" is undependable (see Jack D. Douglas, *The Social Meanings of Suicide* (Princeton, N.J.: Princeton University Press, 1967). Yet until viable alternatives can be presented, the "official statistics" remain our best source for an objective and comprehensive investigation of suicide. Furthermore, there seems to be consensus by independent investigators on the trends described in this paper.

Table 25. Suicide rates per 100,000 population by socioeconomic status ("SES"), among males in Cook County, Illinois, 1959–63.

	SES Scores	Suicide Rates	N
UPPER SOCIAL STATUS	70–100	15.2	220
MIDDLE SOCIAL STATUS	50–70	21.9	566
LOWER SOCIAL STATUS	0–50	33.0*	763
			1,549

*Suicides whose occupation was unknown or who were unemployed were included in the lower social status category.

Source: U.S. Bureau of the Census, *Methodology and Scores of Socioeconomic Status* (Working Paper No. 15) (Washington, D.C., 1963).

County and the Vital Statistics of the United States force us to reject Henry and Short's hypothesis.[17]

Yap discovered that "in Hong Kong not only did the business men have a low fatality (i.e., low frequency of suicide), but their rate was not high; in fact it was lower than that for coolies and amahs (female domestics), clerks, and shop assistants." In London, Sainsbury controlled for the suicide's actual economic status at the time of death and found that the proportion of suicides in poverty was increased. Breed's New Orleans data showed disproportionately high suicide rates in the lower occupational ranks as compared to controls and census figures.[18] In other words, on the basis of the evidence it would be reasonable to assert a hypothesis which directly contradicts that of Henry and Short,

---

[17]The suicide rate increases with increasing age, especially for men. See Dublin, *op. cit.*, p. 27. Breed (*American Sociological Review*, p. 184) found high suicide rates to be associated with decreasing income in 51 percent of New Orleans suicides. Forty-one percent of the suicides had the same income in the last year of their life, compared with their income two years earlier. Eight percent had increased income. Comparable income percentages for nonsuicidal controls were 11, 54, and 35, respectively.

[18]Yap, *op. cit.*, p. 35; Sainsbury, *op. cit.*, p. 73; Breed, *American Sociological Review*, p. 181, table 1, p. 182; Cf. Dublin, *op. cit.*, p. 65.

viz, "low status categories will have higher suicide rates than high status categories."

Nor can the above criticism be averted completely by restating the hypothesis to read that "the probability of suicide varies inversely with the strength of the relational system of the individual."[19] Admittedly, other Cook County data show the highest suicide rates among older, unmarried, white males (who are relatively unrestrained). But if suicide is particularly frequent among those persons who are relatively unrestrained, then why do the occupational data show such high rates of suicide for the lower status groups (i.e., operatives, service workers, and laborers —who are subject to strong vertical restraints; cf. footnote 42)?

In order for it to be true "that the degree of legitimization of other-directed aggression varies positively with the strength of external restraint over behavior" (p. 120, Henry and Short's concluding proposition), research must show that high suicide rates correlate positively both with participation in group relationships and social status. Although the Cook County data substantiate the former correlation, they emphatically contradict the latter. On these grounds Henry and Short's conclusion is reduced to a half-truth. The inverse relationship between social status and suicide is left unexplained. Perhaps a long unused and often overlooked footnote from Durkheim can help us here.[20] The prevalence of high suicide rates among lower status groups suggests the efficacy of a fatalistic (suicide as a reaction to constraint) explanation of a significant proportion of contemporary American suicides.[21]

The alert reader may object that clerical workers are also subjected to hyperregulation but have low suicide rates. This strongly suggests that regulation in itself does not cause suicide. It would appear that a suicidal situation exists only when fatalism combines with egoism and *anomie*. Although both middle and lower status workers are heavily regulated, lower status workers suffer from

---

[19]Henry and Short, *op. cit.*, p. 74. "Relational involvement" does *not* replace "external restraint" as the crucial variable in the etiology of suicide because relational involvement is an indicator of external restraint. Henry and Short write: "The probability of suicide varies inversely with the strength of the relational system *because* persons with strong relational systems are subjected to greater external restraints than persons with weak relational systems" (p. 75) .

[20]Durkheim, *op. cit.*, p. 276.

[21]See Cavan, *op. cit.*, pp. 222 ff., "The Case of the Youth Who Was Prematurely Tired."

egoism and *anomie* to a more marked degree. Middle status workers are more likely to belong to voluntary associations, to have gone to college, to have better chances for upward mobility, and to have more occupational prestige than lower status workers.[22] Among lower status workers

. . . the economic and educational limitations accompanying low status produce a lack of interest in and a lack of self-confidence in dealing with certain important areas in our culture; as a result, there is reduced participation—a *withdrawal from* participation in these areas.[23]

Having withdrawn from societal participation, the lower status workers are less able to achieve common social goals than are middle status workers. Thus, both egoistic and anomic factors are disproportionately present among lower status workers.

On the other hand, since the death certificate calls for the "usual occupation" of the deceased and since unemployment is perhaps underestimated, it could be that a study of pre-suicidal careers would reveal stages and degrees of regulation.[24] For example, at the time of death the suicide indeed may be characterized aptly as fitting primarily an egoistic-anomic suicide pattern (thus salvaging the Henry and Short hypothesis), but at the onset of the suicidal process a fatalistic pattern might predominate. Such an interpretation would be consistent with the assumption that in many instances (sometimes as much as 35 percent error) the death certificate does not report present occupational status but prior occupational status—and would point to the pressing need for an investigation of the dynamics of presuicidal careers.

2. Put into Henry and Short's own language, this criticism reduces to the fact that vertical restraint cannot be bifurcated into high and low status categories without glossing over important variable relationships between social and status levels and the suicide rate (see Table 24). More specifically, (*a*) within the low status category there is a significant difference between the relationship of service workers and laborers and other lower status

[22]Alvin W. Gouldner, *Modern Sociology* (New York: Harcourt, Brace & World, Inc., 1963), pp. 211–63.

[23]Genevieve Knupfer, "Portrait of the Underdog," *The Public Opinion Quarterly*, Vol. 11 (Spring, 1947), pp. 103–14. Cf. C. C. North, *Social Differentiation* (Chapel Hill, N.C.: University of North Carolina Press, 1927), p. 247.

[24]Breed, *American Sociological Review*, p. 182.

occupations to suicide, and (*b*) controlling for other variables produces considerable variation in the relationship of social status to the suicide rate.

a) The suicide rate of service workers (policemen, barbers, housekeepers, nurses, etc.) and laborers is over twice as high as that of either craftsmen *et al.* (carpenters, electricians, jewelers, photographers, plumbers, tailors, etc.) or operatives *et al.* (apprentices, bus and taxi drivers, deliverymen, assemblers, etc.), even though craftsmen and operatives have the third and fourth highest suicide rates overall.

b) Table 26 controls for socioeconomic status and race among males.[25] It is immediately evident that the inverse relationship

Table 26. Suicide rates per 100,000 population by socioeconomic status and race among males in Cook County, Illinois, 1959–63.

	SES Scores	White Males	Nonwhite Males	N
UPPER SOCIAL STATUS	70–100	15.3 (214)	15.0 (6)*	200
MIDDLE SOCIAL STATUS	50–70	22.4 (540)	14.4 (26)	566
LOWER SOCIAL STATUS	0–50	35.7 (665)	22.3 (98)	763
N		1,419	130	1,549

*Admittedly a small number of cases, but there are simply very few upper status nonwhite males who suicide.

between the suicide rate and social status holds only for whites. For nonwhites, social status apparently has little influence on the suicide rate.

The analysis by Henry and Short is limited by the lack of control variables and by the gross indices of social status that were utilized. Since their study assigned "low status" to all nonwhites, females, the elderly, and persons with low incomes, differences

---

[25]Additional controls (such as age and marital status) were impossible since the Bureau of the Census does not have tables of occupation by age or marital status for Cook County. Furthermore, the cost of constructing these tables was prohibitive.

within these categories could not be taken into account. Table 26 demonstrates that such differences are important. Not only is there a difference between the suicide rates of whites and nonwhites but there is also a difference between the suicide rates of whites and nonwhites of different statuses.[26]

3. The distribution of suicide rates in Tables 24 and 25 is perfectly compatible with an interpretation that suicide is characteristic of downwardly mobile populations.[27] Of course, the inverse relationship between social status and the suicide rate tells us nothing of the *process* of status-change of suicides, but it certainly could portray *the last phase* of the process. If downward mobility were characteristic of suicides, then we would expect distributions of suicide rates by occupation or social status to look very much like those of Tables 24 and 25. What evidence is there in recent suicide research for the hypothesis that suicides are downwardly mobile?

Breed discovered that when the occupational level of the suicide and his father are compared, considerable downward mobility appears.[28] In fact, about 75 percent of the New Orleans suicides manifested some form of downward mobility.[29] Peter Sainsbury found in London that the incidence of unemployment (an indicator of downward mobility) was significantly higher among the suicide population, and that the suicide rate among the unemployed was about five times that of the general population.[30] Powell also claimed that unemployment was a primary factor in suicide, especially of the aged male.[31] Sainsbury wrote that:

. . . among the suicides were many who had lost status. . . . The findings support the hypothesis that increased social mobility . . . whether of class, occupation, or neighborhood, conduces to suicide.[32]

---

[26]We are using different criteria for status than Henry and Short use. For them nonwhites as a whole are given a low status rank. Our criterion of status is primarily occupation, which allows us to describe status variation among nonwhites.

[27]This is especially true since there is a tendency to misrepresent the incidence of unemployment on the death certificates. It will be recalled that 35 percent of Breed's New Orleans suicides were recorded as employed (on the official records) when in fact they were either unemployed, retired, or not working full time.

[28]Breed, *American Sociological Review*, p. 183.

[29]*Ibid.*, p. 184.

[30]Sainsbury, *op. cit.*, p. 55.

[31]Powell, *op. cit.*, p. 136.

[32]Sainsbury, *op. cit.*, p. 73.

Although the present data can be considered only exploratory and suggestive, we have sufficient evidence to suspect, first, that Henry and Short's analysis of suicide is too static and, second, that they have obscured the relationship of social status to suicide (perhaps by making business cycles their major independent variable). Henry and Short do not ignore status fluctuations completely. But they tend to consider status change as a mediating variable between the business cycle and the suicide rate. We are urging that attention be focused on the process of status change regardless of its etiology. An *ad hoc* mechanism for losing status (fluctuation in the business cycle) is not so important as the fact of status change. Henry and Short's procedure has the effect of obscuring, of playing down, the relationship between varying social statuses and the suicide rate.

We are advocating a more dynamic analysis of suicidal phenomena. Henry and Short have emphasized structural considerations to the neglect of status dynamics. Perhaps their most glaring oversight is not to have considered in sufficient detail the consequences of status loss for suicide.

Discussion

If we were to reformulate Henry and Short's hypothesis on the basis of the findings of this chapter and our survey of the suicide literature, we would have to assert that low status categories (assumed subject to strong external restraints) have higher suicide rates than high status categories (assumed subject to weak external restraints.)[33] The reformulation appears unacceptable if we assume that *anomie* is especially characteristic of upper social statuses, that strong external restraint necessarily acts as a preventive of suicide, and that *anomie* and external restraint cannot both play a part in the etiology of suicide.[34]

Following Durkheim, Henry and Short tend to assume that

---

[33]Irwin Goffman has suggested in a personal communication that his research on suicide rates and intervention patterns might go a long way in explaining the inverse relationship between social status and suicide. For example, successful suicidal intervention is more likely in the upper social statuses than in the lower social statuses. See James L. Wilkins and Irwin Goffman, "Accomplishing Suicide," paper presented in Miami at the 1966 Annual Meeting of the American Sociological Association.

[34]See Barclay Johnson, "Durkheim's One Cause of Suicide," *American Sociological Review*, Vol. 30, No. 6 (December, 1965), pp. 875–86. If Mr. Johnson is right, what is true of *anomie* is true of egoism.

anomie is likely to victimize especially those in upper social statuses.[35] For example, they do this when they assert that the suicide rate of persons in upper social statuses is more influenced by fluctuations in the business cycle than the suicide rate of persons in lower social statuses. According to Durkheim, anomic suicide results from an abrupt alteration in the norms of a society.[36] Durkheim considers anomic suicide to be a particular attribute of the social situation of those in upper social statuses. He argues that upper status men who tend to look to the future for satisfaction will have no meaningful past. But a past is necessary to endure present crises. Interruptions which prevent pursuit of future goals, especially when permanent, can leave such men in a desperate situation in which they have accomplished nothing (their definition of the situation). These kinds of men are unsatisfied and, furthermore, have no prospects of ever reaching their original goals. Such a situation is highly conducive to suicide. On the other hand, lower status men who tend to value limited, present achievements have something (some accomplishments, and, thus, some satisfactions) when other future needs or goals become unrealizable.

But if we focus on *anomie* per se, ignoring that generated by fluctuations in the business cycle, then it does not necessarily follow that high status categories are more inclined to *anomie* and suicide.[37] *Anomie* simply indicates that there is a disjunction of means and ends, of effort and attainment.[38] Someone experiencing

---

[35]Durkheim, *op. cit.*, pp. 253, 254: "With increased prosperity desires increase. . . . Poverty protects against suicide because it is a restraint in itself. . . . Wealth, on the other hand, by the power it bestows, deceives us into believing that we depend on ourselves only." Cf. p. 165.

[36]Durkheim, *op. cit.*, pp. 246 ff.

[37]Indeed, Robert Merton argues that *anomie* is especially likely among those with the least opportunity for economic success. Using Srole's scale, Wendell Bell found that *anomie* is inversely related to economic status (Wendell Bell, "Anomie, Social Isolation, and the Class Structure," *Sociometry*, Vol. 20 [June, 1957], pp. 105–16). Mizruchi claims that the relatively lower classes have a greater tendency to *anomia* because of the socially structured, differential access to supportive subsystems, in addition to the inaccessibility of means to achieve socially desired ends (Ephraim H. Mizruchi, "Social Structure and *Anomia* in a Small City," *American Sociological Review*, Vol. 25 [October, 1960], pp. 645–54). Richard Simpson argues that in general the higher the status, the lower the *anomie* (Richard Simpson, "A Note on Status, Mobility, and *Anomie*," *British Journal of Sociology*, Vol. 11 [December 1960], pp. 370–72).

[38]Talcott Parsons, *The Structure of Social Action* (New York: The Free Press, 1949), p. 335. Whereas this definition fits Durkheim's and Parsons' conception

anomie does not have the means to meet his perceived needs. According to many writers, the single most pressing contemporary American need is for secular occupational achievement.[39] Certainly low status persons, especially if they are unemployed or downwardly mobile, will experience more occupational *anomie* than high status persons and should be more likely to suicide.

This is exactly what we have found in our researches. Our conclusion is substantiated by Breed, Sainsbury, and Powell, who argue that low-achievement performances of males, particularly lack of competence on the job, promote suicide.[40] It would appear that Henry and Short have generated a pseudo-association between high suicide rates and high social status because they simply bifurcate the status data and because of their criteria for high status.

How is *anomie* related to Henry and Short's concepts of frustration and external restraint? In the above argument we have assumed that frustration is roughly equivalent to Durkheim's meaning of *anomie* since frustration, like *anomie*, is little more

---

of *anomie*, we want to avoid the bugaboo of reductionism. *Anomie* is a major sociological concept and as such has an almost embarrassing wealth of connotations. For example, Robert Merton calls our attention to Durkheim's failure to make a systematic distinction among different kinds of values and opportunity structures (Robert K. Merton, *Social Theory and Social Structure* [New York: The Free Press, 1957], pp. 139–57). When we distinguish between acceptance and rejection of culturally prescribed means and ends, we see that instead of one type of deviant adaptation to *anomie* there are at least four (which Merton labels "innovation," "ritualism," "retreatism," and "rebellion").

Richard Cloward ('Illegitimate Means, *Anomie*, and Deviant Behavior," *American Sociological Review*, Vol. 24 [April, 1959], pp. 164–76) has indicated that *anomie* can apply not only to an individual's opportunity to realize legitimate goals but also to illegitimate goals.

The term *"anomia"* has been coined to designate *personal* disorganization often in spite of social normality (see Robert K. Merton, *"Anomie, Anomia,* and Social Interaction: Contexts of Deviant Behavior," in Marshall B. Clinard [ed.], *Anomie and Deviant Behavior* [New York: The Free Press, 1964], pp. 213–42. Cf. Ephraim H. Mizruchi, *Success and Opportunity* [New York: The Free Press, 1964]) . *"Anomie* has been used to mean isolation, alienation, and despair" (Leo Srole, "Social Integration and Certain Corollaries: An Exploratory Study," *American Sociological Review*, Vol. 21 [1956], pp. 709–16; and Dorothy Meier and Wendell Bell, *"Anomia* and Differential Access to the Achievement of Life Goals," *American Sociological Review*, Vol. 24 [1959], p. 191) .

[39]Robin M. Williams, Jr., *American Society* (New York: Alfred A. Knopf, Inc., 1952) , pp. 389–442; Breed, *American Sociological Review, passim;* and Leonard Pearlin, "Alienation from Work," *American Sociological Review*, Vol. 27 (June, 1962) , pp. 314–26.

[40]Breed, *American Sociological Review*, p. 188; Powell, *op. cit.*, p. 139; and Sainsbury, *op. cit.*, pp. 68 ff. Apparently the crucial role-problems of suicide vary with sex. Breed found that while male suicides were prone to job failure, female difficulties centered around the marital role. See Breed, *The Journal of Social Issues*, p. 43.

than having inadequate means to satisfy needs.[41] However, *anomie* is not equivalent to frustration because *anomie* implies nonpersonal or external failure of means to ends. Thus, a second problem is to explain how lower status persons, who are more externally restrained than upper status persons, can still have a higher suicide rate.[42]

It is not inconceivable that what Durkheim called fatalism operates in conjunction with *anomie,* especially if we consider pre-suicidal events and not just the act of suicide. We have previously noted empirical grounds for suspecting a fatalistic component in the etiology of contemporary suicide.[43] Indeed, Elwin Powell has argued for what he calls "institutionalized *anomie*" or "envelopment," which is defined as meaninglessness arising from normative regulation itself.[44]

We are arguing for a fatalistic-anomic pattern of suicide. On the face of it, such a pattern appears self-contradictory. We have two replies to this objection. First, the fatalistic and anomic factors have their peak influence at different times in the presuicidal career (fatalism early and *anomie* late). Second, institutionalized *anomie,* a mixture of normative deregulation and hyperregulation, is a meaningful concept. It would appear that laborers, service workers, and operatives have experienced downward mobility and loss of occupational prestige, often loss of

---

[41]"Frustration is usually defined as interference with the occurrence of an instigated (incited) goal response at its proper time in the behavior sequence (see J. Dollard *et al., Frustration and Aggression* [New Haven: Yale, 1939], p. 7; cf. Leonard Berkowitz, *Aggression* [New York: McGraw-Hill Book Co., Inc., 1962], p. 26). Suppose a small boy, James, reacts to an ice cream cone vendor's bell by asking his mother for money for an ice cream cone. If she tells James that he cannot have money or the cone, then James will be frustrated. We have cast frustration in terms of means and needs. For example, James does not have the means (money, permission of his mother) to meet his need (to get and eat an ice cream cone; i.e., to react so as to reduce the strength of the instigation).

[42]Lower status occupations typically present fewer alternatives, fewer chances for autonomy and free decisions to the worker than upper status occupations. Laborers and service workers tend to be public or domestic servants. Contrast this situation with that of the professional or manager, both of whom have considerably less coercion regarding what to do, when to do it, and whether to do it. Cf. Henry and Short, *op. cit.,* p. 75; and Leonard I. Pearlin and Melvin L. Kohn, "Social Class, Occupation, and Parental Values: A Cross National Study," *American Sociological Review,* Vol. 31, No. 4 (August, 1966), pp. 466–79.

[43]See footnote 20 and related text in this chapter.

[44]Powell, *op. cit.,* p. 139. Note that Powell claims envelopment is a characteristic of upper status suicides—not lower status suicides.

job, in contemporary industrial society.[45] When a work pattern is evaluated by the larger society as inadequate, self-devaluation follows, with alienative reactions and dissociation as frequent corollaries.[46] One of the possible consequences of alienation from one's work is unemployment and, ultimately, social isolation. Such a disenchanted or disinherited lower status worker is more likely to suicide than the upper and middle status workers who have made more adequate adjustments to a changing work situation.

Although the measures of external restraint give some indication of the characteristics of suicidal populations, many persons experience the failure of external restraint and, yet, do not suicide.[47] It is clear that a more sophisticated treatment of the etiology of suicide would have to include an investigation of differences in the adaptive responses of individuals to external restraint. What determines which lower status workers react to the social forces described above by withdrawing from social participation, becoming alienated, venting their frustration upon themselves rather than aggressing against some external object? Unfortunately, an adequate answer to these questions would take us far beyond the limitations of our data and stated intentions.[48]

Let us simply say that usually those who react to external restraint by suiciding have what Henry and Short call "internal restraint," i.e., suicides have more superego strength than those who do not suicide, as well as a greater ability to objectify their egos.[49] Furthermore, Breed argues that most of those who suicide should show a marked internalization of major societal role expec-

---

[45]Further support for the skidding hypothesis of suicide can be found in preliminary analysis of a current study of 82 suicides by the Los Angeles Suicide Prevention Center. See Harold L. Wilensky and H. Edwards, "The Skidder: Ideological Adjustments of Downwardly Mobile Workers," *American Sociological Review*, Vol. 24 (April, 1959), pp. 215–31. Harold Wilensky, "Orderly Careers and Social Participation," *American Sociological Review*, Vol. 26 (August, 1961), pp. 521–39.

[46]Cf. Knupfer, *op. cit.*, p. 247.

[47]See Karl Menninger, *Man against Himself* (New York: Harcourt, Brace & World, Inc., 1938), p. 17: "Behavior is never determined only by external forces; there are impulses within, the adjustment of which to external reality necessarily brings about stresses and strains which may be highly painful, but endurable except to a very few."

[48]The reader who wishes to pursue this perplexing and important problem is referred to Norman Farberow and Edwin Shneidman, *The Cry for Help* (New York: McGraw-Hill Book Co., Inc., 1961), Part II; and Berkowitz, *op. cit.*

[49]Henry and Short, *op. cit.*, pp. 101–20.

tations, a rigid adherence to these role expectations (leading to an inability to overcome shame), that their significant others define them as failures, and that they are seriously dependent upon the approval of significant others.[50] Those who do not suicide should be more flexible about role expectations, with the result that failure is likely to be accommodated by redefinition of previous goals. It is suggested that nonsuicides would be likely to adjust their friends to fit their changing self-images, to mitigate their failures. Thus, nonsuicides will have more ability to overcome feelings of shame than will suicides.

Conclusions

First, the most dramatic finding of our research is the high suicide rate among persons of lower social status. This discovery casts doubt on Henry and Short's hypothesis asserting a direct relationship between status and suicide, as well as their claim that suicide varies inversely with external restraint. The reasons for the former doubt are that there are exceptions to the hypothesis in Henry and Short's own data (notably the association of high suicide rates with old age and low rent community areas) and that data from Cook County, New Orleans, London, Los Angeles, and China reveal an inverse relationship between suicide and social status. The reason for the latter doubt is that strong (vertical) external restraints in lower status groups are associated with high suicide rates. Our findings have led us to posit a pattern of suicide for lower status persons including the traits of fatalism, egoism, and *anomie*. We have argued that these traits are not incompatible with one another, especially when the possibility of their being dominant at different times in the suicide process is considered.

Two other possible explanations of our data should be entertained. First, intervention might be more successful in the upper social strata. Second, persons of upper social status may be more successful in evading detection and classification as suicides. Future research should be directed to these possibilities.

---

[50]Warren Breed, "On the Social Psychology of the Suicide Process," unpublished manuscript.

Second, one cannot make simplistic statements about the relationship between status and suicide, as Henry and Short do, and expect them to be meaningful. Status has a complicated relationship to suicide which is revealed only by breaking status categories down into occupational and class subdivisions and by controlling for other variables, such as race, age, and marital status. When this is done, crude generalizations about suicide and social status are no longer feasible. Of course, once we have established particular generalizations it is reasonable to proceed inductively to build higher level generalities. But grand generalizations should not be arrived at by fiat, prior to analysis.

Third, one's social status is not constant. Among suicides it appears that status loss is more highly related to the suicide rate than status position. Positional analyses tend to overlook how one came to be in that position. For example, the death certificates may be depicting a true state of affairs at the first stages of a presuicidal "career" but untrue at the time of death. Thus, someone may be listed as employed, married, belonging to voluntary associations, and nonalcoholic, while in fact he is unemployed, estranged from his spouse, belongs to no voluntary associations, and has become an alcoholic.

This type of error would strengthen the Henry and Short hypothesis; i.e., would tend to underestimate the lack of external restraints. However, just because strong restraints are not manifested at the time of death does not rule out their causal relevance. Furthermore, assuming that the occupational data were not substantially in error, the high suicide rates among lower status occupations suggest the presence of strong external restraints even at the time of death. A sociological study of the dynamics of the suicidal process is called for.

Finally, it is imperative that suicide researchers turn their attention to the joint effects of internal and external restraint. This is just another way of saying that psychologists and sociologists need to pool their resources in the study of suicide. Once sociologists have identified the types and extent of external restraint most highly associated with suicide, it remains a problem as to why some individuals respond to these circumstances by suiciding while others continue to affirm life.

Suggestions for further reading

Breed, Warren. "Occupational Mobility and Suicide among White Males." *American Sociological Review*, Vol. 28, No. 2 (April, 1963), pp. 179–88. One of the few studies of suicide based on interviews (with those who knew the suicide) rather than on death certificates. Breed discovered the same inverse relationship between social status and suicide that we found in Chicago. Work problems were the chief cause of suicide.

Durkheim, Emile. *Suicide,* pp. 165 ff. New York: The Free Press, 1962. Durkheim argues that persons in upper classes have more active intellectual lives which in turn leads to greater egoism and higher suicide rates.

Henry, Andrew F., and Short, James F., Jr. *Suicide and Homicide,* N.B. pp. 15, 27, 55, 70. New York: The Free Press, 1954. A social-psychological explanation of suicide and social status. It is claimed that high status types are subject to weak external restraint and strong internal restraint; a situation which tends to encourage self-destructive behavior when frustration occurs. High status types are more subject to frustrations produced by business cycles than are low status types.

Merton, Robert K. *Social Theory and Social Structure,* pp. 139–57. New York: The Free Press, 1957. Develops general theory of the relationship of *anomie* and deviant behavior. One major conclusion is that deviance ensues on a large scale only when common success goals have been internalized but opportunities to achieve those goals have been differentially distributed.

Powell, Elwin. "Occupations, Status, and Suicide." *American Sociological Review,* Vol. 23, No. 2 (April, 1958), pp. 131–39. Compare the fatalistic-anomic suicide pattern we argue for with Powell's concept of "institutionalized *anomie*" or "envelopment."

CHAPTER 8

Community characteristics and
suicidal types

Durkheim believed that the primary causative force determining the suicide rate of a community or nation was its "social environment," i.e., its ideas, beliefs, and customs.[1] He was struck by the constancy of the suicide rate of a nation over time. This suggested that the suicide rate did not depend upon the attributes of individual suicides (which were varied, not constant) but rather upon an external and constraining moral force, a collective conscience, the social environment of the community:

> There must then be some force in their common environment inclining them all in the same direction, whose greater or lesser strength causes the greater or less number of suicides. . . . This force must be collective. In other words, each people has collectively an inclination of its own to suicide, on which the size of its contribution to voluntary deaths depends.[2]

Durkheim's conception of social environment comes very close to Sorokin's conception of "cultural mentalities" or Kroeber's conception of the "superorganic."[3] The procedure in suicide re-

---

[1] Emile Durkheim, *Suicide* (New York: The Free Press, 1962), pp. 299, 302.

[2] *Ibid.*, p. 305.

[3] Pitirim Sorokin, *Social and Cultural Dynamics* (Boston: Porter Sargent Publisher, 1957), pp. 20–53; and Alfred L. Kroeber, *The Nature of Culture* (Chicago: The University of Chicago Press, 1952), pp. 22–30.

search is to determine how the distinguishing socio-cultural traits of a community are associated with the community's suicide rate. One well-known illustration of the community characteristics approach is Herbert Hendin's work on suicide in Scandinavia.[4] Hendin tries to determine the "character differences" of Danes, Swedes, and Norwegians in order to explain their different suicide rates.

In this chapter we will adopt a similar approach. Instead of nations with high and low suicide rates, we propose to investigate community areas within Chicago with high and low suicide rates. From the address on the death certificate each suicide will be placed into one of 76 community areas. Next the areas with the highest and lowest suicide rates will be determined. The University of Chicago publishes a community fact book which gives the social characteristics of 76 community areas.[5] We will use the community characteristics as a rough indicator of what Durkheim called the "social environment" of the suicides.

An effort will be made to guarantee that the areas with common community characteristics are in fact communities. For example, usually aggregated community areas will be spatially contiguous as well as homogeneous in community characteristics. From an analysis of community characteristics, types of suicidal areas within the high and low suicide rate areas will be distinguished.

In effect we will be asking whether there are any significant differences between the social forces operating in the different suicidal areas. We know that *some* forces in the suicidal areas are influencing the suicide rates. Put another way, we will be asking if there are significant differences in community social environment and community suicide rates. We are *not* concerned with why any *one* individual might suicide but why a suicide *rate* might be high in one community and not in another over at least a five-year span. No doubt the suicide rate is partially determined by a subcommunity within the suicidal areas from which the community characteristics are drawn. But if there were no connection between community characteristics and suicide rates, then

---

[4]Herbert Hendin, *Suicide and Scandinavia* (Garden City, N.Y.: Anchor Books, 1965).

[5]Evelyn M. Kitagawa and Karl F. Taeuber (eds.), Chicago Community Inventory, *Local Community Fact Book, Chicago Metropolitan Area, 1960* (Chicago: University of Chicago, 1963).

why would the suicide rate of communities vary systematically with their social characteristics?

Data, methods, and findings

Using a code book provided by the Population Research and Training Center of the University of Chicago, each suicide in Chicago ($N = 1,547$) was placed by street address into 1 of 76 "community areas."[6] Suicide rates were then computed for each area. Figure 8 presents the results. Table 27 gives the same information in nongraphic form and adds the 1960 population of the area.

It is informative to compare the results of the present investigation with those obtained by Ruth S. Cavan in 1928.[7] The North Side (especially those areas immediately adjacent to Lake Michigan), the Loop, and the Near West Side remain the areas with the highest suicide rates. The suicide rate of the Near South Side has declined since 1928, probably because of the heavy influx of Negroes. Negroes are known to be much less likely than whites to suicide.[8] The incidence of suicide on the North and West Sides of Chicago has spread from the core of the city toward the periphery. Generally the greater the distance from the core of the city, the lower the suicide rate.[9] Finally, the secular decline in Chicago's suicide rates should be noted. Cavan's "highs" were between 35 and 87 per 100,000; ours were between 12 and 23. Twenty-five percent of Cavan's community area had suicide rates above 17;

[6]Chicago Community Inventory, *Guide for Coding Street Addresses to Community Area and Census Tract, Chicago, 1960* (Chicago: University of Chicago, 1961).

[7]Two well-known ecological studies first published in 1928 were Ruth Shonle Cavan, *Suicide* (New York: Russell & Russell, Inc., 1965); and Calvin F. Schmid, *Suicides in Seattle, 1914 to 1925* (Seattle, Wash.: University of Washington Press, 1928). In such studies it is easy to fall into the trap of "the ecological fallacy." (See William S. Robinson, "Ecological Correlations and the Behavior of Individuals, *American Sociological Review*, Vol. 15 [1950]; Edward L. Thorndike, "On the Fallacy of Imputing the Correlations Found for Groups to the Individuals or Smaller Groups Composing Them," *American Journal of Psychology*, Vol. 52 [1929]; and Otis Dudley Duncan, Ray P. Cuzzort, and Beverly Duncan, *Statistical Geography* [New York: The Free Press, 1961]). That is, it is easy to make inferences about individuals on the basis of group data. We have scrupulously avoided such inferences by confining attention to the suicide *rate* as a community characteristic.

[8]Louis I. Dublin, *Suicide: A Sociological and Statistical Study* (New York: The Ronald Press Co., 1963), chap. iv.

[9]Cf. Schmid, *op. cit.*

Figure 8.   Suicide rates by community areas, City of Chicago, 1959–63.

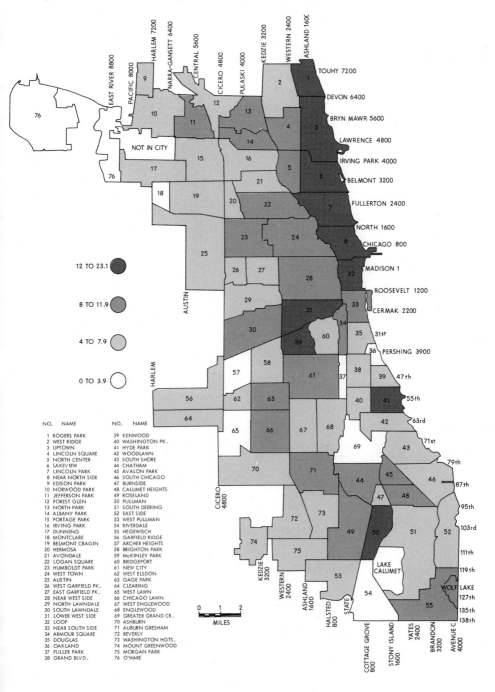

12 TO 23.1

8 TO 11.9

4 TO 7.9

0 TO 3.9

NO.	NAME	NO.	NAME
1	ROGERS PARK	39	KENWOOD
2	WEST RIDGE	40	WASHINGTON PK.
3	UPTOWN	41	HYDE PARK
4	LINCOLN SQUARE	42	WOODLAWN
5	NORTH CENTER	43	SOUTH SHORE
6	LAKEVIEW	44	CHATHAM
7	LINCOLN PARK	45	AVALON PARK
8	NEAR NORTH SIDE	46	SOUTH CHICAGO
9	EDISON PARK	47	BURNSIDE
10	NORWOOD PARK	48	CALUMET HEIGHTS
11	JEFFERSON PARK	49	ROSELAND
12	FOREST GLEN	50	PULLMAN
13	NORTH PARK	51	SOUTH DEERING
14	ALBANY PARK	52	EAST SIDE
15	PORTAGE PARK	53	WEST PULLMAN
16	IRVING PARK	54	RIVERDALE
17	DUNNING	55	HEGEWISCH
18	MONTCLARE	56	GARFIELD RIDGE
19	BELMONT CRAGIN	57	ARCHER HEIGHTS
20	HERMOSA	58	BRIGHTON PARK
21	AVONDALE	59	McKINLEY PARK
22	LOGAN SQUARE	60	BRIDGEPORT
23	HUMBOLDT PARK	61	NEW CITY
24	WEST TOWN	62	WEST ELSDON
25	AUSTIN	63	GAGE PARK
26	WEST GARFIELD PK.	64	CLEARING
27	EAST GARFIELD PK.	65	WEST LAWN
28	NEAR WEST SIDE	66	CHICAGO LAWN
29	NORTH LAWNDALE	67	WEST ENGLEWOOD
30	SOUTH LAWNDALE	68	ENGLEWOOD
31	LOWER WEST SIDE	69	GREATER GRAND CR.
32	LOOP	70	ASHBURN
33	NEAR SOUTH SIDE	71	AUBURN GRESHAM
34	ARMOUR SQUARE	72	BEVERLY
35	DOUGLAS	73	WASHINGTON HGTS.
36	OAKLAND	74	MOUNT GREENWOOD
37	FULLER PARK	75	MORGAN PARK
38	GRAND BLVD.	76	O'HARE

0   1   2

MILES

Table 27. Suicide rates per 100,000 population by community areas, city of Chicago, 1959–63.

Number	Name	Rate*	Frequency	1960 Population
1	Rogers Park	14.4	41	56,888
2	West Ridge	7.2	23	63,884
3	Uptown	13.3	85	127,682
4	Lincoln Square	11.6	29	49,850
5	North Center	11.9	26	43,877
6	Lakeview	15.0	89	118,764
7	Lincoln Park	15.3	68	88,836
8	Near North Side	19.3	73	75,509
9	Edison Park	6.4	4	12,568
10	Norwood Park	5.9	12	40,593
11	Jefferson Park	10.9	15	27,494
12	Forest Glen	7.3	7	19,228
13	North Park	10.1	9	17,866
14	Albany Park	10.1	25	49,450
15	Portage Park	7.3	24	65,925
16	Irving Park	6.5	19	58,298
17	Dunning	7.2	15	41,626
18	Montclare	3.4	2	11,802
19	Belmont Cragin	6.9	21	60,883
20	Hermosa	4.7	5	21,429
21	Avondale	7.5	15	39,748
22	Logan Square	10.8	51	94,799
23	Humboldt Park	8.1	29	71,609
24	West Town	11.5	80	139,657
25	Austin	7.4	46	125,133
26	West Garfield Park	7.5	17	45,611
27	East Garfield Park	6.7	23	66,871
28	Near West Side	11.4	72	126,610
29	North Lawndale	4.2	26	124,937
30	South Lawndale	10.8	33	60,940
31	Lower West Side	14.9	36	48,448
32	Loop	23.1	5	4,337
33	Near South Side	9.7	5	10,350
34	Armour Square	8.9	7	15,783
35	Douglas	6.1	16	52,325
36	Oakland	1.6	2	24,378
37	Fuller Park	0.0	0	12,181
38	Grand Boulevard	5.0	20	80,036
39	Kenwood	7.7	16	41,533
40	Washington Park	6.4	14	43,690
41	Hyde Park	12.3	28	45,577
42	Woodlawn	6.2	25	81,279
43	South Shore	6.8	25	73,086
44	Chatham	8.1	17	41,962
45	Avalon Park	11.0	7	12,710
46	South Chicago	7.6	19	49,914
47	Burnside	5.8	1	3,463
48	Calumet Heights	8.3	8	19,352
49	Roseland	9.2	27	58,750
50	Pullman	14.3	6	8,412

Table 27 (continued)

Number	Name	Rate*	Frequency	1960 Population
51	South Deering	4.3	4	18,794
52	East Side	6.9	8	23,214
53	West Pullman	5.7	10	35,397
54	Riverdale	0.0	0	11,448
55	Hegewisch	9.0	4	8,936
56	Garfield Ridge	6.4	13	40,449
57	Archer Heights	1.9	1	10,584
58	Brighton Park	5.8	11	38,019
59	McKinley Park	13.0	11	16,908
60	Bridgeport	7.2	15	41,560
61	New City	8.6	29	67,428
62	West Elsdon	4.2	3	14,215
63	Gage Park	9.2	13	28,244
64	Clearing	6.4	6	18,797
65	West Lawn	3.0	4	26,910
66	Chicago Lawn	9.0	23	51,347
67	West Englewood	7.9	20	58,516
68	Englewood	5.5	27	97,595
69	Greater Grand Crossing	3.8	12	63,169
70	Ashburn	4.1	8	38,638
71	Auburn Gresham	8.1	24	59,484
72	Beverly	7.3	9	24,814
73	Washington Heights	7.4	11	29,793
74	Mount Greenwood	4.6	5	21,941
75	Morgan Park	5.7	8	27,912
76	O'Hare	0.0	0	Unknown
			N = 1,547	

*Some of the rates are unreliable due to the small number of suicides in some community areas. Any N under 5 should be suspected.
    Source: Evelyn M. Kitagawa and Karl F. Taeuber (eds.), Chicago Community Inventory, *Local Community Fact Book, Chicago Metropolitan Area, 1960* (Chicago: University of Chicago, 1963).

only 3 percent (2) of ours did, the Loop (area No. 32) and the Near North Side (area No. 8).

In an effort to determine the associations of high and low suicide rates with other community variables, 10 tables (not presented here) were constructed in which the community areas (9 areas) with the highest suicide rates (a dependent variable) were contrasted with the community area (six areas) with the lowest suicide rates (a dependent variable) with respect to age, median school years completed, median family income, percentage of white-collar workers, percentage unemployed, percentage of Negroes, percentage of foreign stock, percentage of population per household, percentage of substandard housing, and percentage in different house in 1955 (the independent variables).[10] The definition of and the information for the independent variables were taken from the *Local Community Fact Book, Chicago Metropolitan Area, 1960*.[11] Table 28 presents the summarized findings.

In Table 28 it can be observed that high suicide areas have an older population than low suicide areas (sig. at 0.01); that the median school years completed is slightly higher in the high suicide areas than in the low suicide areas (sig. at 0.10); that the median income in high suicide areas is about $1,000 higher per year than in low suicide areas (sig. at 0.30); that there are far more white-collar workers in high suicide areas than in low suicide areas (sig. at 0.01); that there are slightly fewer unemployed people in high suicide areas than in low (sig. at 0.30); that there are far fewer Negroes in high suicide areas than in low (sig. at 0.02); that high suicide areas have more foreign stock than low suicide areas (sig. at 0.15); that in high suicide areas the population per household is smaller (roughly a ratio of 2 to 3) than in low suicide areas (sig. at 0.01); that substandard housing is about twice as prevalent in high suicide areas as in low (sig. at 0.15); and, somewhat surprisingly, that the amount of residential mobility in high suicide areas is about the same as that in low suicide areas (sig. at 0.30).[12]

It is worth noting that suicide is not primarily an act committed by transients but by people who have resided at their present addresses for quite some time (almost 30 percent for 41 or more years; see Tables 29 and 30). This finding is contrary to those of Calvin Schmid and Peter Sainsbury who found on the basis of their studies of Seattle (1928) and London (1955) that suicide

---

[10]The decision on how many cases to include in the high and low suicide rate categories was somewhat arbitrary. Basically what we did was to compare the two poles of the suicide rate distribution, i.e., the community areas with the highest and lowest suicide rates. The number of community areas included in the high and low categories was determined by inspection of the natural breaks in the distribution. Inspection of social characteristics of additional community areas revealed that no new patterns would emerge by adding more cases. One exception to the above rule should be noted. The Loop was omitted from analysis since it presented a highly anomalous patterning which we were not prepared to explain.

[11]See footnote 5 above.

[12]By refusing to specify a single significance level we hope to call attention to differences that would otherwise be obscured. Cf. James F. Skipper *et al.*, "The Sacredness of 0.05: A Note Concerning the Uses of Statistical Levels of Significance in Social Science," *The American Sociologist*, Vol. 2 (February, 1967), pp. 16–18.

Table 28. Means for selected variables of community areas with highest and lowest suicide rates, city of Chicago, Illinois, 1959-63.

	Areas with Highest Suicide Rates ($N_1 = 9$)	Areas with Lowest Suicide Rates ($N_2 = 6$)	Results of Two-Tailed T-Test* Significant at—	Zero-Order Correlations with Suicide Rates of All Areas†
Percentage 65 and older	12.1	7.0	0.01	0.56
Median school years completed	10.6	9.6	0.10	0.10
Median family income	$6,898.	$5,819.	0.30	0.01
Percentage white-collar workers	44.6	25.1	0.01	0.34
Percentage unemployed	5.6	8.6	0.30	0.15
Percentage Negro	8.2	52.9	0.02	-0.31
Percentage foreign stock	38.6	24.4	0.15	0.20
Population per household	2.50	3.70	0.01	-0.72
Percentage in substandard housing	25.1	12.0	0.15	-0.28
Percentage in different house in 1955	58.0	51.7	0.30	0.20

*
$$t = \frac{\bar{X}_1 - \bar{X}_2}{\hat{\sigma}_{\bar{X}_1} - \bar{X}_2} \qquad \hat{\sigma}_{\bar{X}_1} - \bar{X}_2 = \sqrt{\frac{N_1 s_1^2 + N_2 s_2^2}{N_1 + N_2 - 2}} \sqrt{\frac{N_1 + N_2}{N_1 N_2}}$$

$$\sigma^1 = \sigma^2 \qquad \text{d.f.} = N_1 + N_2 - 2 = 13$$

†Pearson product-moment correlation for 76 community areas of Chicago.
Source: Evelyn M. Kitagawa and Karl F. Taeuber (eds.), Chicago Community Inventory, Local Community Fact Book, Chicago Metropolitan Area, 1960 (Chicago: University of Chicago, 1963).

Table 29.   Percentage of suicides by age and length of residence in Cook County, Illinois, 1959–63.

Age Group	Less than 1	1	2	3	4	5–10	11–20	21–30	31–40	41+	Unknown	Total
0–14	0	0	0	0	—*	0	—	0	0	0		0
15–24	—	—	—	—	—	—	1	1	0	0		—
25–34	—	—	—	—	—	2	3	2	1	0		—
35–44	—	—	—	—	—	4	3	—	3	2		—
45–54	—	—	—	—	—	3	2	2	1	6		—
55–64	—	—	—	—	—	1	1	2	3	6		—
65–74	—	—	—	—	—	—	—	1	2	7		—
75–84	—	—	—	—	—	—	—	—	—	3		—
84 and over	0	0	0	0	0	—	—	—	—	—		0
Unknown	0	0	0	0	0	0	0	0	0	—		0
Percentage	4	3	4	3	2	15	14	11	14	28	2	100

*The symbol "—" is used here to indicate less than 1 percent.

Table 30.   Percentage of Cook County, Illinois, population by length of residence, 1960.

Years of Residence	Percentage	N
1–7	45	2,322,011
8–10	20	1,010,123
11–14	13	654,490
15–25	11	582,900
25 or more	6	312,350
Unknown	5	245,862
	100	5,129,736

Source: U.S. Bureau of the Census, *U.S. Census of Population: 1960. Vol. I, Characteristics of the Population. Part 15, Illinois* (Washington, D.C.: U.S. Government Printing Office, 1963), table 82, pp. 15, 382.

was related directly to high rates of residential mobility.[13] Even though horizontal mobility, a change of physical position (e.g., residence) without a change of social position, does not seem to be characteristic of suicidal areas, this does not preclude the

---

[13]Schmid, *op. cit.;* and Peter Sainsbury, *Suicide in London* (London: Chapman & Hall, Ltd., 1955).

possibility of a high association of vertical mobility, a change of social position up or down the class hierarchy, and suicidal types or areas.[14]

As the reader might suspect, the grand means (data in Table 28) of the high and low suicide areas obscure the diversity of means of the individual areas from which grand means were computed. The presence of variety suggests that in order to gain a clearer picture of suicide and its causes it will be necessary to probe beneath the facade of the bipartite typology of high and low suicide rate areas. Durkheim, Cavan, Menninger, and others have noted numerous types of suicide.[15]

The adjectives "low," "medium," and "high" used below refer to the ranks of particular community areas *within* the 15 community areas comprising the zones of highest (9 areas) and lowest (6 areas) suicide rates. "Low," "medium," and "high" are defined as follows:

	Low	Medium*	High
Percentage 65 and older	Below 5%	5–9.9%	10% and above
Median school years completed	Below 9%	9–9.9%	10% and above
Median family income	Below $5,000	$5,000–6,999	$7,000 and above
Percentage white-collar workers	Below 30%	30–39%	40% and above
Percentage unemployed	Below 5%	5–14.9%	15% and above
Percentage Negro	Below 20%	20–79%	80% and above
Percentage foreign stock	Below 10%	10–39%	40% and above
Percentage per household ..	Below 2.5%	2.5–3.3%	3.4% and above
Percentage in substandard housing	Below 10%	10–23%	24% and above
Percentage in different house in 1955	Below 40%	40–59%	60% and above

*The "medium" category contains the mean score of all 76 of Chicago's community areas. Thus, minimally "high" and "low" indicates scores that are above and below the grand mean.

Table 31 lists selected sets of community areas according to similarity of ranks on the 10 variables being studied.

[14]Indeed Warren Breed's work in New Orleans suggests a strong positive association between vertical mobility and the suicide rate.

[15]Durkheim, *op. cit.;* Cavan, *op. cit.;* and Karl Menninger, *Man against Himself* (New York: Harcourt, Brace & World, Inc., 1938) .

Table 31. Ranks on specific variables of selected sets of community areas, Chicago, Illinois, 1959–63.

	Community Areas with Highest Suicide Rates			Community Areas with Lowest Suicide Rates		
	Gold Coast	Skid Row	Total	Suburban	Negro	Total
Percentage 65 and older	H*	M	H	H	L	M
Median school years completed	H	L	H	M	L	M
Median family income	M	M	M	H	L	M
Percentage white-collar workers	H	L	H	M	L	L
Percentage unemployed	L	L	L	L	H	M
Percentage Negro	L	L	L	L	H	M
Percentage foreign stock	M	H	M	H	L	M
Percentage per household	M	M	M	L	H	M
Percentage in substandard housing	M	M	M	L	H	M
Percentage in different house in 1955	H	M	M	M	H	M

*"H," "M," and "L" mean high, medium, and low (see footnote to preceding table for the meaning of "high," "medium," and "low").

The gold coast area

Rogers Park, Uptown, Lakeview, Lincoln Park, Near North Side, and Hyde Park (community areas Nos. 1, 3, 6, 7, 8, and 41) seem to form a high suicidal area subtype, which will be called the *gold coast* type. This type is characterized by a high population 65 and older, high educational level, medium income, a high percentage of white-collar workers, a low amount of unemployment, a low proportion of Negroes (with the exception of the Near North Side, which is about 31 percent Negro, and Hyde Park, which is about 38 percent Negro), a medium amount of foreign stock, medium population per household, a medium amount of substandard housing, and high residential mobility.

It is no surprise to find that the so-called "gold coast" areas have high suicide rates. Whereas the low suicide areas are characterized by strong external constraints, the high suicide areas appear to be characterized by weak external constraints. *Anomie* is common to areas with high suicide rates. As we saw in Chapter 2, anomic suicide usually results from a temporary but abrupt alteration in the norms of a society. To review: Durkheim mentions the following three indices (among others) of anomic suicides. First, abrupt social changes, such as the Great Depression in the United States in the 1930's, seem to be associated with high suicide rates. Second, on a more general plane Durkheim suggests that *any* disturbances in the collective order can lead to an increased suicide rate.[16] Under normal conditions social and personal equilibrium prevail; that is, legitimate means of attaining gratifications are sufficiently proportioned to felt or actual needs. With *anomie* the relationship between means and ends, between effort and attainment, is upset. The result is confusion, a loss of orientation. Crises often reduce means without a corresponding reduction in needs. With the constraining force of society temporarily disrupted, individuals are thrown back upon themselves and often are unable to maintain personal equilibrium.

It is crucial to realize that for Durkheim, these general disturbances of the collective order affect the upper social classes

[16]Durkheim, *op. cit.,* p. 246.

more than the lower social classes.[17] Andrew Henry and James Short, Jr., make a similar point when they demonstrate that the suicide rate of upper status categories is more highly related to fluctuations in the business cycle than is the suicide rate of lower status categories.[18] Durkheim argues that the upper status man who tends to look to the future for satisfaction (a pattern of deferred gratification) will have no past (his definition of the situation). But a past is necessary to endure present crises. Interruptions which prevent pursuit of future goals, especially when permanent, can leave a man in a desperate situation in which he feels that he has accomplished nothing. On the other hand, the lower status man, who tends to value limited, present achievements (a pattern of immediate gratification), has something (some feeling of accomplishment, and thus, of satisfaction) when other future goals become unrealizable.[19]

Third, liberal occupations should serve as an index for anomic suicide.[20] For example, managers of industry should have higher suicide rates than their employees. Furthermore, members of modern, urban industrial societies should have higher suicide rates than members of traditional, agrarian societies since urban industrial societies display more *anomie* than agrarian societies.

Anomic suicide is characterized by unregulated emotions. It is always accompanied by a morbid desire for the infinite, violence, irritation, and disgust. Poverty restrains it.

Several variables indicate that high suicide areas tend to have a disproportionate share of *anomie*. For example, the high suicide areas are located in the core of Chicago. As Cavan, Faris and

---

[17]See Durkheim, *op. cit.*, pp. 246 ff., 253–54: "With increased prosperity desires increase. . . . Poverty protects against suicide because it is a restraint in itself. . . . Wealth, on the other hand, by the power it bestows, deceives us into believing that we depend on ourselves only."

[18]Andrew F. Henry and James F. Short, Jr., *Suicide and Homicide* (New York: The Free Press of Glencoe, Inc., 1954), p. 27: "Suicide of high status categories will be more highly associated with the business cycle than suicide of lower status categories."

[19]Ephraim H. Mizruchi, *Success and Opportunity* (New York: The Free Press, 1964), found that *anomia* (Srole's scale) was associated with perception of limited opportunities for the middle classes but not for the lower classes. The following sentence appears on page 127: "We suggested that the effects of disparity between aspiration and achievement may possibly be smaller in the lower classes than in the higher classes, because there is a greater familiarity with failure among the former and a greater opportunity to rationalize."

[20]Durkheim, *op. cit.*, p. 257.

Dunham, Sainsbury (in London), and others have noted, this area has more social and personal disorganization than other areas of the city.[21] The population of the gold coast areas has high amounts of education, white-collar workers, and horizontal mobility. All of these attributes fit the anomic pattern.

In *Suicide,* Durkheim writes that

> . . . as a rule suicide increases with knowledge. Knowledge does not determine this progress. It is innocent; nothing is more unjust than to accuse it. . . . Man seeks to learn and man kills himself because of the loss of cohesion . . . ; he does not kill himself because of his learning.[22]

Nonetheless, the greater the education level, the less the regulation by traditional norms, and the higher the suicide potential. Likewise, in the gold coast area (*but not* in the skid row area) being higher in the socioeconomic hierarchy is associated with a high suicide rate. It is appropriate that we should find an empirical association between high social class, high levels of education, and high suicide rates. Durkheim predicted just such an association.

> The liberal professions and in a wider sense the well-to-do classes are certainly those with the liveliest taste for knowledge and the most active intellectual life. Now although the statistics of suicide by occupations and classes cannot always be obtained with sufficient accuracy, it is undeniably exceptionally frequent in the highest classes of society.[23]

Thus, we find in the gold coast area the higher the socioeconomic status, the greater the educational level, the more social disorganization, the greater the horizontal mobility, the less regulation by traditional norms, and the higher the suicide rate.[24]

The skid row area

Among the high suicide areas, the characteristics of the Lower West Side (No. 31), Pullman (No. 50), and McKinley Park (No.

---

[21]Cavan, *op. cit.;* R. E. L. Faris and H. Warren Dunham, *Mental Disorders in Urban Areas* (Chicago: The University of Chicago Press, 1965) ; and Sainsbury, *op. cit.*

[22]Durkheim, *op. cit.,* pp. 168–69.

[23]*Ibid.,* p. 165. Cf. p. 245. Note that the direct relationship between social class and suicide predicted by Durkheim was *not* found to hold in the skid row area.

[24]See Robert K. Merton, *On Theoretical Sociology* (New York: The Free Press, 1967) , pp. 213–42.

59) suggest the existence of a second type of suicidal area, the attributes of which are: a medium percentage of the population 65 and older, low educational attainment, medium family income, a low percentage of white-collar workers, low unemployment, almost no Negroes, high proportion of foreign stock, medium population per household, medium amount of substandard housing, and a medium amount of residential mobility. This type of suicide *approximates* what Emile Durkheim called "egoistic suicide." It characteristically is found in the metropolitan slum, such as the population of Madison and Halsted Streets in Chicago. Thus, it will be designated the *skid row* type.

The social characteristics of the skid row population stand in marked contrast to those of the gold coast population. The gold coast area is characterized primarily by an anomic suicide model while the skid row area also manifests strong "egoistic" factors.[25] According to Durkheim, the egoistic suicide is marked by excessive individuation and apathy (whereas anomic and altruistic suicides are marked by activity). It results from man's no longer finding a basis for existence in life.

The skid row area populations are low in educational attainment, low in percentage of white-collar workers, and high in percentage of foreign stock—all attributes which should contribute to excessive individuation in a modern urban-industrial society. As we have seen in Chapter 7 members of the upper and middle classes are more likely to belong to voluntary associations, to have gone to college, to have better chances for upward mobility, and to have more occupational prestige than members of the lower classes.[26] Thus, in the skid row area, the lower the educational attainment, the lower the socioeconomic status, the higher the number of foreign-born, the greater the alienation and withdrawal from societal participation and norms, and the higher the suicide rate. In spite of some important differences, both of the areas with high suicide rates tend to have more egoism (excessive individuation) and *anomie* than the areas with low suicide rates.

---

[25]See Durkheim, *op. cit.*, pp. 152–216. This does not preclude the possibility that *on another level* of analysis egoistic and anomic suicide may be considered unicausal. Cf. Barclay D. Johnson, "Durkheim's One Cause of Suicide," *American Sociological Review*, Vol. 30, No. 6 (December, 1965) , pp. 875–76.

[26]Alvin W. Gouldner, *Modern Sociology* (New York: Harcourt, Brace & World, Inc., 1963) .

The suburban area

The community areas with the lowest suicide rates also demonstrate the possibility of subtypes. Montclare (No. 18), Archer Heights (No. 57), and West Lawn (No. 65) form what will be called the *"suburban syndrome."* The most remarkable difference of these areas from the remaining areas in the lowest suicide rate category is that they have no Negroes in their populations whereas Oakland (No. 36), Fuller Park (No. 37), and Riverdale (No. 54) are about 95 percent Negro. The suburban communities have a high proportion of people 65 and over, medium educational attainments, high income, a medium number of white-collar workers, a low number of unemployed, a low percentage of Negroes, a high amount of foreign stock, low population per household, a low percentage of substandard housing, and medium residential mobility. The suburban area, unlike the high suicide rate areas, is characterized by strong external constraints. We argue that the style of life of the Negro community and the suburban community are functionally equivalent with respect to the intensity of external constraint. Research by Whyte, Riesman, and others testifies to the intense relational involvement of suburban life.[27] The presence of strong external constraints in both the suburban and the Negro communities suggests that they fit Durkheim's fatalistic pattern and that fatalistic suicide is more rare than anomic or egoistic suicide.[28]

Furthermore, suburban areas are well insulated from high suicide areas, being on the periphery of the city. Physical isolation could be a factor contributing to the low suburban suicide rate. The geographical isolation of suburbanites should not be confused with the personal isolation of the skid row pariah. Suburbanites are far from excessively individuated. When they occur, their suicides are characterized by *insufficient* individuation. Social integration is high in suburbia but low in skid row. Suburbanites

[27]William H. Whyte, Jr., *The Organization Man* (Garden City, N.Y.: Doubleday & Co., Inc., 1957), esp. Part VII; and David Riesman *et al., The Lonely Crowd* (Garden City, N.Y.: Doubleday & Co., Inc., 1953). Cf. Henry and Short, *op. cit.,* pp. 74 ff.

[28]Durkheim, *op. cit.,* p. 276. See Cavan, *op. cit.,* pp. 222 ff., "The Case of the Youth Who Was Prematurely Tired."

are isolated spatially and *as a group* from high suicide rate areas in Chicago. Skid row dwellers are isolated socially from significant others within high suicide rate areas.

Thus, we find that the more suburban the community, the greater the relational involvement of the residents and the lower the suicide rate.

The Negro area

Evidence has accumulated that *Negroes* are not prone to commit suicide. The results of the ecological investigation offer additional confirmation of this tendency. Three of the six areas of lowest suicidal incidence are Negro communities. Nonetheless, Riverdale (No. 54) presents some striking dissimilarities from Oakland (No. 36) and Fuller Park (No. 37), and, thus, will be described separately.

Oakland and Fuller Park have a low percentage of people 65 and older, a low educational level,[29] low income, a low percentage of white-collar workers, a high amount of unemployment, a very high amount of Negroes and very low amount of foreign stock, a high population per household, a high amount of substandard housing, and high amount of residential mobility.

Riverdale is a dramatic partial confirmation of Emile Durkheim's contention that instead of causing suicide, poverty actually protects against it. Riverdale combines a very low suicide rate with a highly deprived style of life. It is a young community; indeed, the youngest of the 15 studied. Strangely enough, Riverdale has a high educational level (much higher than areas 36 and 37) but a low income (about the same to somewhat lower than areas 36 and 37), a low proportion of white-collar workers (but more than areas 36 and 37), a high number of unemployed persons (higher than that of areas 36 and 37), a population which is 90 percent Negro (compared with 98 percent for Oakland and 96 percent for Fuller Park), a low amount of foreign stock (but higher than areas 36 and 37), the highest population per household of any area, the lowest amount of substandard housing (a com-

---

[29]The educational attainment of these two Negro communities is about the same as that of the skid row communities.

pletely unanticipated result), and a medium amount of residential mobility (lower than that of areas 36 and 37).

In reading the history of Riverdale, probable explanations for some of the peculiarities of the community emerged. Since 1940 Riverdale has become heavily industrialized. Most of the population influx is a result of the immigration of Negro laborers. This would account for the low percentage of white-collar workers, the relatively low income, and the youth of the Riverdale population. In 1943–44 the Chicago Housing Authority (CHA) constructed 1,500 apartments, called "Altgeld Gardens," for the Negro population. In 1954 the CHA finished the Philip Murray Homes (500 dwelling units). The presence of public housing accounts for the community's low amount of substandard housing. Since the Negro population is young and the housing units are superior, it is not surprising that Riverdale should have the highest population per household.

In Chapter 7 we argued that Negroes tend to experience more frustration than do whites, particularly in their efforts to realize vocational aspirations. Negro aggression is more likely to be other-directed rather than self-directed, primarily because they undergo a *status* deprivation relative to most whites and because they have a higher degree of relational involvement than do most whites.[30] In other words, Negroes as a group are externally constrained more than are whites as a group. Earlier researchers have demonstrated that the suicide rate varies inversely with the strength of the relational system.[31] When people are subjected to strong external constraint, by virtue either of subordinate status or intense involvement in social relationships with other persons, it is easier to blame others when frustration occurs. But when the external constraints are weak, the self must bear a greater burden of responsibility for frustration. Thus, it has been hypothesized that Negroes are more likely than whites to commit homicide and less likely than whites to commit suicide.[32] The Chicago ecological data adds further confirmation of this hypothesis.

The suicide rate of nonwhites is uniformly low in the South

[30]The South Side of Chicago is a huge Negro ghetto with a high degree of relational involvement. For example, the three Negro communities in the low suicide rate areas (No. 36, No. 37, and No. 54) have a high population per household.

[31]Henry and Short, *op. cit.*

[32]*Ibid., passim.*

and the South-Central states, ranging from 2.0 in South Carolina to 4.8 in Tennessee. Arkansas, Louisiana, Mississippi (which is over 50 percent Negro), Alabama, Texas, and South Carolina have lower suicide rates than any other states, except for Massachusetts and New Jersey.[33] Given that a large proportion of the Negro population in Chicago is made up of southern migrants,[34] it is to be expected that the rates would be lower among Negroes than among the Chicago whites, who for the most part are not southern migrants.

Durkheim has argued that there is an inverse relationship between poverty and suicide rate.[35] The poorer a population is, the less likely it is that its suicide rate will be high. The Negroes of community areas 36, 37, and 54 all have relatively low incomes.

As a rule, the older a person is the more likely he or she is to commit suicide.[36] The three Negro communities all had a lower percentage of their populations in the 65 and older bracket than did the suburbanites or the high suicide rate areas.

Thus, the more Negroes in a community, the lower the median family income, the higher the population per household, the younger the population, the higher the degree of relational involvement, the more externally directed aggression, and the lower the suicide rate.

Conclusion

An analysis of community characteristics of 1,547 Chicago, Illinois, suicides indicates that areas with high suicide rates can be distinguished from areas with low suicide rates on selected variables. Radically different scores on these variables suggest the existence of at least four types of suicidal areas and that these four types have different associations with the suicide rate.

More specifically the high suicide rate areas can be distinguished from the low suicide rate areas by an older population, slightly more education and income, far more white-collar workers, fewer

---

[33]Dublin, *op. cit.*, pp. 220–21.

[34]See U.S. Bureau of Census, *U.S. Census of Population: 1960. Subject Reports. Mobility for States and State Economic Areas. Final Report PC (2)-2B* (Washington, D.C.: U.S. Government Printing Office, 1963) , pp. 256 ff.

[35]Durkheim, *op. cit.*, pp. 245 ff. Cf. Sainsbury, *op. cit.*, *passim*.

[36]Dublin, *op. cit.*, chap. iii.

unemployed, far fewer Negroes, more foreign stock, much lower population per household, more substandard housing, and slightly more residential mobility.

Among the high suicide rate areas, gold coast and skid row subtypes were discovered and their attributes outlined. Suburban and Negro subtypes were found in the low suicide rate areas. The analysis of the social characteristics of the subareas *suggested* that gold coast suicides were predominantly anomic, skid row suicides were predominantly egoistic, and suburban and Negro suicides were predominantly fatalistic.[37] It also suggested that fatalistic suicide was rarer than the anomic or egoistic varieties. Finally, generalizations were made concerning the relationships between salient social characteristics and the suicide rate for each of the four suicidal subtypes.

It should be emphasized that anomic, egoistic, and fatalistic suicides undoubtedly occurred in all four of the sets of community areas discussed. What distinguished one type of community area from another was the probable *disproportionate* occurrence of one type of suicidal area in relation to the other three types. Figure 9 summarizes the implications of our argument.

Figure 9. A hypothetical distribution of *anomie*, egoism, and fatalism in four suicidal areas.

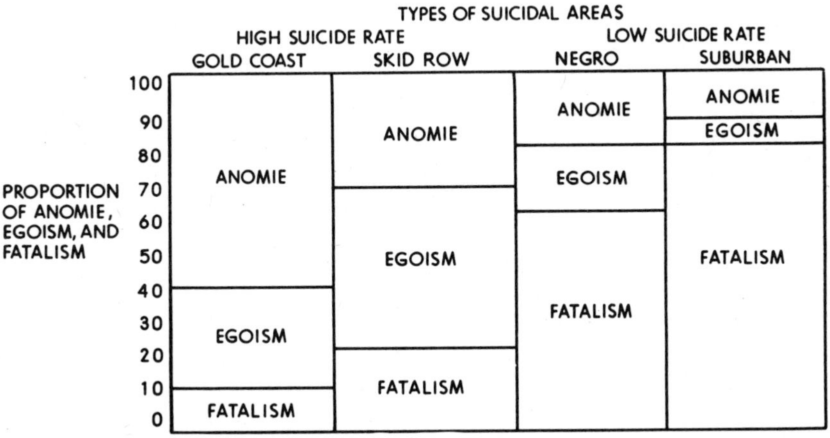

[37]We have no way of knowing the exact relationship between community characteristics and suicides who resided in a community. Thus, the data in this chapter are only "suggestive."

Suggestions for further reading

Douglas, Jack D.   *The Social Meanings of Suicide.* Princeton, N.J.: Princeton University Press, 1967. See pages 95–108 for a critical review of ecological theories of suicide.

Cavan, Ruth Shonle.   *Suicide.* New York: Russell & Russell, Inc., 1965. Pages 77–105 offer materials (late 1920's) for a direct comparison with our recent ecological work in Chicago.

Sainsbury, Peter.   *Suicide in London.* London: Chapman & Hall Ltd., 1955. Permits cross-cultural ecological study. Sainsbury is a researcher at the Institute of Psychiatry, Maudsley Hospital, London.

Schmid, Calvin F.   *Suicides in Seattle, 1914 to 1925.* Seattle, Wash.: University of Washington Press, 1928. A representative ecological study of suicide common to the sociology of the 1920's.

Selvin, Hanan S.   "Durkheim's *Suicide*: Further Thoughts on a Methodological Classic," *Emile Durkheim* (ed. Robert A. Nisbet), pp. 113–36. Englewood Cliffs, N.J.: Prentice-Hall, Inc., 1965. Examines some of the methodological pitfalls in the ecological study of suicide.

Wechsler, H.   "Community Growth, Depressive Disorders, and Suicide," *The American Journal of Sociology,* Vol. 67 (July, 1961), pp. 9–17. A study of the relationship of population growth to the frequency of hospitalized mental illness and suicide.

PART III

Evaluation and conclusion

CHAPTER 9

Major implications: a critical evaluation of Durkheim's theory of suicide

So much for the empirical analysis. The question now is "What can we make of it?" We ought to be in a better position to criticize and suggest reformulations of Durkheim's theory of suicide and to be loyal to the radical spirit in which this book was conceived. Paradoxically, however, the major explanatory postulate of our work *supports* Durkheim. In the next and last chapter we argue that the suicide rate varies inversely with external constraint. Yet, the inconsistency is more apparent than real. Championing the heuristic value of irreverence in science does not require heretical results. It could be that Durkheim was in some measure right about the causes of suicide.

On the other hand, our explanatory postulate is tentative, as, indeed, any explanation is. The criticism of Durkheim when fully developed may yet lead to additional or revised postulates. It could be that using data sources similar to Durkheim's made our results too conservative. Perhaps a different approach to the problem of suicide is necessary. For example, future research should include interviews with attempted suicides who ordinarily would have died, "psychological autopsies," and interviews with

159

"gatekeepers" like coroners and the police.[1] A synthesis of socio-logical, psychological, and psychoanalytical techniques seems espe-cially promising.

It is likely that the criticisms which follow will lead to an extension of Durkheim's theory of suicide rather than to an elimination of it. In effect our research affirms the importance of the concept of external constraint in explaining suicide but sensi-tizes us to the need for additional postulates, such as Henry and Short's concept of internal restraint. We turn now directly to the criticisms deriving from our own and supporting research.

Socioeconomic status and the suicide rate

In direct contradiction to Durkheim, many recent investiga-tions of suicide (including our own) have discovered that the lower the socioeconomic status, the higher the suicide rate.[2] Our data on suicide and status suggest that vertical restraint (restraint deriving from being in a subordinate status) aggravates suicide and casts doubt on Durkheim's major conclusion, and that suicide varies inversely with social integration. Additional questions must be raised about the association of suicide with education and income. It is now more difficult to accept that poverty protects against suicide and that increased education aggravates it. The United States Census Bureau index of socioeconomic status (utilized to analyze our data) incorporated occupation, income, and education as measures and still revealed an inverse relation-ship between status and suicide.

We conclude that Durkheim's theory of suicide underestimates the importance of fatalistic suicide; i.e., suicide in response to

---

[1]Herbert Hendin, "The Psychodynamics of Suicide," in Jack P. Gibbs (ed.), *Suicide* (New York: Harper & Row, 1968). For references to the psychological autopsy see *Suicide and Depression* (mimeographed; New Hampshire Department of Health and Welfare).

[2]It could be argued that the relationship of SES and the suicide rate is an artifact of the data; e.g., that death certificates are unreliable. However, the difference be-tween the suicide rates of the upper and lower classes are so large (roughly 15 versus 50 per 100,000 population) that numerous upper class suicides could have gone undetected without changing the relationship between class and suicide. It strains credulity to contend that so many upper class suicides were able to avoid the stigma of being classified as suicides in the several separate studies we referred to. Furthermore, Durkheim used comparable data and got opposite results.

hyperregulation. Such a conclusion would appear to be sufficient grounds for rejecting Durkheim's general theory of suicide. However, there are at least three reasons why the time is not yet ripe for rejection. First the relationship of social restraint and suicide is still unclear. For example, the Chicago data show a strong negative relationship between what Henry and Short call "horizontal restraint" (restraint deriving from relational involvement) and the suicide rate. Second, high suicide rates occur in two very different types of communities: what we have called the "gold coast" areas and "skid row" areas, respectively. In the gold coast areas, high SES is associated with high suicide rates, as Durkheim predicted. Third, since the death certificate calls for "usual occupation," the SES pattern derived from our data is somewhat questionable. For example, the Chicago data might be portraying an SES pattern true a year or two *before* the time of death. At the time of death, the social situations of suicides may indeed be primarily egoistic and anomic.

This brings us to another criticism of Durkheim. Perhaps the crucial variable in predicting the suicide rate is not status position but rather status change.[3] Any study of suicide based on death certificates is unable to deal adequately with questions of social mobility or suicidal careers. For example, one possible suicidal career pattern would involve initially strong vertical restraints leading eventually to alienation from prevailing social norms. If the withdrawal of legitimacy from social norms is pervasive, *anomie* can result. In any event alienation does lead to egoism. Thus, both egoism and *anomie* can result from a fatalistic social situation. Such a hypothetical suicidal career demonstrates how it is possible for the suicide rate to vary both positively and negatively with social integration over time.

Probably the relationship between social integration, SES, and suicide is much more complex than Durkheim thought it was. It is clear that adequate treatment of the problem awaits data on the social histories of suicides. It would be premature to propose final solutions to a problem whose dimensions we do not yet fully understand.

---

[3]See Warren Breed, "Occupational Mobility and Suicide among White Males," *American Sociological Review,* Vol. 28, No. 2 (April, 1963), pp. 179–88.

Sex and age

Whereas Durkheim found about a 3 to 1 ratio for male and female suicides at all ages, the Chicago data show increasing disparities in the male-female suicide rates with aging. For young adults the ratio is 2 to 1, in middle age it increases to 3 to 1, and at age 65 and after it soars to about 5 to 1. For the most part Durkheim ignored the relationship between age and sex roles and the suicide rate. Age and sex were marginally social variables at best for Durkheim. Even a cursory reading of *Suicide* will reveal that Durkheim considers age and sex directly only in Book I, which is concerned with extrasocial factors. In Book II, the heart of *Suicide,* Durkheim focuses upon religion, family, economy, politics, and the military. Age and sex are considered only indirectly; for example, when Durkheim discusses the coefficient of preservation of married men *vis-à-vis* married women.

We argue that Durkheim failed to consider adequately the social causes of suicide in various age and sex roles. Our study of suicide in Chicago suggests that the age differences in male and female suicides can be explained in large part by a malfunctioning of occupational and marital and family careers respectively. The male suicide rate shows a sharp increase at about age 65. This made us suspect that male suicides were particularly the result of work problems, retirement, unemployment, and downward mobility. Data from secondary sources have supported this suspicion.[4]

Female suicides, on the other hand, are stable or declining at age 65. From approximately ages 35 to 75, female suicides occur at about the same rate. The sharpest increases are from ages 15 to 35. One of the most significant events in this time period is marriage and the raising of children. Thus, we speculated that female suicides are related to marital and family problems. This hypothesis was given considerable support in the "literature."[5]

---

[4]*Ibid.* Cf. I. R. C. Batcheor, "Suicide in Old Age," in Edwin S. Shneidman and Norman L. Farberow (eds.), *Clues to Suicide* (New York: McGraw-Hill Book Co., Inc., 1957), p. 149; and Andrew Henry and James F. Short, Jr., *Suicide and Homicide* (New York: The Free Press, 1954), p. 31.

[5]Leonard M. Moss and Donald M. Hamilton, "Psychotherapy of the Suicidal Patient," *Clues to Suicide,* p. 107; Pow Meng Yap, *Suicide in Hong Kong* (Hong Kong: Hong Kong University Press, 1958), pp. 28 ff.; and Calvin F. Schmid, *Suicides in Seattle, 1914 to 1925* (Seattle, Wash.: University of Washington Press, 1928), pp. 39 ff.

Errors of omission

Perhaps Durkheim's gravest error was his refusal to admit that race, alcoholism, physical and mental health, and psychological variables in general were required for an adequate explanation of the suicide rate. Subsequent research has made it clear that no theory of suicide which neglects these variables can hope to explain the suicide rate. The great service of Andrew Henry and James Short, Jr., is to call attention to the interrelationships of social and psychological variables in determining the suicide rate.[6] Figure 10 predicts that the suicide rate will be high when external

Figure 10.   Reactions to restraint.

External Restraint

		High	Low
Internal Restraint	High	Anxiety	Suicide
	Low	Homicide	Undetermined

restraint is low (i.e., when what we have called "vertical and horizontal restraint" is low) and internal restraint is high (generally, the stricter the superego, the greater the internal restraint). Such typologies cover a dimension that was missing in Durkheim's theory of suicide. Durkheim's theory of suicide is unable to account for why some people suicide when external restraint is low and others do not. By bringing in the psychological dimension of internal restraint a step has been made in the right direction. It is encouraging that recently sociologists have begun to devote attention to the social psychology of suicide.[7]

Race

Durkheim thought of race as a biological or extrasocial variable. However, contemporary sociologists have fixed upon the crucial

---

[6]Henry and Short, *op. cit.*, p. 121.
[7]See Anthony Giddens, "A Typology of Suicide," *European Journal of Sociology,* Vol. 7, No. 2 (1966) , pp. 276–95.

importance of the societal reaction to race. Biological factors are not so significant in determining race relations as in the perception of biological factors. With this shift in the connotation of "race" it has become easier to see how race can be a social cause of suicide. Since Durkheim did not investigate the relationship of race and the suicide rate, all of our findings in Chicago constitute increments to his empirical results. If Durkheim's general theory of suicide is adequate, then our findings must be derivable from his general explanatory propositions. Among our major findings were that whites were over twice as likely to suicide as non-whites (primarily Negroes); that most nonwhite suicides were under age 45; and that young, nonwhite females were more likely to suicide than young, white females. It appears that most of these findings can be fitted into Durkheim's general theory of suicide.

An examination of the social situation of Chicago Negroes revealed that they were subjected to strong external constraints and that this was a primary factor in their low suicide rate. Noteworthy were their status deprivation (strong vertical restraint) and the high population per household of their communities (which suggests strong horizontal restraint). We also noted the relative youth of the Negro communities and that their suicides were often the product of retroflexed anger rather than the product of hopelessness. Since Negro suicides occurred under conditions of strong social constraint, some questions must be raised about Durkheim's claim that suicide and social restraint are negatively related. According to Durkheim, many Negro suicides occur under circumstances that should serve as a suicidal prophylactic. For example, Breed found in New Orleans that Negro suicides were disproportionately associated (in relation to white suicides) with authority problems, especially problems with the police.[8] However, these questions do not pose a serious threat to Durkheim's general theory since the Negro suicide rate is in fact very low, and this is exactly what Durkheim would have expected.

The anomaly among young, nonwhite females was explained in terms of the differential roles of young, white and nonwhite females. Nonwhite females were more likely than white females

---

[8]Warren Breed, "The Negro and Fatalistic Suicide," unpublished manuscript.

to assume the responsibility of breadwinner for the family. Thus, it is probable that they were subjected to many of the same stresses and strains associated with work that white males were and that this contributed to their high suicide rate.

Alcoholism

Given Durkheim's sociological bias, it is understandable that he should focus on the relative independence of alcoholism and suicide rates. However, in his own data (especially those from Denmark) there was considerable overlap between high suicide rate areas and areas of alcoholism. Furthermore, recent evidence shows significant interaction between rates of alcoholism and suicide.[9] For example, George Murphy and Eli Robins report that 75 percent of the suicides in one of their studies suffered from either depression or alcoholism.[10] This statistic becomes particularly impressive when it is realized that no other diagnosis was present in more than 5 percent of the suicides. Alcoholic suicides were less likely to be married and more likely to live alone than a comparable control group drawn from the United States population. Finally, Durkheim apparently was unaware that psychoanalytically alcoholism is of the same *genre* as suicide. Karl Menninger labels alcoholism as a kind of "chronic suicide"; i.e., a partial suicide with a general focus.[11] Alcoholism can be viewed as a form of self-destruction short of suicide which atones for feelings of guilt generated from one's aggression. Since Durkheim was not interested in functional equivalents of suicide and since his sociological blinders prevented him from considering the causal relevance of a partially physical condition, he overlooked an important variable in the aetiology of suicide.

Physical and mental health

While it is no doubt true that some suicides are committed by completely healthy persons, it is absurd to hold that social

---

[9]Charles R. Snyder, "Inebriety, Alcoholism, and *Anomie*," in Marshall B. Clinard (ed.), *Anomie and Deviant Behavior* (New York: The Free Press, 1964), pp. 189–223.

[10]George E. Murphy and Eli Robins, "Social Factors in Suicide," *The Journal of the American Medical Association*, Vol. 199 (January, 1967), pp. 303–8.

[11]Karl Menninger, *Man against Himself* (New York: Harcourt Brace & World, Inc., 1938), p. 161.

factors alone are the determining causes of suicide.[12] It makes much more sense to speak in terms of the interaction effects of social and nonsocial forces. Dorpat and Ripley claim that 70 percent of the suicides they studied had one or more serious physical diseases at the time of death or within one year of death.[13] Bohannan's investigation of African suicides revealed that physical illness played a prominent role in suicide—accentuating what Menninger called "the wish to die."[14] We found some evidence of a similar pattern among old, white male suicides in Chicago.

Similarly, mental illness appears to be disproportionately high among suicides. In one sample of suicides 98 percent were diagnosed as "psychiatrically ill." Of these, 50 percent were depressed at the time of death.[15] Other works by Hendin, Batchelor, Menninger, Henry and Short, Sainsbury, and Shneidman and Farberow testify to the importance of psychological and psychoanalytical variables in determining the suicide rate.[16] The evidence is clear. Durkheim would have been able to account for more of the variance in the suicide rate if he had acknowledged the interplay between social and nonsocial causes.

The above discussion of substantive weaknesses in Durkheim's theory of suicide should make us suspect that the distinguishing attribute of Durkheim's work was its conceptual framework, not its substantive conclusions. Durkheim was no fool. He was aware that alcoholism, race, and physical and mental health had some effect on the suicide rate. However, Durkheim denied their direct causal role and insisted that they only influenced social integration, which in turn was the real general cause of suicide. Only social integration was consistently associated with the suicide rate. All of this suggests that Durkheim differed from his predecessors primarily because of his conceptual bias and that no evaluation

---

[12]Emile Durkheim, *Suicide* (New York: The Free Press, 1962) , p. 69.

[13]T. L. Dorpat and H. S. Ripley, "A Study of Suicide in the Seattle Area," *Comparative Psychiatry*, Vol. 1 (December, 1960) , pp. 349–59.

[14]Paul Bohannon (ed.) , *African Homicide and Suicide* (Princeton, N.J.: Princeton University Press, 1960) .

[15]Murphy and Robins, *op. cit.*

[16]Herbert Hendin, *Suicide and Scandinavia* (Garden City, N.Y.: Anchor Books, 1965) ; Batchelor, *op. cit.;* Menninger, *op. cit.;* Henry and Short, *op. cit.;* Peter Sainsbury, *Suicide in London* (London: Chapman & Hall, Ltd., 1955) ; and Norman L. Farberow and Edwin S. Shneidman (eds.) , *The Cry for Help* (New York: McGraw-Hill Book Co., Inc., 1961) .

of Durkheim's theory of suicide would be complete without a critical look at conceptual problems in *Suicide*.

The strain toward generalization

Durkheim's *Suicide* stands out from most other works on suicide because a systematic theoretical framework accompanies and undergirds the empirical study of suicide. In a very real sense, suicide is a vehicle, one substantive area among numerous possibilities, for Durkheim's pioneering construction of social theory. Like it or not, Durkheim was a philosopher as well as a sociologist. Accordingly, any attempt to transcend *Suicide* must come to grips with conceptual problems as well as empirical problems. Another student of Durkheim has written:

. . . overemphasis on the quantitative aspects of *Suicide* would be as dangerous as total neglect, if it furthered the current tendency to substitute technical virtuosity for hard thinking about empirical data that is guided by theory and directed toward enriching theory. This, after all, is the essential message of *Suicide*: that methodology is valuable insofar as it springs from the needs of theory and that theory is most fruitful when it is continually tested and refined in methodologically adequate research.[17]

One of the troublesome conceptual problems in *Suicide* is how to formulate general explanatory propositions which account for the full diversity of the research findings. Of course, this is a dilemma facing all scientists. On the one hand we have the need to generalize, ultimately to discover laws. Yet, at the same time, we want to avoid generalizing prematurely before it is clear what our generalizations must subsume. Given Durkheim's compulsion to construct a general theory of suicide, he was particularly prone to gloss over subtleties in the data. Durkheim's approach to the study of suicide was primarily "realistic," not nominalistic (what Alpert calls "associational realism").[18]

The effect of Durkheim's realism is to ignore important details;

[17]Hanan C. Selvin, "Durkheim's *Suicide*: Further Thoughts on a Methodological Classic," in Robert A. Nisbet (ed.), *Emile Durkheim* (Englewood Cliffs, N.J.: Prentice-Hall, Inc., 1965), p. 136.

[18]Harry Alpert, *Emile Durkheim and His Sociology* (New York: Russell & Russell, Inc., 1961), pp. 147 ff. Cf. Jack D. Douglas, *The Social Meanings of Suicide* (Princeton, N.J.: Princeton University Press, 1967), p. 177.

findings which might call for revision of the general theory. For example, we were surprised with the neatness of the curve of suicide by seasons. Every other analysis of suicide by season revealed a much more complex relationship between month of the year and the suicide frequency. Once the complexities in the data are admitted, then simple explanations become less tenable. In another case we were told that the old are more likely to suicide than the young. But why should this be especially true for white males? One writer has noted that the striking differences between white and nonwhite male suicides are manifested in old age.[19] Whereas the usual ratio of white to nonwhite suicides is about two to one, after age 65 it soars to eight to one.

In what may be (Durkheim's data seemed to fit the explanation) the classic case of Durkheim's forcing the data to fit the explanation, it was claimed that high SES groups had higher suicide rates than low SES groups. Most recent evidence indicates that the opposite is true, as we have seen above. Considering marital status, Durkheim discovered that the never-married had higher suicide rates than the married. Nevertheless, never-married females and married females had similar suicide rates at certain ages. We could go on.

Two questions need to be raised about Durkheim's generalizations. First, do they account for the data? As hard as he tried, we have presented evidence that Durkheim did not always get the facts clear before he generalized. Furthermore, he seemed to see especially clearly those facts which substantiated his general theory. For example, we have seen that he probably underestimated the incidence of fatalistic suicide. Even though his generalizations about suicide are basically sound, there are certain pesky inconsistencies in his and recent data that call for a closer look. Finally, there were entire sets of data such as that on race which Durkheim simply wrote off as irrelevant.

Second, are Durkheim's general explanations of suicide meaningful? Durkheim's use of "abstract meanings" (like egoism and *anomie*) has prompted Jack Douglas to call for "situated meanings." He writes that:

---

[19]Lee N. Robins, "Suicide and Violence: Explaining the Low Negro Suicide Rate," paper read at the Annual Meeting of the American Sociological Association, San Francisco, California, 1967.

What is called for is a whole new sociological method for determining and analyzing the communicative actions which can be observed and replicated in real-world cases of suicide. This method must retain the emphasis on observation and description of the earlier case-study methods, but it must also retain the emphasis on comparative studies of patterns of meanings of the statistical method.

The ideal method would involve, at the first step of observation, the exact recording of all verbal and non-verbal communicative acts involved in a case of suicide. The next step would be the preliminary analysis of the patterns of invariant linguistic items (i.e., words, phrases, sentences, facial expressions, etc.). Following this, one would next analyze such communications to determine the varying structures in which these linguistic items appear: that is, one would determine the usages (or constructions . . .) made with these linguistic items. One would then attempt to determine the relationships between the general situations or contexts of the social actors, as defined by the actors, and the constructions appearing. Lastly, one would be ready to attempt a more general theory relating meanings to each other and to actions.[20]

In part Douglas' criticism is a just plea for different sources of data. Of course, most of us realize the limitations of using official statistics. Hopefully, through the use of hospital case histories, interviews with suicide attempters (especially those who would have died except for intervention, etc.), interviews with survivors (i.e., significant others of the suicide), coroners' inquest records, and suicide notes we can begin to get at the situated meanings of suicide which we have previously ignored.

On the other hand, Douglas seems to be unaware that "abstract meanings" (like egoism or *anomie*) or general social conditions are a necessary ingredient in predicting the suicide rate. Suicidal motivations are not sufficient indicators of the suicide rate. One could predict the suicide rate fairly accurately on the basis of general social conditions, even if all suicides did not mention or were unaware of these conditions. Thus, the expressions "anomic" or "egoistic" suicides are far from meaningless. One gets the impression that Douglas is suspicious of *all* abstraction and that he is elevating a necessary condition for understanding suicide to the level of sufficient condition.[21]

---

[20] Jack D. Douglas, "The Sociological Analysis of Social Meanings of Suicide," *European Journal of Sociology,* Vol. 7, No. 2 (1966) , p. 265.

[21] Even though Douglas denies it (cf. Douglas, *The Social Meanings of Suicide,* p. 242) .

The relationship between society and individuals

Perhaps the single most important theoretical problem in Durkheim's work is the ambiguity of the relationship between society and individuals. In *Suicide,* Durkheim rules out certain variables as possible causes of the suicide rate because they are attributes of individuals, not of groups. No amount of research can reverse this judgment of Durkheim's because it is based not only on facts but also on how Durkheim *saw* facts. To delineate social facts from nonsocial facts is a conceptual as well as an empirical problem. For example, we have seen that Durkheim eliminated race, alcoholism, and physical and mental health as causes of the suicide rate because he regarded them as nonsocial facts.

Durkheim emphasized the distinction between the suicide *rate* of a group and the suicide of an individual. Rates were attributes of collectivities, such as nations. Durkheim argued that associated individual suicides were transformed into a new entity, viz, the suicide rate. Thus, rates were qualitatively as well as quantitatively different from individual acts of suicide. Durkheim claims only that he has explained the suicide *rate*.

If what Durkheim says is true, then it becomes a problem as to how one goes back from the explanation of suicide rates to the explanation of individual suicides. Furthermore, if the transition cannot be made, then of what value is the explanation? Durkheim seems to have explained the behavior of a nonentity. Logically, if the basis for the explanation of suicide rates was derived from individual suicides, then the explanations of the causes of suicide rates should have some relationship to the explanation of the causes of individual suicides.

Alpert maintains that Durkheim's exclusive concern with generalization led him to consider only the "impersonal forces" in social situations.[22] Durkheim ignored what Max Weber called *verstehen*, the investigation of a social situation or process from the viewpoint of the motivation of the human agents involved.[23]

---

[22]Alpert, *op. cit.,* pp. 109 ff.

[23]Max Weber, *The Theory of Social and Economic Organization,* trans. A. M. Henderson and Talcott Parsons (New York: Oxford University Press, 1947), pp. 8–29, 87–114.

Even if as Durkheim claims all internal life draws its primary material from "without," this does not mean that "internal life" is not capable of generating novelty; i.e., affecting the external world as well as being affected by it.

Durkheim has generated needless problems in part because he failed to clarify the distinction between real and ideal types. Perhaps the most conspicuous example of this failure occurs in Durkheim's celebrated discussion of social facts.[24] Here Durkheim claims that social facts are external and constraining. They are external in the sense that they are outside (physically and epistemologically) and a product of the association of individuals. They are constraining in that by virtue of their collective aspects, they require one to fulfill certain obligations (such as those deriving from being a brother, a husband, or a citizen).

But by concentrating on social *facts* Durkheim is committed to say that the social is also internal and liberating. This seriously compromises the descriptive power of the attributes "external" and "constraining." As an example of how social facts are liberating, consider Durkheim's book *The Elementary Forms of the Religious Life.*[25] Admittedly we find that the negative cult functions to make religious and profane lives mutually exclusive and that social organization into clans coerces one into having restricted cross-clan social relationships. But religious rites also serve to revivify the most essential elements of the collective conscience. Religious rites are a means whereby groups reaffirm themselves periodically (as Malinowski has shown in respect to funeral rites.)[26] Given that the individual participates in this group revivification, it can be argued that social organization liberates the individual as well as constrains or coerces him.

Social facts are not only external either. In a significant sense social facts are operative within the confines of the inner, private life of the individual. Given that the individual has been successfully socialized (i.e., has internalized the norms of his society or community), his private and unspoken responses even to highly abstract situations constitute social acts. For example, one coercive

---

[24]Emile Durkheim, *The Rules of Sociological Method* (New York: The Free Press, 1962) .

[25]New York: Collier Books, 1961.

[26]Bronislaw Malinowski, *Crime and Custom in Savage Society* (Paterson, N.J.: Littlefield, Adams & Co., 1962) , pp. 33 ff.

agent of the private social act is the superego. The internal struggles between the id and the superego are properly labeled as social situations, as social facts.[27]

Thus, social facts (such as suicide) are not only external and coercive but are also internal and liberating. However, this is an unhappy situation because it can lead to a distorted and ambiguous definition of the concept of the social. By dealing exclusively with social facts, Durkheim is obliged to characterize the concept of the social with epithets that grate against each other—whose meanings conflict with one another. To say that the concept of the social has the attributes of externality and internality, constraint and liberation sounds more like a riddle than a definition. Would it not be clearer to say that the ideal social type is characterized by externality and constraint, while the ideal nonsocial type is characterized by internality and liberty, *and* that every real situation (e.g., suicide) has both social and nonsocial components?

Two methodological problems

The ecological fallacy

When Durkheim used characteristics of society (such as egoism or *anomie*) to explain the behavior of suicides, he was guilty of the ecological fallacy.[28] Attributes of groups are not necessarily applicable to the individuals or subsets of individuals who compose these groups. Notice though that community characteristics can be used to predict the suicide rate when the suicide rate is taken as an attribute of the community. However, in this case we run into another of Durkheim's old nemeses—the relationship between social facts and individual characteristics. Thus, with Durkheim's method we are forced into two apparently equally unpalatable alternatives. Either our analysis procedure is invalid and our results dubious or our conclusions are accurate but too abstract.

It is more profitable to regard egoism or *anomie* as highly gen-

---

[27]Some readers might agree that social facts influence the inner life of the individual but prefer to think of id-superego struggles as socially derived and socially defined psychological processes. Even allowing this interpretation it remains true that social facts are not wholly external, since social conditioning of the internal dialogue of the self has occurred.

[28]Selvin, *op. cit.*, p. 126.

eral conditions of the larger social situations of suicides. In themselves they tell us little about the suicide potential of an individual. Let us assume that you were an insurance agent for Metropolitan Life and that you had two applicants for $100,000 life insurance policies. If part of your job was to assess the risk of your clients' deaths by suicide, it would not be much help to know that suicide varied inversely with the degree of social integration of the social groups of which your clients formed parts. But given the particular research findings of *Suicide* and of subsequent research, you would know that you had better deny the application of the 75-year-old white male who is divorced, lives in skid row in Chicago, is an Austrian immigrant, is a manual laborer, is a Protestant, is depressed, and has cancer. You, no doubt, would approve the application of your other client who is a 22-year-old Negro female, is married and has five children, lives in Winnetka, Illinois, is a ninth-generation African immigrant, is the housewife of a prosperous farmer, is Jewish, and is in fine health.

One way of minimizing the danger of committing the ecological fallacy is to make your generalizations less general; i.e., to construct more particularistic typologies of suicide. In effect this is to assume that there are many different types of suicide and many suicide rates. If there are different types of suicide, then why should their explanations be the same? Perhaps it is still premature and presumptuous to try to explain the general suicide rate of a nation. More nominalistic typologies of suicide are called for.

It is a long way from the community at large to the suicidal subcommunity and to a particular suicide. Social facts like egoism or *anomie* merely sensitize us to suicide potential. To use a distinction first made by Aristotle, they are the "material" causes of suicide ("that out of which something arises"), not the "efficient" causes ("the forces producing an effect"). In order to explain suicide we need not only to know about general social forces associated with the suicide rate but also to know about individual characteristics (e.g., the level of internal restraint of a specific person, the situational variables, etc.).

Multivariate analysis

Durkheim was one of the pioneers in multivariate analysis, but he lacked the techniques to carry it through. If Durkheim had been able to use multiple and partial correlation, his analysis would have been more sophisticated. For example, in our study of the suicide rate as a community characteristic we looked at the various relationships of age, population per household, and the suicide rate. The zero-order correlations were as Durkheim might have predicted. Age and the suicide rate were correlated 0.56; population per household and the suicide rate were correlated − 0.72. But computing a partial correlation for age and the suicide rate, controlling for population per household, we found that the correlation went negative (− 0.18). However, the partial between population per household and the suicide rate, controlling for age, was still strongly negative (− 0.60). This suggests that population per household may be a more important determinant of the suicide rate than age.

Obviously it is senseless to criticize Durkheim for not using tools that were not available to him. The point of our remarks is that the opportunity now exists for someone to "tease out" the interaction effects of the variables Durkheim considered. We would expect that such an analysis would permit more subtle generalizations, call for qualifications in Durkheim's generalizations, and point to the more important variables affecting the suicide rate.

Conclusions

On the basis of suicide research since the publication of Durkheim's *Suicide,* including our own study in Chicago, we have outlined some of the weaknesses in Durkheim's approach to suicide. A summary of these weaknesses and our recommendations for their correction is given in Figure 11. It is hoped that by this and similar analyses we can transcend Durkheim and get on to fresh approaches to the study of suicide.

Certainly Durkheim's *Suicide* has its strengths, too. In fairness we must concede that much of its homage is justified. But that homage is unhealthy when it borders on idolatry. In order to meet the challenge of *Suicide* we must transcend it, even as we build on it. It is hard to believe that suicide is so simple or Durkheim so insightful that the definitive sociological word could have

Figure 11. A summary of current research results indicating weaknesses in Durkheim's *Suicide* with recommendations for their remedy.

Type of Weakness	Research Results	Recommendations
SUBSTANTIVE	1. SES is related inversely to the suicide rate. 2. The suicide rate is related to social mobility as well as social position. 3. The suicide rate is related to age and sex roles. 4. Durkheim omitted variables relevant to the suicide rate.	1. Investigate the possibility that hyperregulation may cause suicide. 2. Consider the social histories of suicides (their "suicidal careers"). 3. Probe the importance of occupational problems for males and marital problems for females. 4a. Look at the interaction effects of internal and external restraint. 4b. Think of race as a social phenomenon. 4c. Alcoholism should be regarded as a partial suicide. Think of suicide as a species of self-destructive behavior. 4d. Since poor health increases hopelessness or the "wish to die," it is relevant to the suicide rate. Determine the role of depression in suicide.
CONCEPTUAL	5. Durkheim made Procrustean generalizations; did not account for his data. 6. Discussion of social facts confuses real and ideal types.	5. Be more sensitive to details; avoid premature closure. 6. Any fact is determined by social and non-social forces.
METHODOLOGICAL	7. Durkheim committed the ecological fallacy. 8. Multivariate analysis performed by Durkheim was rudimentary and perhaps resulted in gross misinterpretations of data.	7. Concentrate on the attributes of suicides; avoid exclusive preoccupation with the social environments of suicides; construct more nominalistic typologies of suicide. 8. Use modern multivariate analysis techniques; control and assess interaction of variables; get at core variables.

been written in 1897. The spirit of *Suicide* is radical. It is part of a grand dialectical tradition which merits an equally radical reaction.

Suggestions for further reading

Douglas, Jack D.   *The Social Meanings of Suicide.* Princeton, N.J.: Princeton University Press, 1967. Any serious student of the sociology of suicide should read this book carefully from cover to cover. It is a serious, scholarly challenge to the Durkheimian approach to the study of suicide. At the very least, Douglas' book is importantly wrong.

Gibbs, Jack P. (ed.).   *Suicide.* New York: Harper & Row, 1968. This collection of essays does admirably to fill in many of the *lacunae* in Durkheim's *Suicide.*

Giddens, Anthony.   "A Typology of Suicide," *European Journal of Sociology,* Vol. 7, No. 2 (1966), pp. 276–95. A thoughtful attempt to combine sociological and psychological variables into a single typology of suicide.

Farberow, Norman L., and Shneidman, Edwin S. (eds.).   *The Cry for Help.* New York: McGraw-Hill Book Co., Inc., 1961. Since Durkheim wrote nothing of the psychoanalytic contributions to the understanding of suicide, the reader should study Part II of Farberow and Shneidman's book. Part I is a valuable resource for those engaged in suicide prevention.

CHAPTER 10

Towards a systematic theory
of suicide

All too often readers become giddy from being deluged with raw research results. It would seem natural for authors to attempt to systematize their research, to explain their results, to construct at least a modest theory of their subject. Unfortunately, even modest theories are usually not forthcoming. Vertigo induced by elliptical statements, lack of operational definitions, and a dearth of explanatory postulates is the rule rather than the exception. Most of us "play it safe" by confining ourselves to what one writer has dubbed "the Statistical Ritual."[1] On the other hand, premature generalization is little more than dogma. Since we do not have the data from which to construct a systematic theory of suicide, our compromise is to offer a single postulate which we argue should constitute a part of any explanation of suicide. Our basic conclusion is that all the propositions resulting from the Chicago research can be logically deduced from the concept of external constraint. Thus, the least we can do in this last chapter is to define "external constraint," give at least one example of the deduction of our research findings, and to illustrate how the postulate of external constraint might be incorporated into a more comprehensive theory of suicide.

[1]C. Wright Mills, *The Sociological Imagination* (New York: Grove Press, Inc., 1961), pp. 71–73.

Before going forward let us back up a little. It will be recalled that Durkheim's general explanation of the suicide rate was that it varied inversely with the degree of social integration of social groups.[2] What most commentators on Durkheim fail to notice is that this famous generalization comes at the conclusion of his consideration of *egoistic* suicide. Thus, there is a serious question as to how the generalization relates to altruistic, anomic, and fatalistic suicides.[3] For example, since *anomie* signals a failure of *regulation,* how can an explanation based on the concept of *integration* account for anomic suicides? Fatalistic suicide is even more of a problem since it varies *directly* with the degree of social integration (not indirectly, as the explanation predicts). Such internal inconsistencies cannot be tolerated in a systematic theory of suicide.

One solution to this problem is to claim that since there are different types of suicide, no single explanation can account for them all; i.e., that a single proposition cannot explain the suicide rate. Such an approach would be an improvement on Durkheim's treatment of the problem. In effect he simply sweeps it under the rug. For example, we are convinced that one reason why fatalistic suicide is mentioned only in a footnote is that it contradicts Durkheim's generalization about social integration and the suicide rate. Durkheim *says* that the reason for the footnote is that fatalistic suicide is a rare event; one which does not require an explanation. On the contrary we have presented evidence that fatalistic suicide occurs with sufficient regularity to require an explanation.[4]

Durkheim's general explanation of suicide does have the advantage of satisfying one of the fundamental laws of theory construction—the laws of parsimony.[5] Loosely interpreted this law

---

[2]Emile Durkheim, *Suicide* (New York: The Free Press, 1962), p. 209.

[3]For a provocative consideration of the relationships of Durkheim's types of suicide with each other and with psychological variables, see Anthony Giddens, "A Typology of Suicide," *European Journal of Sociology,* Vol. 7, No. 2 (1966), pp. 276–95.

[4]See especially Chapter 7.

[5]One of the most famous statements of the law of parsimony was made by William of Ockham: *Entia non sunt multiplicanda praetor necessitatem.* For example, Thomas S. Kuhn argues (*The Copernican Revolution* [New York: Vintage Books, 1959], p. 166) that Copernicus' theory of planetary motion was more parsimonious than Ptolemy's because Copernicus' theory required no major epicycles to explain the apparent retrogression of the planets.

states that one should never postulate the existence of a greater number of entities or factors when fewer will suffice (to explain). It follows that the most desirable resolutions of the problem would be one which offered a general explanation of suicide but avoided the inconsistencies which plagued Durkheim.

Barclay Johnson has tried to salvage Durkheim's unicausal explanation of the suicide rate.[6] First, he argues that altruism and fatalism must be eliminated because they occur almost exclusively in primitive and non-Western societies and they are not explained in purely social terms (remember that Halbwachs contended that altruistic suicide was so different from egoistic and anomic suicide that there could be no common explanation for the three types).[7] Thus, altruistic and fatalistic suicide are inconsistent with Durkheim's premises.[8] Second, Johnson claims that *anomie* and egoism are equivalent since regulation and integration are different indicators of a single dimension. In fact, Durkheim himself writes that *anomie* and egoism "are usually merely two different aspects of one social state."[9] Furthermore, since one definition of "egoism" is lack of social regulation, we can consider *anomie* as a species or aspect of egoism. Thus, Johnson concludes that Durkheim actually arrived at only one cause of suicide: viz, "The more integrated (i.e., regulated) a society, group, or social condition is, the lower its suicide rate."[10]

The reader will notice that our postulate of external constraint used to explain the Chicago data is basically the same as Johnson's interpretation of Durkheim. For example, we argue that the single dimension which *anomie* and egoism refer to is external constraint (viz, the *lack* of it). Integration is the structural aspect and regulation the normative aspect of external constraint. An externally constraining social situation is one in which the members of a society or community behave in a certain way (e.g., do not suicide) because of structural interdependency or normative regulation. External constraint exists when there is a high amount of cohesion (what Durkheim called *solidarité*) in social

---

[6]Barclay D. Johnson, "Durkheim's One Cause of Suicide," *American Sociological Review*, Vol. 30, No. 6 (December, 1965), pp. 875–86.

[7]*Ibid.*, p. 881.

[8]*Ibid.*, p. 879.

[9]Durkheim, *op. cit.*, p. 288.

[10]Johnson, *op. cit.*, p. 886.

relationships and when these relationships regulate or prescribe the individual.[11] For example, we can describe the social situation of married couples with children as generally more externally constraining than that of the never-married individual. Notice that marriage, especially when children are produced, involves more interpersonal dependency and normative prescriptions on behavior. We use "integration" to connote the number of interpersonal dependency relationships. The more interpersonal dependency relationships, the greater the integration in one's social situation. "Regulation" means that there are subordinate-superordinate relationships (i.e., it indicates the existence of power).[12] The more subordinate one is, the less power he has, the more prescriptions he is subjected to and the more regulated he is. For example, we argue that the young, white married female is more externally constrained than the adult, white single male.

To be sure there are several problems in the operationalization of the concept of external constraint which we cannot hope to resolve in a theoretical epilogue such as this. For example, someone might raise the question as to how one would *measure* (on an interval scale) the relative amounts of external constraint in various specific cases. Our reply is that a *rough* indication of the social integration of a particular individual could be obtained by simply *counting* the number of direct interpersonal dependency

---

[11]In Durkheim's *Suicide*, "solidarity" or "cohesion" refers to a type of relationship between the whole (society, a group) and its parts (individuals). If there is mechanical or organic solidarity, then society is an integer, a whole, integrated.

[12]For Durkheim a "regulated" social situation is one in which there is *nomia* ("a condition in which rules prevail") or morality. *"Anomie"* connotes varying degrees of normative chaos, of immorality. N.B., in actual social situations regulation and integration *interact;* e.g., if several people depend on you (or vice versa), i.e., your integration is high, then your behavior is also more regulated. Although the converse is less certain, it is probably true that the more subordinate you are in a group, the higher your interpersonal dependency. Thus, the strength of external constraint would be expected to be distributed as follows:

REGULATION

		Low	High
	High		Maximum
INTEGRATION			
	Low	Minimum	

relationships. For purposes of simplicity we could assume that ego's being dependent upon alter was equivalent to alter's being dependent upon ego. In other words, two-way dependencies score the same as one-way dependencies (a more subtle measure might want to differentiate types of dependency). We limit "dependency" to a nonpsychological connotation. "Dependency" refers to our various familial, friendship, and occupational associations (i.e., to relationships or involvements with "significant others"). We assume that interaction persists only when some dependency need is being gratified.[13] Sociometric analysis could be performed on individual cases of suicide. For example, two hypothetical cases might be graphed as follows:

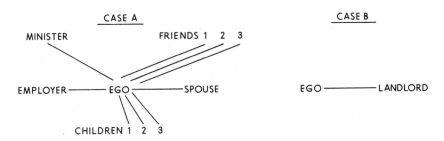

CASE A   CASE B

MINISTER   FRIENDS 1 2 3

EMPLOYER———EGO————SPOUSE   EGO————————LANDLORD

CHILDREN 1 2 3

Clearly A (integration score = 9) is more socially integrated than B (integration score = 1). The reader could quarrel with this measure. For example, eventually some weighting procedure would have to be implemented to measure the quality of the relationships (i.e., whether they indicated liking or disliking; how important one relationship was *vis-à-vis* others, etc.). Such difficulties should not be insurmountable.

A similar measuring procedure could be devised for regulatory relationships. Points could be assigned for being a particular sex or age, in a specific social class or occupation. These points would reflect the amount of dominance exerted on the individual (the lack of freedom he has with respect to observing common norms). For example, census occupational categories could be scored from 1 (professionals, etc.) to 11 (laborers). Thus, the more regulated, the higher one's score. Finally, a total could be computed which

---

[13]George C. Homans, *Social Behavior: Its Elementary Forms* (New York: Harcourt, Brace & World, Inc., 1961) , pp. 30–50.

would indicate an individual's external constraint score. The theoretical scheme could be tested by calculating external constraint scores for known suicides and a control group of non-suicides. It would be hypothesized that the external constraint scores of the experimental group (the suicides) and the control group would reveal statistically significant differences. The suicides would be expected to have lower external constraint scores than the controls. Note that external constraint could be measured ordinally in *any* group by estimates of integration and regulation (such as the proportion of young, married females—a group with relatively high external constraint). We would predict that external constraint and the suicide rate would vary inversely.

Reservations about a unicausal theory of suicide

Some reservations about a unicausal theory of suicide need to be stated. To begin with, our study of suicide in Chicago leads us to believe that fatalistic suicide has a significant incidence in contemporary America. It follows that a serious *apparent* contradiction has been introduced into our theory of suicide. How can it be true that both greater and less external constraint cause a high suicide rate? In Chapter 7 we suggested that Durkheim had trouble with fatalistic suicide in part because his data, certificates of death, depicted the suicide at one point in time (viz, at his death). If we look at the careers of suicides, we see that external constraint *diminishes* as the suicidal act approaches. There is no contradiction in saying that excessive regulation can lead to alienation from societal norms, *anomie,* and, finally, suicide. *At the time of death* it is still true that the less external constraint, the higher the suicide rate. Furthermore, fatalistic exceptions to the external constraint explanation of suicide were found in groups where the suicide rate was very low, such as among Negro females and young people. Thus, in these groups it is still true that external constraint and the suicide rate vary inversely.

Secondly, although failure of external constraint is a necessary condition for the occurrence of a high suicide rate, it is not a sufficient condition. In a book to which we have often referred, *Man against Himself,* Karl Menninger writes: "Behavior is never determined only by external forces; there are impulses from within, the adjustment of which to external reality necessarily brings about stresses and strains which may be highly painful, but endurable except to a very few."[14] All we are claiming is that most of the variation in the sociological variables considered in the Chicago study can be accounted for by the concept of external constraint. There remains the further question as to why many people experience failure of external constraint and yet *do not suicide*. In order to answer this question we would have to consider "impulses from within" or what Henry and Short call "internal restraint."[15] Although we have speculated on the relationship between external and internal constraint, we have no data which bear on the problem. As important as internal restraint is, a thorough treatment of it transcends the research problem which we have set down for ourselves.

Relationship between the concept of external constraint and a systematic theory of suicide

Although our investigations are too incomplete and preliminary to support the construction of a systematic theory of suicide, at least we can point to the form such a theory might take. To begin with, concepts like external constraint are merely component variables of systematic theory. What, then, is a theory? A theory is a deductively connected set of laws.[16] Some of the laws, the axioms or postulates, logically imply others, the theorems or corollaries. A theory functions to provide an explanation of research findings. A good example of a sociological theory is presented in George Homans' book, *Social Behavior: Its Elementary Forms*.[17] The postulates of the theory are the five general propositions given in Chapter 4. The function of the theory is to

---

[14]Karl Menninger, *Man against Himself* (New York: Harcourt, Brace & World, Inc., 1938) , p. 17.

[15]Andrew F. Henry and James F. Short, Jr., *Suicide and Homicide* (New York: The Free Press, 1954) , pp. 101–20.

[16]Mary Brodbeck, "Models, Meanings, and Theories," in Llewellyn Gross (ed.) *Symposium on Sociological Theory* (Evanston, Ill.: Row, Peterson and Co., 1959) , pp. 377–78. One of the real problems is whether or not there are any sociological laws. See pp. 491 ff. of Gross.

[17]Homans, *op. cit.*, especially chaps. i–iv.

deduce the descriptive propositions arrived at in the five field studies in *The Human Group* and in the so-called "small-group" researches of Festinger, Bales, Blau, and others.[18]

A law is an empirical generalization on a high level of generality. For example, "the distance a released body falls varies directly with the square of its time" or "Person's liking for Other varies with the frequency of interaction with him (provided that Person may interact with some third man, that Person's costs of interacting with Other do not exceed his rewards, and that Person and Other do not have radical status differences)." An empirical generalization "refers to the kind of categorical proposition that describes what has actually been observed and enumerated under limited circumstances."[19] A classic example of an empirical generalization is Durkheim's proposition that social integration and suicide rates are related inversely.[20]

A deductive argument involves the claim that its premises provide conclusive evidence for the truth of its conclusion.[21] Validity is a question of *form.* Various common valid argument forms have been enumerated by logicians under the rubric of "rules of inference."[22] When used in conjunction with true premises, rules of inference guarantee the validity of the deductively connected propositions or laws, and thus of the soundness of the theory.

Take this relatively simple argument:

A man can have many friends only if he respects them as individuals. If he respects them as individuals, then he cannot expect them all to behave alike. A man does have many friends. Therefore, he does not expect them all to behave alike.

Add two important rules of inference known respectively as *"modus ponens"* ($p \supset$ ["implies"] q, p, therefore, q) and "hypothetical syllogism" ($p \supset q$, $q \supset r$, therefore, $p \supset r$) and the above argument can be proved easily to be valid:

---

[18]George C. Homans, *The Human Group* (New York: Harcourt, Brace & World, Inc., 1950). Unfortunately Homans fails to deduce descriptive propositions in any strict sense of "deduce."

[19]Llewellyn Gross, "Theory Construction in Sociology; A Methodological Inquiry," in Gross (ed.), *Symposium on Sociological Theory,* p. 543.

[20]Durkheim, *op. cit.,* p. 209.

[21]Irving M. Copi, *Introduction to Logic* (New York: The Macmillan Co., 1961), chaps. v–x.

[22]*Ibid.,* pp. 275–83, 315–22.

1. $F \supset R$
2. $R \supset - E$
3. F/Therefore, $- E$
4. $F \supset - E$ By premises 1 and 2 and hypothetical syllogism
5. $- E$ By theorem 4 and premise 3 and *modus ponens*

Our explanation of suicide is a modest attempt to begin to construct a formal theory of suicide as outlined above. Our theory of suicide is similar to that offered by George Homans of elementary social behavior. Homans writes that:

> Science has been built by some of the damndest methods, but the strategy that I follow starts with scanning of the literature within a particular field in search of sheer, approximate empirical propositions, and with an effort to state them in some single set of concepts, that is, some single set of terms.
>
> This was as far . . . as *The Human Group* went, but it is no place to stop forever. Once you have established that the higher a man's rank in the group, the more closely his activities conform to its norms, you will ask *why* it should be so. The only way to get an answer is to borrow from somebody else's work, if you can, or invent for yourself, if you must, a set of general propositions, still *of the same form* as the empirical ones, from which you *can logically deduce* the latter under specified given conditions [italics mine]. To deduce them successfully *is* to explain them.
>
> The new propositions are more general in the sense that empirical propositions other than the ones you started with can also be derived from them under other givens. . . . The process of borrowing or inventing the more general propositions I call induction, . . . the process of deriving the empirical propositions from the more general ones I call explanation. . . . The second process has definite rules, *the rules of logic* [italics mine].[23]

Our crucial postulate or general proposition is that the external constraint in a group (or of an individual) varies inversely with its suicide rate (his suicide potential). Fortunately we have been able to derive this proposition from Durkheim's writings in much the same way that Homans derived his postulates from the writings of B. F. Skinner and the classical economists.

Like Homans we have scanned the literature for empirical propositions about suicide. These propositions and the research findings of the Chicago study could be deduced from the postulates

---

[23]Homans, *Social Behavior: Its Elementary Forms*, pp. 8 ff.

of external constraint and definitions (such as "integration," "regulation," "suicide rate," etc.) by the use of logic or rules of inference. If the research findings are deduced successfully, they become theorems of the theory. To deduce the research findings is to explain them. Schematically the procedure can be represented as follows:[24]

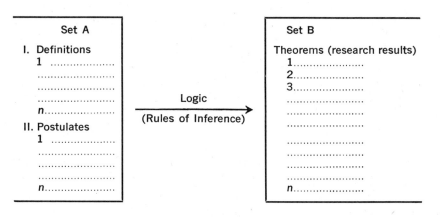

For example, we found that the greater the proportion of married persons in a population, the lower the suicide rate. Generally we postulated that the more external constraint, the lower the suicide rate. By definition it can be said that the more married persons in a population, the greater the external constraint. It follows from the postulate and the definition that the more married persons in a population, the lower the suicide rate. Formalized, the argument looks like this:

1. $+ EC \supset - SR$ postulate
2. $+ M \supset + EC$ by definition

3. $+ M \supset - SR$ premises 2, 1, and hypothetical syllogism

By the rule of transposition $[(p \supset q) \supset (- q \supset - p)]$, if any of the Chicago research findings cannot be transformed into theorems, then something is wrong with the theory. The postulate may not be correctly conceived, more postulates may be needed, an inference may be fallacious, or a research finding may be false.

[24]W. H. Werkmeister, "Theory Construction and the Problem of Objectivity," in Gross (ed.) , *Symposium on Sociological Theory*, p. 487.

A modest systematic theory of suicide

We are proposing a *modest* systematic theory of suicide. There are several indications that the time is not ripe for a thorough-going, formal sociological theory of suicide. For example, Clarence Schrag has noted that:

> It may . . . be unwise for most sociologists to devote their energies to the attempted construction of abstract and comprehensive theories such as those found in the more advanced sciences. Perhaps the greater need in sociology today is for more of the modest "inference chains," "explanation sketches," and embryo theories that aim primarily at organizing selected research findings and suggesting further avenues of inquiry.[25]

Anyone who has studied the history of science, such as that of astronomy or physics, is well aware of the theoretical and methodological hurdles that needed to be cleared prior to the emergence of a full-blown science. The youth of social science alone should make us skeptical of the propitiousness of a formal theory of suicide. Before such a theory of suicide can be constructed, we need more confirmed hypotheses to settle the question of the existence and nature of sociological laws (can social behavior be generalized in the same manner as physical behavior?), to develop a common vocabulary and common definitions of terms, and to gain more logical and mathematical skills. Until these needs are met it would seem to be more appropriate to construct modest "inference chains."

On the other hand, there are certain distinct advantages to constructing a modest systematic theory of suicide. In order to construct a theory one is forced to differentiate and classify the elements of the theory. Certain confusions are resolved simply by distinguishing definitions (theoretical and operational, nominal and real) from generalizations (theoretical and empirical on different levels), from hypotheses (null and alternative, accepted and rejected), from laws (are there any?) from concepts, from facts, from theorems, etc. Perhaps one of the most important latent

[25]Clarence Schrag, "Elements of Theoretical Analysis in Sociology," in Llewellyn Gross (ed.), *Sociological Theories: Inquiries and Paradigms* (New York: Harper & Row, 1967), p. 244.

functions of such distinctions is that it forces the development of operational definitions and enables the theory to be tested.

Once the elements of the theory have been classified, it becomes possible to interrelate formerly isolated and unintegrated propositions.[26] By imaginatively combining propositions it is often possible to generate new propositions, which may not have been revealed yet by empirical observation. Reversing the process of inference, general propositions or laws can be discovered.

Finally, a systematic theory tends to sift out the relevant phenomena from the irrelevant.[27] If the propositions of the theory are true and the arguments are sound, then prediction and control of suicide are enhanced. Both our reservations and hopes for a systematic sociological theory of suicide are summed up well by W. H. Werkmeister:

> To be sure, the phenomena which are the subject matter of the social sciences are so complex that as yet it is not possible to obtain that degree of precision in description and the formulation of laws which is requisite to the ultimate integration. In fact the descriptive phase of scientific inquiry will predominate in the social sciences for a long time to come. Without theory construction, however, the social sciences will never reach full scientific maturity. Even statistically disclosed uniformities are at best only descriptive of "what is the case." As in any other science, their explanation depends upon their being derivable as theorems or laws from a set . . . of definitions and postulates.[28]

Summary

It is our contention that there is a need for a much more rigorously constructed theory of suicide than Durkheim envisaged. While we have not developed one here, we have supported a major postulate (that of external constraint), provided new empirical generalizations, and outlined a logic of procedure. Any systematic theory of suicide will probably be modified by the development of new empirical generalizations on suicide. However, it would have the advantage of being a theory in the strict sense of the term, i.e., a set of logically interrelated, empirically

[26]Hans L. Zetterberg, *On Theory and Verification in Sociology* (Totowa, N.J.: The Bedminster Press, 1965) , p. vii.

[27]Schrag, *op. cit.*, p. 230.

[28]Werkmeister, *op. cit.*, p. 493.

substantiated propositions. Should future research contest the adequacy or usefulness of such a theory (prove the findings false, the postulates poorly conceived, or the argument invalid), at least there would be some formal theory to modify.

Suggestions for further reading

Costner, Herbert L., and Leik, Robert D. "Deductions from 'Axiomatic Theory,'" *American Sociological Review,* Vol. 29, No. 6 (December, 1964), pp. 819–35. Discusses the problems of deductive inferences from associational relationships (such as r or Q) where the correlations are less than perfect.

Gross, Llewellyn (ed.). *Symposium on Sociological Theory.* Evanston, Ill.: Row, Peterson and Co., 1959. A first-rate collection of essays on sociological theory (especially theory construction). See articles by Hempel, Brodbeck, Hochberg, Werkmeister, and Gross. Cf. Gross' latest book, *Sociological Theories: Inquiries and Paradigms,* Part IV. New York: Harper & Row, 1967.

Homans, George C. *Social Behavior: Its Elementary Forms,* esp. chaps. i–iv. New York: Harcourt, Brace & World, Inc., 1961. Homans is one of the few modern theorists who has attempted to construct a systematic theory of his subject. Chaps. i–iv provide a paradigm of the logic of procedure for constructing a systematic theory of suicide. The book reads well and is thoroughly documented.

Zetterberg, Hans L. *On Theory and Verification in Sociology.* 3d ed. Totowa, N.J.: The Bedminster Press, 1965. The pioneering work on methods of "propositional theory." Costner and Leik's article should be read after Zetterberg's book.

Appendixes

APPENDIX A

FILL IN WITH TYPEWRITER OR LEGIBLE PRINTING

STATE OF ILLINOIS

CORONER'S CERTIFICATE OF DEATH

STATE FILE NUMBER

REGISTRATION DISTRICT NO.

REGISTERED NUMBER

DECEDENT'S BIRTH NO.

1. PLACE OF DEATH		2. USUAL RESIDENCE (Where deceased lived. If institution, residence before admission.)	
a. STATE **ILLINOIS**	b. COUNTY	a. STATE	b. COUNTY

c. ☐ INSIDE corporate limits and in City, Village, or Incorporated Town

c. ☐ INSIDE corporate limits and in City, Village, or Incorporated Town

d. ☐ OUTSIDE corporate limits and in Township name..................... Road District No.....................	e. LENGTH OF STAY IN 1c or 1d	d. ☐ OUTSIDE corporate limits and in Township name................... Road District No...................	e. LENGTH of RESIDENCE AT 2c or 2d

f. NAME OF HOSPITAL OR INSTITUTION	g. LENGTH OF STAY IN 1f	f. RESIDENCE ADDRESS (Street & No. or R.F.D. and Post Office)

h. If not in hospital or institution, give Street & No. or R.F.D. and Post Office

g. Did decedent reside ON A FARM?   YES ☐   NO ☐

3. NAME OF DECEASED a. (FIRST) b. (MIDDLE) c. (LAST)	4. DATE OF DEATH (MONTH) (DAY) (YEAR)

5. SEX	6. RACE	7. MARRIED, NEVER MARRIED, WIDOWED, DIVORCED (specify)	8. DATE OF BIRTH	9. AGE (in years last birthday)	if under 1 year MONTHS | DAYS	if under 24 hrs. HOURS | MIN.

10a. USUAL OCCUPATION	10b. KIND OF BUSINESS OR INDUSTRY	11. BIRTHPLACE (City and state or foreign country)	12. Citizen of what country?

13. FATHER'S FULL NAME	14. MOTHER'S FULL MAIDEN NAME

15. Was deceased ever in U. S. Armed Forces? (Yes, no, or unknown) (Give war or dates of service)	16. SOCIAL SECURITY NUMBER	17. INFORMANT a. SIGNATURE

b. ADDRESS	c. RELATIONSHIP TO DECEASED

18. MEDICAL CAUSE OF DEATH

PART I. DEATH WAS CAUSED BY. [Enter only one cause per line for (A), (B) and (C).]

INTERVAL BETWEEN ONSET AND DEATH

IMMEDIATE CAUSE (A) ....

Conditions, if any, which gave rise to the above IMMEDIATE CAUSE (A), stating the UNDERLYING cause last.

▶due to (B) ....

▶due to (C) ....

PART II. OTHER SIGNIFICANT CONDITIONS CONTRIBUTING TO DEATH BUT NOT RELATED TO THE TERMINAL CONDITION GIVEN IN PART I(A).

20. AUTOPSY?

19a. DATE OF OPERATION	19b. MAJOR FINDINGS OF OPERATION	
		YES ☐ NO ☐

21a. ACCIDENT ☐ SUICIDE ☐ UNDETERMINED ☐ HOMICIDE ☐	21b. PLACE OF INJURY (e.g., in or about home, farm, factory, street, office bldg., etc.)	21c. INJURED AT (CITY, TOWNSHIP, OR LOCATION) (COUNTY) (STATE)

21d. TIME OF INJURY (HOUR) (MONTH) (DAY) (YEAR) A.M. P.M.	21e. INJURY OCCURRED WHILE AT WORK ☐ NOT WHILE AT WORK ☐	21f. HOW DID INJURY OCCUR?

22a. Upon medical investigation I find this death was caused as stated above. DATE: SIGNED:	22b. Upon official investigation I find the person described died as stated above. DATE: SIGNED:
M. D. CORONER'S PHYSICIAN.	COUNTY CORONER.

23. DISPOSITION: BURIAL-REMOVAL-CREMATION Date.............. CEMETERY .... LOCATION	24. FUNERAL DIRECTOR SIGNATURE .... ADDRESS ....License ....Number.............

25. Received for filing on (Signed)	
	LOCAL REGISTRAR

APPENDIX B

A brief history of a data access problem

It was no easy matter to secure the suicide records we needed to do this study. Our initial effort to gain access to some 2,153 death certificates was met with the following response from a state official:

I have been weighing the problem of making vital records available to Mr. Maris for his study of Cook County suicides for a period of five years. After much deliberation and the desire to support worthwhile research studies, I find that I cannot in good conscience approve Mr. Maris' request.

This decision has nothing to do with Mr. Maris personally, or the possible value of his study. Rather, it is based primarily upon the fact that death by suicide is a traumatic experience for the next of kin; that interrogation of the Coroner's informant would mean the reopening of old sorrows; and that the persons so involved have a right to privacy which the State should not negate. Moreover, the demands and requests upon the Department for assistance in various projects have grown beyond our operational ability to cooperate fully and still keep up with our primary statutory responsibilities [October 7, 1964].

Frankly, we were puzzled by the denial of permission to copy the state's records. Such an act was not prohibited by law. Furthermore, we were convinced that the research could be conducted in such a manner as not to reopen old wounds and that it was a

194

significant enough problem to justify other attempts to gain the needed information.

Our reply to this letter conceded not to interview the suicide's next of kin, but it denied the legitimacy of the state's "operational ability." Previous arrangements had been made with the head of the records department, and he had assured us that such operations were rather routine and that there really was no mechanical barrier to procuring the death certificates.

Rather than reply to the same state official who had refused to cooperate on what he considered just grounds, we decided to employ indirection. Another state official in a different but related department was contacted, and an interview was conducted. The results of this confrontation were successful enough to prompt the second state official to telephone personally the man who originally denied us access to the data.

On November 13, 1964, the man who had made the refusal sent a letter which read, in part:

> The subject of making certain vital records available to you for a study of Cook County suicides has again reached me through Dr. X. It may well be that the advantages of your study may outweigh the disadvantages which were mentioned in my letter of October 7, 1964.

Upon arriving in Springfield for an interview with this official, we were greeted cordially and granted complete license to conduct the project at our own professional discretion, including interviewing the survivors of the decedents.

This brief episode is included only because it might be of some benefit to would-be researchers of taboo topics. The moral of these events may be summarized in the following manner. First, you must be convinced that the unorthodox research which you are proposing will be primarily beneficial to the majority of those persons involved. Second, once convinced of the value of your study, explore different means of attaining the desired end and try all of those which are within the limits of good judgment (clearly, the end does not always justify the means). In our case, bringing mild pressures, from various sources, to bear upon the person with the power to grant permission was the most successful avenue.

Third, do not be discouraged by setbacks and delays. Especially when dealing with subjects such as suicide, it is best to go slowly. It could well be that the state was correct in assuming that a personal interview with the coroner's informant would be too traumatic. We have not decided the point yet, nor have we conducted any interviews (although the funds were available). Furthermore, the wheels of large bureaucratic organizations turn slowly, as we all know. However, a delayed decision is not always unfavorable. It took six months from the onset of negotiations to get the permission needed.

Fourth, be sure that you are well accredited. We carefully identified ourselves with the University of Illinois and with the National Science Foundation. We learned in these data-gathering adventures that vital statistics sometimes are exploited by those with crass economic motives. For example, dealers in baby products occasionally try to get addresses of new parents from birth certificates. Suicide records may have a bearing on lawsuits, insurance claims, wills, etc.

Finally, do not make it hard on those who will follow. We never really knew why permission was refused in the first place. It might have been a utilitarian consideration on the part of the official (a state election was near and a large and touchy investigation like ours might have caused unfavorable public opinion). It might have been that the official did not want to risk angering 2,153 survivors for the sake of one researcher. It might have been for the reasons actually stated in the first letter or for any one of a number of other reasons.

Bibliography

Bibliography

The focus in this bibliography is on *recent sociological* works; especially those referred to in the text of this manuscript. Accordingly, several items noted are not yet in print. The list of sociological works is most comprehensive. There is also a large number of recent publications on suicide prevention. The psychiatric, psychological, and medical references on suicide are only token. Readers should be aware of Norman L. Farberow and Edwin S. Shneidman's excellent bibliography in *The Cry for Help* and the more recent list in Jack P. Gibbs' (ed.) *Suicide (infra)*.

Alpert, Harry. *Emile Durkheim and His Sociology.* New York: Russell & Russell, Inc., 1961.

Appelbaum, Stephen A. "The Problem-Solving Aspect of Suicide," *Journal of Projective Techniques,* Vol. 27, No. 3 (1963), pp. 259–68.

Berkowitz, Leonard. *Aggression.* New York: McGraw-Hill Book Co., Inc., 1962.

Blachly, P. H., *et al.* "Suicide by Physicians." Paper read at the First Annual National Conference on Suicidology, Chicago, Illinois, March 20, 1968.

Bohannan, Paul (ed.). *African Homicide and Suicide.* Princeton, N.J.: Princeton University Press, 1960.

Bonnafous, M. "Le Suicide: thése psychiatrique et thése sociologique," *Revue philosophique,* Vol. 115 (May–June, 1933), pp. 456–75.

Breed, Warren. "Occupational Mobility and Suicide among White Males," *American Sociological Review,* Vol. 28, No. 2 (April, 1963), pp. 179–88.

————. "On the Social Psychology of the Suicide Process." Mimeographed. New Orleans, La.: Tulane University, 1966.

————. "Suicide, Migration, and Race: A Study of Cases in New Orleans," *The Journal of Social Issues,* Vol. 22, No. 1, pp. 30–43.

————. "The Negro and Fatalistic Suicide." Mimeographed. New Orleans, La.: Tulane University, 1967.

Bruyn, Henry B., and Seiden, Richard H. "Student Suicide: Fact or Fancy?" *The Journal of the American College Health Association,* Vol. 14, No. 2, pp. 69–77.

Camus, Albert. *The Myth of Sisyphus.* Trans. Justin O'Brien. New York: Alfred A. Knopf, Inc., 1964.

Cantor, Joel M. "Alcoholism as a Suicidal Equivalent." Mimeographed. Los Angeles, Calif.: Veterans Administration Center, 1967.

Cavan, Ruth Shonle. *Suicide.* New York: Russell & Russell, Inc., 1965.

Chambliss, William J., and Steele, Marion F. "Status Integration and Suicide: An Assessment," *American Sociological Review,* Vol. 31 (August, 1966), pp. 524–32.

Clinard, Marshall B. (ed.). *Anomie and Deviant Behavior.* New York: The Free Press, 1964.

Cutter, Fred, *et al.* "Suicide in Art." Paper read at the Fourth International Conference for Suicide Prevention, Los Angeles, California, October, 1967.

Dahlgren, K. G. *On Suicide and Attempted Suicide.* Lund, Sweden: Lindstadts, 1945.

De Fleury, M. *L'Angoisse Humaine.* Paris: Editions de France, 1924.

Delmas, F. Archille. *Psychologie pathologique du suicide.* Paris: Alcan, 1932.

Demographic Yearbook. Published annually by the United Nations.

Devries, A. G. "Identification of Suicidal Behavior by Means of the MMPI," *Psycholgical Reports,* Vol. 19 (1966), pp. 415–19.

Dollard, J., *et al. Frustration and Aggression.* New Haven: Yale, 1939.

Dorpat, T. L., and Ripley, H. S. "A Study of Suicide in the Seattle Area," *Comparative Psychiatry,* Vol. 1 (December, 1960), pp. 349–59.

Douglas, Jack D. *The Social Meanings of Suicide.* Princeton, N.J.: Princeton University Press, 1967.

————. "The Sociological Analysis of Social Meanings of Suicide," *European Journal of Sociology,* Vol. 7, No. 2 (1966), pp. 249–75.

Dublin, Louis I. *Suicide: A Sociological and Statistical Study.* New York: The Ronald Press Co., 1963.

Dublin, Louis I., and Bunzel, Bessie. *To Be or Not to Be.* New York: Harrison Smith and Robert Hass, 1933.

Durkheim Emile. *Sociology and Philosophy.* New York: The Free Press, 1953.

————. *Suicide.* New York: The Free Press, 1962.

————. *The Division of Labor in Society.* New York: The Free Press, 1960.

————. *The Elementary Forms of the Religious Life.* New York: Collier Books, 1961.

————. *The Rules of Sociological Method.* New York: The Free Press, 1962.

Farberow, Norman L. (ed.). *Vita.* Official Newsletter for the International Association of Suicide Prevention, 2521 West Pico Boulevard, Los Angeles, California.

————, and Shneidman, Edwin S. *The Cry for Help.* New York: McGraw-Hill Book Co., Inc., 1961.

Firth, Raymond. "Suicide and Risk-Taking in Tokopia Society," *Psychiatry,* Vol. 24 (February, 1961), pp. 2–17.

Ford, R., and Moseley, A. L. "Motor Vehicular Suicides," *Journal of Criminal Law, Criminology, and Police Science,* Vol. 54 (September, 1963), pp. 257–59.

Frederick, Calvin J. "Suicide and Handwriting: A Study of Suicide Notes." Paper read at the First Annual National Conference on Suicidology, Chicago, Illinois, March 20, 1968.

Freud, Sigmund. "Mourning and Melancholia," *Collected Papers,* Vol. IV. London: The Hogarth Press, 1925.

————. *The Ego and the Id.* Trans. Joan Riviere. London: The Hogarth Press, 1947.

Gargas, S. "Suicide in the Netherlands," *The American Journal of Sociology,* Vol. 37 (March, 1932), pp. 697–713.

Gibbs, Jack P. "Suicide," in *Contemporary Social Problems* (eds. R. K. Merton and R. A. Nisbet). New York: Harcourt, Brace & World, Inc., 1961.

———— (ed.). *Suicide.* New York: Harper & Row, 1968.

————, and Martin, Walter T. *Status Integration and Suicide.* Eugene, Ore.: The University of Oregon Press, 1964.

Giddens, Anthony. "A Typology of Suicide," *European Journal of Sociology,* Vol. 7, No. 2 (1966), pp. 276–95.

————. "The Suicide Problem in French Sociology," *British Journal of Sociology,* Vol. 16 (March, 1965), pp. 3–18.

Gold, Martin. "Suicide, Homicide, and the Socialization of Aggression," *The American Journal of Sociology,* Vol. 63 (1958), pp. 651–61.

Gross, Llewellyn (ed.). *Symposium on Sociological Theory.* Evanston, Ill.: Row, Peterson and Co., 1959.

Hagedorn, Robert, and Labovitz, Sanford. "A Note on Status Integration," *Social Problems,* Vol. 14 (Summer, 1966), pp. 79–94.

Halbwachs, Maurice. *Les Causes du Suicide.* Paris: Alcan, 1930.

Hendin, Herbert. *Suicide and Scandinavia.* Garden City, N.Y.: Anchor Books, 1965.

Henry, Andrew F., and Short, James F., Jr. *Suicide and Homicide.* New York: The Free Press, 1954.

Homans, George C. *Social Behavior: Its Elementary Forms.* New York: Harcourt, Brace & World, Inc., 1961.

Illinois Department of Public Health. *Vital Statistics Illinois.* Springfield, Illinois.

Jensen, V. W., and Petty, T. A. "The Fantasy of Being Rescued in Suicide," *Psychoanalytical Quarterly,* Vol. 27 (1958), pp. 327–39.

Johnson, Barclay D. "Durkheim's One Cause of Suicide," *American Sociological Review,* Vol. 30, No. 6 (December, 1965), pp. 875–86.

Kitagawa, Evelyn M., and Taeuber, Karl E. (eds.). Chicago Community Inventory. *Local Community Fact Book; Chicago Metropolitan Area, 1960.* Chicago: University of Chicago, 1963.

Kobler, A. L., and Stotland, Ezra. *The End of Hope.* New York: The Free Press, 1964.

Lendrum, F. C. "A Thousand Cases of Attempted Suicide," *American Journal of Psychiatry,* Vol. 13 (1933), pp. 479–500.

Litman, Robert E., *et al.* "Emergency Response to Potential Suicide," *The Journal of the Michigan State Medical Society,* Vol. 62 (January, 1963), pp. 68–72.

————. "Investigations of Equivocal Suicides," *Journal of the American Medical Association,* Vol. 184 (June, 1963), pp. 924–29.

————. "Suicide-Prevention Telephone Service," *Journal of the American Medical Association,* Vol. 192 (April, 1965), pp. 21–25.

————, and Tabachinick, Norman. "Fatal One-Car Accidents," *The Psychoanalytic Quarterly,* Vol. 36 (1967), pp. 248–59.

————, and Kramer, Jan. "Some Hypnotics Commonly Used in Suicide Attempts." Mimeographed. Los Angeles, Calif.: Los Angeles Suicide Prevention Center, 1964.

Lunden, Walter A. "Suicides in France, 1910–1943," *The American Journal of Sociology,* Vol. 37 (January, 1947), pp. 321–34.

Metropolitan Life Insurance Company. "International Rise in Suicide," *Statistical Bulletin,* Vol. 48 (March, 1967), pp. 4–7.

Maris, Ronald. "Age, Sex, Marital Status and the Suicide Rate," *Yale Scientific,* Vol. 42, No. 4 (January, 1968), pp. 6–24.

————. "Suicide, Status and Mobility in Chicago," *Social Forces,* Vol. 4, No. 2 (December, 1967), pp. 246–56.

————. "Suicide: The Nondiminishing Rate," *Minnesota Medicine,* Vol. 51, No. 5 (May, 1968), pp. 723–26.

_____. "The Sociology of Suicide Prevention: Policy Implications of Differences between Suicidal Patients and Completed Suicides." Paper read at the Annual Meeting of the American Sociological Associaion, Boston, Massachusetts, 1968.

Meerloo, J. A. M. *Suicide and Mass Suicide*. New York: Grune & Stratton, Inc., 1962.

Menninger, Karl. *Man against Himself*. New York: Harcourt, Brace & World, Inc., 1938.

Merton, Robert K. *On Theoretical Sociology*. New York: The Free Press, 1967.

Morselli, Henry. *Suicide: An Essay in Comparative Moral Statistics*. New York: D. Appleton, 1903.

Murphy, George E., and Robins, Eli. "Social Factors in Suicide," *The Journal of the American Medical Association*, Vol. 199 (January, 1967), pp. 303–8.

Neuringer, Charles. "Rigid Thinking in Suicidal Individuals," *Journal of Consulting Psychology*, Vol. 28, No. 1 (1964), pp. 54–58.

O'Neal, P., *et al.* "A Psychiatric Study of Attempted Suicide in Persons over Sixty Years of Age," *Archives of Neurology and Psychiatry*, Vol. 75 (1956), pp. 275–84.

Palmer, Stuart. "Murder and Suicide in Forty Non-Literate Societies," *The Journal of Criminal Law, Criminology and Police Science*, Vol. 56, No. 3, pp. 320–24.

Parsons, Talcott. *The Structure of Social Action*, chaps. viii–xi. New York: The Free Press, 1949.

Pearlin, Leonard. "Alienation from Work," *American Sociological Review*, Vol. 27 (June, 1962), pp. 314–26.

Pierce, Albert. "The Economic Cycle and the Social Suicide Rate," *American Sociological Review*, Vol. 32, No. 3 (June, 1967), pp. 457–62.

Pokorny, A. D. "Characteristics of 44 Patients Who Subsequently Committed Suicide," *A. M. A. Archives of General Psychiatry*, Vol. 2 (March, 1960), pp. 314–23.

Porterfield, Austin L. "Indices of Suicide and Homicide by States and Cities: Some Southern-Non-Southern Contrasts with Implication for Research," *American Sociological Review*, Vol. 14 (June, 1959), pp. 481–90.

_____. "Suicide and Crime in Folk and in Secular Society," *The American Journal of Sociology*, Vol. 57 (1952), pp. 331–38.

————. "Suicide and Crime in the Social Structure of an Urban Setting: Fort Worth, 1930–1950," *American Sociological Review,* Vol. 17 (June, 1952), pp. 341–49.

————. "Traffic Fatalities, Suicide and Homicide," *American Sociological Review,* Vol. 25 (1960), pp. 897–901.

————, and Gibbs, Jack P. "Occupational Prestige and Social Mobility in Suicides in New Zealand," *American Journal of Sociology,* Vol. 66 (September, 1960), pp. 147–52.

Powell, Elwin. "Occupations, Status, and Suicide," *American Sociological Review,* Vol. 23, No. 2 (April, 1958), pp. 131–39.

Quetelet, A. *Sur l'homme et le développement de ses facultés.* Paris, 1835.

Quinney, Richard. "Suicide, Homicide, and Economic Development," *Social Forces,* Vol. 43, No. 3 (March, 1965), pp. 401–6.

Robins, Lee N. "Suicide and Violence: Explaining the Low Negro Suicide Rate." Paper read at the Annual Meeting of the American Sociological Association, San Francisco, California, 1967.

Sainsbury, Peter. *Suicide in London.* London: Chapman & Hall, Ltd., 1955.

Schrut, Albert. "Suicidal and Self-Destructive Adolescents and Children." Mimeographed. Los Angeles, Calif.: Los Angeles Suicide Prevention Center, 1965.

Schmid, Calvin F. *Suicides in Seattle, 1914 to 1925.* Seattle, Wash.: University of Washington Press, 1928.

Seiden, Richard H. "Campus Tragedy: A Study of Student Suicide," *Journal of Abnormal Psychology,* Vol. 71, No. 6 (1966), pp. 389–99.

Selvin, Hanan C. "Durkheim's *Suicide*: Further Thoughts on a Methodological Classic," *Emile Durkheim* (ed. Robert A. Nisbet), pp. 113–36. Englewood Cliffs, N.J.: Prentice-Hall, Inc., 1965.

Shneidman, Edwin S. (ed.). *Essays in Self-Destruction.* New York: Science House, Inc., 1967.

————. "Orientations Toward Death," *The Study of Lives* (ed. Robert W. White). New York: Prentice-Hall, Inc., 1963.

————. "Suicidal Phenomena: Their Definition and Classification." Mimeographed. Los Angeles, Calif.: Los Angeles Suicide Prevention Center, 1965.

————, and Farberow, Norman L. (eds.). *Clues to Suicide.* New York: McGraw-Hill Book Co., Inc., 1957.

————, and Mandelkorn, Philip. *How to Prevent Suicide.* Public Affairs Pamphlet No. 406. New York, 1967.

————, and Swenson, David D. (eds.). *Bulletin of Suicidology,* National Clearinghouse for Mental Health Information, National Institute of Mental Health, Chevy Chase, Maryland, 20203.

Simpson, George. "Methodological Problems in Determining the Aetiology of Suicide," *American Sociological Review,* Vol. 15 (October, 1950), pp. 658–63.

Simpson, Richard. "A Note on Status, Mobility, and *Anomie,*" *British Journal of Sociology,* Vol. 11 (December, 1960), pp. 370–72.

Spiegel, Donald E., and Neuringer, Charles. "Role of Dread in Suicidal Behavior," *Journal of Abnormal and Social Psychology,* Vol. 66, No. 5 (1963), pp. 507–11.

Steinmetz, S. R. "Suicide among Primitive People," *American Anthropologist,* Vol. 7 (January, 1894), pp. 53–60.

Stengel, Erwin. *Suicide and Attempted Suicide.* Great Britain: Penguin Books, 1964.

————, and Cook, N. G. *Attempted Suicide: Its Social Significance and Effects.* New York: Oxford University Press, 1958.

Tabachnick, N. "Interpersonal Relations in Suicidal Attempts," *A. M. A. Archives of General Psychiatry,* Vol. 4 (January, 1961), pp. 16–21.

————, *et al.* "Comparative Psychiatric Study of Accidental and Suicidal Death," *A. M. A. Archives of General Psychiatry,* Vol. 14 (January, 1966), pp. 60–68.

Trautman, E. C. "The Suicidal Fit," *A. M. A. Archives of General Psychiatry,* Vol. 5 (July, 1961), pp. 76–84.

United Nations, World Health Organization. *Epidemiological and Vital Statistics Report,* Vol. 9, No. 4 (1956).

U.S. Bureau of the Census. *United States Census of the Population: 1960, Illinois.* Washington, D.C.: U.S. Government Printing Office, 1963.

U.S. Department of Health, Education and Welfare. *Vital Statistics of the United States, 1963,* Vol. II: Mortality, Parts A and B. Washington, D.C.: U.S. Government Printing Office, 1965.

Wechsler, H. "Community Growth, Depressive Disorders, and Suicide," *The American Journal of Sociology,* Vol. 67 (July, 1961), pp. 9–17.

Wetzel, Richard D. "Suicide Prevention, Inc. of St. Louis." Paper read at the First Annual National Conference on Suicidology, Conrad Hilton Hotel, Chicago, Illinois, March 20, 1968.

Wilensky, Harold L., and Edwards, H. "The Skidder: Ideological Adjustments of Downwardly Mobile Workers," *American Sociological Review,* Vol. 24 (April, 1959), pp. 215–31.

Wilkins, James L., and Goffman, Irwin. "Accomplishing Suicide." Paper read at the Annual Meeting of the American Sociological Association, Miami, Florida, 1966.

Williams, Robin M., Jr. *American Society.* New York: Alfred A. Knopf, Inc., 1952.

Wolf, Carl I. "The Cry for Help." Mimeographed. Los Angeles, Calif.: Los Angeles Suicide Prevention Center, 1965.

————. "Who Calls the Suicide Prevention Center?" Paper read at the First Annual National Conference on Suicidology, Chicago, Illinois, March 20, 1968.

Wolfgang, Marvin E. *Patterns of Criminal Homicide.* New York: John Wiley & Sons, Inc., 1966, pp. 269–83.

Wood, A. L. "A Socio-Structural Analysis of Murder, Suicide, and Economic Crime in Ceylon," *American Sociological Review,* Vol. 26 (1961), pp. 744–53.

World Health Organization. *World Health Statistical Annuals.*

Yap, Pow Meng. *Suicide in Hong Kong.* Hong Kong: Hong Kong University Press, 1958.

Zilboorg, Gregory. "Differential Diagnostic Types of Suicide," *Archives of Neurology and Psychiatry,* Vol. 35 (January, 1935), pp. 270–91.

Index

Index

This book has been set in 11 and 10 point Baskerville, leaded 2 points. Part titles and numbers and chapter titles are in 18 point Record Gothic Bold. Chapter numbers are in 14 point News Gothic. The size of the type page is 26 by 43⅔ picas.